From Tea Cakes to Tamales

NUMBER SIXTEEN

Clayton Wheat Williams Texas Life Series

From Tea Cakes to Tamales

Third-Generation Texas Recipes

Nola McKey

Illustrated by Cora McKown

TEXAS A&M UNIVERSITY PRESS
COLLEGE STATION

This paper meets the requirements of ANSI/NISO Z39.48–1992
(Permanence of Paper).
Binding materials have been chosen for durability.
Manufactured in China by Everbest Printing Co.
through FCI Print Group

Library of Congress Cataloging-in-Publication Data

Names: McKey, Nola, 1946– author.
Title: From tea cakes to tamales : third-generation Texas recipes / Nola
   McKey ; illustrated by Cora McKown.
Other titles: Clayton Wheat Williams Texas life series ; no. 16.
Description: First edition. | College Station : Texas A&M University Press,
   [2016] | ?2016 | Series: Clayton Wheat Williams Texas life series ; number
   sixteen | Includes bibliographical references and index.
Identifiers: LCCN 2015044740| ISBN 9781623494094 (pbk. (with flaps) :
(alk. paper) | ISBN 9781623494100 (ebook)
Subjects: LCSH: International cooking. | Cooking—Texas. | Texas—Social life
   and customs—20th century. | Texas—Social life and cusoms—21st century.
   | Food habits—Texas—History—20th century. | Food
   habits—Texas—History—21st century. | LCGFT: Cookbooks.
Classification: LCC TX725.A1 M3935 2016 | DDC 641.59764—dc23
LC record available at http://lccn.loc.gov/2015044740

For my grandmother

Ailcy Elizabeth "Bessie" Hall McKey

—whose tea cakes delighted me as a child
and inspired me as an adult

Contents

Acknowledgments

Writing this cookbook has been an adventure, complete with challenges and discoveries, and I'm grateful to many people for their help along the way. First, I'm indebted to the cooks who trusted me with their treasured recipes, photographs, and family histories. Some of them are friends and family members, but many others I've never met. Without their contributions, this book would not exist. I hope they find it a worthy tribute to the ancestors whose recipes are the heart of this endeavor.

Next in line for gratitude is my multitalented collaborator, friend, and former professor Cora McKown. I'm thankful for her vibrant watercolors and artistic vision, as well as her enthusiasm for this project. She's no longer my teacher, but I continue to learn from her.

I also owe a huge thank-you to my friend Susan Nelson and her nutrition and wellness classes at Ell-Saline Middle/High School in Brookville, Kansas, who tested numerous recipes for me. Specific thanks go to the following students during the spring and fall semesters of 2014: Kassidy Chalmers, Sierra DeArvil, Elany Edgerton, Katie Edgerton, Austin Funk, Kachina Harrington, Riley McKain, Fallyn Morrical, Tabitha Newton, Marlene Nunez, Kiva Phelps, Adriena Rodriguez, Amanda Schneider, and Sivonna Williams. Susan also tested many recipes for me at home, as did her mother, Norma Roesner. I greatly appreciate their generosity.

Specific thank-yous go to others as well: to Kathleen Martin, for loaning me a wonderful collection of vintage dishes for use as props in the watercolors (and for testing Oyster Stew in the middle of August); to Lana Beyer, for loaning me her pizzelle press so that I could test the Pizzelle recipe; to Kathleen Niendorff, for providing publishing advice early in the process; to Michael Traweek, for grilling a gorgeous brisket that served as a model in one of the watercolors and for providing a venison tenderloin so that I could test the venison recipe; to Jo Ann Andera, for providing contact information for Texas Folklife Festival volunteers; to Martha Hartzog, for letting members of the Daughters of the Republic of Texas know about the opportunity to submit third-generation Texas recipes; to Linda Wolff, for lending me copies of the two Texas Settlement Region cookbooks she edited; to reporter Manuella Libardi of the *Beaumont*

Enterprise, for solving the mystery of the origin of Jailhouse Rolls; to Anne Popolizio, for translating Italian ingredients and refining recipes; to Patsy Weiser, for helping procure the Wild Mustang Grape Wine recipe; and to Joyce Bise, executive director of the Texas Wendish Heritage Museum, for linking me with Hattie Schautschick, who contributed the recipe for Wendish Noodles.

On a broader scale, I'm grateful to the Texas A&M University Press staff, especially TAMUP director Shannon Davies and associate editor Patricia Clabaugh, for their expertise in producing this book, as well as their enthusiasm throughout the process. I'm particularly indebted to my copyeditor, Cynthia Lindlof, for her careful, respectful editing and skillful handling of the manuscript.

I am also grateful to my family and friends for their steadfast support. My mother, Helen McKey, provided a number of family photographs, as well as frequent encouragement. Long before I started writing this book, she taught me that the most important ingredient in any recipe is the care that goes into making it. My sister Laura McKey also deserves special mention. The booklet she compiled for the 1997 McKey reunion, McKey Stories, is the source of two stories adapted and included here. She has also been my genealogical touchstone in sorting out my own family recipes. My other sister, Becky Braddock, found my late aunt Thelma's chess pie recipe among a forgotten collection of letters and photos and encouraged her daughter to make it, in addition to testing several recipes herself. My brother, Doyle McKey, volunteered to sample my first attempt at testing Mama's Green Grape Cobbler, which unfortunately included hard seeds because I picked the mustang grapes too late that year. (He "ate around the seeds" and pronounced the dessert a winner anyway.) An ecology professor when he's not taste-testing, he also helped immeasurably with proofreading. Special appreciation goes to fellow writer and friend Linda Ellis, who has been a source of inspiration and advice from the onset of this project.

Saving the best for last, I'm eternally grateful to my son, Clay Eads, for his help with photo editing, graphic-design advice, and computer expertise (some of which he patiently provided during the last half of Super Bowl 2015), and most of all, for believing in me. No matter what happens in my life, Son, you make the journey worthwhile.

Recipe Contributors

Margaret Martin Beabout

Elizabeth "Liz" Henneke Boenig

Courtney Crawford Braddock

Kaitlyn "Kaitie" Marie Braddock

Karey Patterson Bresenhan

Nicholas Carona, Rachel Carona Fishback, and Jennifer Carona Phelan

Sylvia Cásares

Cathy "CC" Moore Chaloupka

Lareatha Honette "Nette" Clay

Brandy Bresenhan Craig

Cynthia "Cindy" Robinson English

Geneva Allen Finstad

Irma Soto Galvan

Toni McCloskey Gustafson

Wilma Dell Strickland Halbert

Tasha Harper-Werner

Stephen Harrigan

Jill Mickelson Henderson

Nadine "Dee" Vernell Rosenberg Henneke

Cheryl Ann Hertz

Kate Martin Howell

Sarah Joy Emerson Huebel

Anne Shannon Lewis Isham

Stacy Shanafelt Johnson and Marianne Shanafelt Hudiburg

Jenny Lynn Paul Kier

Danny Koop
Genevieve "Genny" Agnes Scheel Kraus
Mary Alice Graves Liles
Janet "Jan" Pritchett Litvin
Randy Mallory
Kathleen Shanafelt Martin
Meredith McClain
Nola McKey (author)
Julia Ann Huddleston Moseley
Peggie Elizabeth Hogan Moseley
Linda Frances Hill Mozisek
Otto Franklin Mozisek Jr.
Harold Odom Jr.
Camille Parmesan
Jean Evelyn Matula Paul
Nancy Walters Powell
Nancy Helen O'Bryant Puentes
Jeri Lyn Rieken-Speer
Kathryn Nell Roberts

Bob Ruggiero Jr.
Peggy Sterling Scarborough
Janice Lloyd Schacherl and Josie Lloyd Davis
Hattie Mitschke Schautschick
David Schnitz
Jean Granberry Schnitz
Julie Catherine Puentes Schrab
Amy Grones Snelgrove
Candy Spaulding
Cheryl Jean "CJ" Stephenson
Shannon Smith Stilwell
Tracy Becker Thronburg
Toni Hamilton Tipton-Martin
Lucy Brianna Wu Weberlein
Denver Lee Weiser
Suzanne Marie Halbert Wohleb
Vada Marie Morton Wolter
Anna Volkmer Zahn

Ancestor Cooks

*Stella Baker Dolen Becker
*Bertha Lee Hester Bustin
Mary Elois Kelly Bresenhan
Lillian Piazza Cappello
Gwen Provost Carona
Rosa "Rose" Catalina Carona
Margaret Ann Abercrombie Carroll
Sara Isassi Cásares
Savannah Barnes Clark
Onie Lee Johnson Cooper
Carolyn Tate Drum
Annie Owens Dunbar
*Ima McKey Fenner
Frankie Jones Gerhard
Noelie Marie Hebert Gilbert
Edith "Egy" Nolting Karoline Glaeser Goodrich
Mary Francis Parker Graves
Artie Metia Collier Greenhill
Brigid Snoga Gwosdz
Lucille Lucy Aletha Crider Harrison
Augusta Margeta Kneupper Heitkamp
Rosa Karow Henneke
Elsie Mae Brice Hill

Lorene Scott Hulse

Edythe Shafer Jackson

Ellen Sprott Kelly

Karrina "Carrie" Swenson Knudson

*Annie Dusek Kossa

Agnes Mary Ploch Kosub

Dorothy McCarter Martin

Averil Babb McCarter

Rita Cook McClain

Bessie Kolonko McClosky

Anna Earle Armstrong McCreight

Ailcy Elizabeth "Bessie" Hall McKey

Authemia "Tennie" Brown McKey

Helen Smiles Jones McKey

Lillie Loucindy Lee McKey

Anna Mattijehtz Mitschke

Estelle Reese Morton

Josef Mozisek

Addie Jane Lewis Odom

Rose Mortellaro Parmesan

Emily Novosad Patek

Myrtle Augusta Loomis Patterson

Ruby S. Patterson

Honora Sloma Paul

Ella Wilhelmina Glaeser Pearce

Glenda Hulse Pope

Kunigunda "Kuni" Schirmer Rieken

Bertha Heitkamp Rosenberg

Jerusha "Jo" Love Clark Schnitz

Dora Belle Lee Scudder

Adolph Charles "A. C." Sevcik

Anastasia Caroline Svetlik Sevcik

Bessie Hackney Shanafelt

Thelma Ulala West Shannon

Lena Belle Hill Shelton

Betty White Smith

Juanita Cruz Soto

Hilda "Jack" Ross Spencer

Minnie Frances McKey Smith Spittler

Marie Sophie Victoire Lebel Commins Stewart

Alpha Mae McLendon Amerine Stone

Claudia Stripling Strickland

Dora Ann Love Stripling

Mildred Faye Jones Tipton

*Maggie Verena Carroll Tucker

Hulda Pfeuffer Weidner

*Ethel Juanita Hunter Weiss

Melissa Alice Autrey West

Baird Dorothea Jackson Wheat

Hettie Louise Hoffman Wiede

Thelma McKey Williams

Thalia Pauline Pearson Chasteen Windham

Lucia "Lucy" Ching-On Lee Wu

Caroline Barak Zeman

*Photo not available

From Tea Cakes to Tamales

Stirring Up Memories

For most families, the links to generations past are few and somewhat tenuous: DNA, at least in the case of biological families. Surnames, usually, but not always. Given names, sometimes (bestowed in honor of ancestors the namesakes may never meet). Faded photographs. Perhaps a few antiques. Tombstones in a distant plot . . .

In some families, however, the ties that bind include a vibrant connection, one they celebrate often: food. The food of their parents and grandparents and, for a rare few, of generations before that. As family members savor dishes associated with their ancestors, they're linked to the past in a tangible way, through the taste, smell, and texture of food.

I've always been intrigued by old family recipes, but it was a surprise visit from my late grandmother that inspired the idea for this book. Let me explain.

One evening some twenty years ago, my then-eight-year-old son announced that he needed a "traditional family dish" to take to school (the next day) for a class project. I hadn't thought about Grandma McKey's tea cakes in years, but my son's homework assignment brought them to mind immediately.

When I was growing up, Grandma always had a supply of these soft, not-so-sweet cookies on hand when my family visited her house in the country near Sublime in Lavaca County. She kept the tea cakes in a ceramic container on the table, right next to the spoon jar, and I could have one whenever I liked, whether it was between meals or not. They weren't the fanciest cookies, but even then I understood that their dependable presence in Grandma's modest home was a symbol of love.

One of the smarter things I've done in my life was to copy down some of Grandma's recipes while she was still alive. I found the card titled "Grandma's Old-Fashioned Tea Cakes" in my recipe box, unused since I had filed it away in the 1960s. I began mixing up the ingredients, and it wasn't long before I got a whiff of *memories*. Baking the cookies brought more. It felt like a visit from Grandma, especially after we sampled the tea cakes—thick, pillowy, with a hint of lemon—just the way I remembered them. I could almost see Grandma standing in the kitchen with her long braid coiled at the back of her head and her apron tied around the waist of her long-sleeved, print dress.

I later learned that the sensation I experienced isn't uncommon. People often describe this type of involuntary memory as "Proustian," a reference to early twentieth-century French writer Marcel Proust's detailed description of suddenly being carried back to his childhood upon tasting a madeleine (*Remembrance of Things Past*, 1913–1927). I also learned that there's a logical explanation for this phenomenon—scientists have long known that scents can trigger powerful memories, especially nostalgic or emotional memories. Because the senses of taste and smell are intertwined, it's not surprising that the tea cakes rekindled fond memories of my beloved grandmother. No matter; the mechanics are unimportant. The seed was planted.

I began reflecting on the significance of heirloom recipes and the power they have to link us to past generations. I wondered how many people were cooking with recipes that had been passed down through their families. Wouldn't it be amazing to honor those cooks and their ancestors and at the same time encourage others to keep their own family culinary traditions alive? Flash-forward a couple of decades— after raising my son and saying good-bye to a satisfying career in journalism, the idea still intrigued me, and I began working on the book in earnest.

Three Generations and Counting

When I began collecting recipes, I opted not to include those that had merely been passed down from one generation to the next. That was too easy; the recipes hadn't proved their staying power. I decided to include only third-generation (and older) recipes, which I defined as recipes that had been passed down from a grandparent, a great-aunt, or a great-uncle, or their counterparts in earlier generations. I included in-laws in the criteria, too.

Marie Denis Hebert cradles her great-granddaughter Peggy Ann Sterling, with Peggy's mother (right), Lillie Mae Gilbert Sterling, and her grandmother Noelie Marie Hebert Gilbert. Courtesy of Peggy Scarborough.

The third-generation minimum requirement has several things going for it. First, recipes that have lasted at least three generations are time-tested and usually represent some tasty dishes. Second, those recipes usually have some interesting stories associated with them, and I wanted to collect the stories as well as the recipes. Third, those recipes often represent links to a family's ethnic roots— sometimes the last remaining links—and I wanted the cookbook to reflect a broad spectrum of cultures.

The Texas Connection

I admit it—I'm a bit of a chauvinist when it comes to my native state. In the 1980s, I lived in Alabama for two years, thought it was beautiful, enjoyed many things about it, liked the people there, and was homesick the entire time. Coming back home and eventually working for *Texas Highways*, "the official travel magazine of Texas," for eighteen years only reinforced my bias. Simply put, my roots are here. So I added two other requirements for the recipes—the contributors must live in Texas, and the "ancestor cooks" must have lived in the state at some time during their lives. I figured this would ensure that most recipe/story combos offered a little slice of Texas history.

To document the generational and Texas links, I devised a common format for the recipe pages: (1) at the top of each recipe, some brief information about the ancestor cook (full name, year of birth and year of death [if deceased], and all the Texas counties in which he or she lived or has lived to date); (2) immediately following the recipe, a few details about the contributor (full name, relationship to the ancestor cook, and the Texas county in which he or she resides today); and (3) following these details, stories or anecdotes relating to the recipe, the ancestor cook, or family history. I hoped having this template in place would allow readers to grasp the historical context and family connections at a glance.

Picturing the Past

To make the stories come alive, I requested that contributors send me photos of the ancestor cooks. In most cases, they sent copies, but several trusted me with their original family photographs, which I promptly scanned and then returned. I wasn't sure how many photos I would receive—after all, the contributors had to go to some trouble to do this—but I eventually obtained a photo for all but six of the ancestors.

The diversity of the photos I received surprised and delighted me. They range from snapshots taken outdoors to formal portraits created in a studio. Some photos were taken when the ancestors were young and show period dress, accessories, and hairstyles. Others were taken when the subjects were older, their wrinkled faces testimony to their years. In some cases, the only photo available included other family members, so those are in the mix, too. One of my favorites includes the family dog.

Expanding the Search

When I began my quest, I turned first to family and friends, who generously contributed recipes, stories, and photos. However, I wanted a collection that represented all parts of Texas and a variety of foodways, so I widened my search. I enlisted the help of Jo Ann Andera at the

University of Texas at San Antonio (UTSA) Institute of Texan Cultures (ITC). Since 1981, Jo Ann has directed the annual Texas Folklife Festival, which involves volunteers from more than forty cultural groups. Thanks to her contacts, I found many contributors eager to share their culinary heritage.

I contacted other groups and talked to friends of friends and eventually amassed a collection of 104 recipes, which includes not only third-generation recipes, but also fourth-, fifth-, and sixth-generation Texas recipes. (A few of the contributors can trace their recipes even further back, to a time before the first generation arrived in the state.) There's an additional recipe in the third chapter from a grandmother who *almost* made it to Texas but stopped short of the Red River. When you read the backstory, you'll understand why I included it.

Amelia (Emily) Marie Margaret Danish Kossa Moore and her granddaughter Katharina Marie Chaloupka. Courtesy of Cathy "CC" Moore Chaloupka.

A Sampling of Watercolors

Not long after I began work on the cookbook, my friend and former professor Cora (Kandi) McKown offered to provide watercolor illustrations for some of the recipes. I happen to love watercolors, so I took her up on the offer right away. Her thirty-nine images provide a splash of color in contrast to the black-and-white photos that populate most of the book. Best of all, Kandi's spare, allusive style suggests rather than defines the dishes, in keeping with the historical theme.

Definitions, Details, and Other Disclaimers

As mentioned earlier, my intent was to present recipes that represent a broad swath of Texas cultures, and more than a dozen ethnic groups are included (fifteen if you allow both Scotch-Irish and Scottish). While that's a respectable showing, it's only a fraction of the ethnicities found in Texas.

Definitions of "ethnic group" vary, so most researchers shy away from citing an exact number. The UTSA Institute of Texan Cultures features twenty-six different cultures and ethnic groups on its main exhibit floor. However, Sarah Gould, lead curatorial researcher with the ITC, notes that the number of ethnic groups in Texas has grown substantially since the ITC opened in 1968. "This was only a few years after the 1965 immigration law overhaul that opened our nation's doors to immigrants from Central and South America, Asia, and Africa," she says. "Thus, our exhibit floor is missing many, many ethnic groups that have become important to Texas. These include Vietnamese, Nigerians, Saudis, Filipinos, Koreans, South Asian Indians, Pakistanis, Colombians, Iranians, Brazilians, Peruvians, and on and on.

"I hope that we will soon undertake the enormous task of reinventing our main exhibit floor to be more inclusive of Texas' greatly diverse population," she adds. "In the meantime, the monthly naturalization ceremonies held at the ITC offer a more accurate picture. These ceremonies welcome new US citizens from almost every country in the world to Texas. For example, in the 2014 ceremonies alone, more than one hundred countries were represented."

While third-generation Texas descendants may be in short supply or nonexistent in families who hail from some of these countries, no doubt there are many heirloom Texas recipes not associated with the fifteen ethnic groups included here; those await discovery.

Most of the recipes in the book make no claim of belonging to any particular culture. (Maybe they were never associated with the family's ethnic roots. Or maybe they were at one time but lost their cultural identity somewhere along the way.) While the origins of some recipes were clear, others were difficult to categorize. Is a cold-oven pound cake (Vanilla, Butter, and Nut Pound Cake) once made by a Polish ancestor representative of the traditional Polish pound cake even if the descendant who makes it today doesn't connect it with her heritage? Is Apple Strudel a Czech or German recipe? People in both groups make strudels, as do those in other cultures. Is Sicilian Pizza an example of Sicilian cuisine, or should it fall in the Italian camp? I decided to go with the recipe contributor's assessment and label the recipe accordingly. In most cases of dueling ethnicities, the recipe was associated with the ancestor cook's country of origin or ancestry, which trumped any other factor.

Another interesting issue arose in the case of categorizing the recipe for Purple Hull Peas from an African American contributor. Should it be labeled African American when my (white) family also enjoyed purple hull peas and our grandmothers' methods of preparing them were virtually the same? In the end, I decided the answer was yes. Purple hull peas, as well as black-eyed peas, are varieties of cowpea, a species native to Africa that came to America through the slave trade.

Chapter 1

Latecomers and Indigenous Peoples

In striving for a diverse mix of ethnic groups, I learned that some groups, such as Chinese Americans and Asian groups in general, haven't been in Texas as long as others, so the pool of third-generation cooks is simply more limited. Marilyn Dell Brady writes in *The Asian Texans* (Texas A&M University Press, 2004) that the first influx of Asians didn't arrive in Texas until 1870, when they came to work on the railroads. (Even after 1870, immigration laws in effect during various periods of the nation's history restricted the number of Asians that could come to the United States.)

Conversely, American Indians—another broad group of underrepresented cultures—were in Texas long before any other groups arrived. James M. Smallwood writes in *The Indian Texans* (Texas A&M University Press, 2004), "Over the centuries, at least forty different tribes have resided within the borders of Texas. Each had its own unique culture. . . . As distinct cultural groups, some tribes did not survive into the twentieth century." He cites several reasons for this, including warring Indian tribes and new diseases brought by the first Europeans that killed thousands. In addition, he writes, "As pioneers from the United States began moving into the area that became Texas, they claimed more and more Indian land. The settlers and the government's Indian policy almost destroyed the many vibrant native cultures. They forced several tribes to leave Texas and move into the Indian Territory, today's Oklahoma, while others moved to Mexico."

While third-generation Texas recipes associated with these groups exist, they're more difficult to find. After several failed attempts at locating a third-generation Chinese American who cooked with an heirloom recipe, I felt fortunate to finally find a contributor who submitted her grandmother's recipe for Fried Rice.

The Asian Texans and *The Indian Texans* are part of a five-book set, Texans All, produced by the UTSA Institute of Texan Cultures and published by Texas A&M University Press. The other books in the series are *The Mexican Texans*, *The European Texans*, and *The African American Texans*. Each offers insights into the state's diverse cultures.

In sorting this out, I was reminded that many dishes thought of as "soul food" are also representative of dishes widely consumed throughout the South. Increasingly, culinary historians are advancing the case that African American cooks working in the kitchens of their slave masters influenced Southern cuisine to a far greater extent than has been acknowledged. Longtime food journalist Mark H. Zanger writes in *The American Ethnic Cookbook for Students* (Oryx Press, 2001), "Because Africans had more experience with hot-climate farming and produce than their French or English masters, and were plantation cooks during and after slavery, they developed much of what is now thought of as southern regional cooking."

The problems associated with classifying dishes by ethnic groups aside, readers will no doubt notice certain idiosyncrasies in these recipes. For example, going against all the accepted rules of recipe writing, many of the titles include not only proper names but also pet names, such as Maw-Maw, NanNan, Bomo, Momo, GMommy, and Memommie, in addition to the usual variations of Grandmother and Grandma. Sometimes the names add confusion, as in the case of Mama and Big Mama. Aren't these supposed to be at least *third-generation* recipes? Well, it turns out that in some families, those *are* grandmother or great-grandmother names. I opted to keep the names in the title because to the families represented, those names are an integral part of the recipe and they're often repeated in the stories that follow it. To save confusion, I added the pet name in parentheses after the ancestor cook's name at the top of the recipe unless it was the standard "Grandma" or "Grandmother." (For whatever reasons, the grandfathers didn't have pet names.)

Journalists will note that I refer to both recipe contributors and ancestor cooks by their first names. This was a matter of practicality as well as tone—using last names would simply have been too complicated.

Cookbook enthusiasts may also notice the use of brand names in some recipes, considered bad form by most food writers. However, when brand loyalty appeared to be important to either the ancestor cook or the contributor, as in the case of Crisco or "Slap Ya Mama" Cajun Seasoning, I let the brand names stand.

Likewise, some cooks may notice that the procedures given in the recipes are all over the map. For example, the five different tea cake recipes included list three different methods of mixing up the dough. Best practice in food writing would be to adjust the recipes so that the

Three Generations: Leon and Agnes Kosub (middle couple in top row) with their children, their married children's spouses, and their grandchildren. Courtesy of Genny Kraus.

procedures are the same. However, I chose not to make any changes in the recipes except when changes were needed for clarity or to adjust the basic format for consistency.

Sometimes it was tempting to veer away from this hands-off policy, as in the case of Momo's Caldo. Like most stews, it's cooked in one pot, which allows the flavors to meld. And in the case of this caldo recipe at least, all of the vegetables are put into the pot at the same time as the meat and everything is cooked for two hours, or until the meat is tender. A modern recipe would call for adding the vegetables toward the end, so that their color and texture don't suffer. However, the flavor wouldn't be the same, and it certainly wouldn't be the same recipe that the contributor's grandmother once made.

With that in mind, I recommend reading through each recipe carefully before making it in case it involves a process that's new to you. Also note the traditional recipe style (in keeping with the traditional recipes) — it's assumed that readers know to look within the instructions to find out the size of the pan and how to prepare it beforehand, at what point to preheat the oven, and that all spices are ground unless otherwise noted.

Finally, there's the matter of the disproportionate number of dessert recipes in the book. This reflects what I found while collecting the recipes: Dessert recipes are more prevalent than any other type of heirloom recipe.

Perhaps ancestor cooks just didn't bother to write down the recipes for dishes they prepared every day. Or perhaps the reason is the formula-like nature of desserts; other types of recipes are more forgiving. At any rate, our ancestors took pride in making special desserts and were often identified with certain ones. These dishes were likely passed down to family members more often.

Concluding Thoughts

Compiling this cookbook involved a number of difficulties, especially in gathering and confirming details about family history with sixty-five contributors. However, along the way, I tasted some delicious food, learned how to make classic dishes from dirty rice to dumplings, heard some fascinating stories, and made new friends. (Several contributors shared experiences they had while making an ancestor's signature dish, echoing my experience while baking my grandmother's tea cakes. One contributor even sent me a package of *his* grandmother's tea cakes.) I also learned some new things about my family, including the fact that my great-grandmother was a midwife, that one aunt specialized in making cakes while another's forte was pies, and that my mother's Jailhouse Rolls really did originate in a jailhouse kitchen.

On another level, this project has allowed me to explore one of my favorite topics—the traditions that connect food and family. Some of the things I've learned are specific to Texas—like the recipe for Brisket with Chuckwagon Hollandaise and the fact that one of the best places to find ribbon cane syrup is at Henderson's annual Heritage Syrup Festival. However, I've also learned about dishes that emigrants brought from foreign lands that are still reflected in the foodways of today—Wendish noodles, Mexican caldo, Sicilian pizza, Norwegian rosettes, and many more. Each of these dishes endures because someone bothered to preserve a family recipe. I feel even more passionately now about the importance of preserving these special heirlooms.

As a result of writing this book, I also have new respect for the cooks in previous generations who often had few resources to draw on yet managed to prepare satisfying, delicious food that their descendants still savor today. The following recipes testify to this ability and to the importance of preserving a family's culinary heritage.

If you'd like to share your
heirloom Texas recipes
and stories, see
www.Nola-McKey.com

2

Recipes

*Whether typed neatly on an index card, written on the back
of an envelope, or scribbled on a scrap of paper, an heirloom
recipe has magical powers: It allows you to re-create a loved
one's signature dish after that person is gone. Taken a step
further, an heirloom recipe is a link to a legacy, one that lives
on when a cook in the present generation makes the same dish
that a departed cook prepared decades earlier.*

Breads

Mama Smith's Cornbread

You'll need a large cast-iron skillet to make this scrumptious bread. (A cast-iron cornbread wedge pan or cornstick pan also works, but you'll have to cut the recipe in half or bake two separate batches.) Don't bother looking for the fat in the recipe; there isn't any except for the vegetable oil that greases the skillet. You're on your own, however, when it comes to adding butter once a chunk of hot cornbread lands on your plate.

Vegetable oil
Sprinkling of stone-ground yellow cornmeal
Additional 1½ cups stone-ground yellow cornmeal
½ cup unbleached flour
1 tablespoon baking powder
1 teaspoon baking soda
¼ teaspoon salt
1 egg, beaten
2 cups buttermilk
Butter or margarine

Preheat oven to 450°F. Coat the bottom and sides of a 10-inch cast-iron skillet with vegetable oil; sprinkle liberally with cornmeal. Place skillet in the oven and lightly brown cornmeal while mixing up the batter.

Mix dry ingredients with a whisk. Add egg and buttermilk and stir thoroughly. Pour mixture into the hot skillet. Return skillet to hot oven and cook 15 to 20 minutes, or until top is brown and crisp. Serve with butter or margarine. *Makes 8 large servings*

Contributed by Randy Mallory
Betty White Smith's grandson
Smith County

Betty White Smith (Mama Smith)
1886–1985
Van Zandt and Smith Counties

Betty White Smith. Courtesy of Randy Mallory.

*R*andy says he has made this cornbread for twenty years, five to six times per year, especially in the spring and summer, when he and his wife, Sallie, enjoy it with fresh peas, squash, cantaloupe, and other local fare.

Originally an unwritten recipe that Randy's grandmother (Mama Smith) probably learned from her mother, the written version of this cornbread was developed in the 1970s by Randy's mother, Betty Ruth Smith Mallory (Nanee), who made notes as she observed Randy's grandmother making it. "This is Southern 'soul food' for whites and blacks," says Randy, adding that his grandmother added chitlins when they were available, but for reasons of health, the family doesn't add chitlins today.

Chitlins may have fallen out of favor, but another tradition has evolved over the years that dictates the way the cornbread is removed from the skillet. "Once it's done," explains Randy, "you tap the opposite edge of the skillet from the handle on a wooden cutting board, and the whole shebang pops right out (as there's so much lube on the bottom) . . . pretty classy . . . [that sound] tells everybody that 'cornbread's ready.'

"When my mother makes cornbread, all other items on the menu are prepared and waiting on the table as she takes out the hot cornbread . . . and only when perfectly browned," he continues. "Waiting on the cornbread is a long-standing tradition in my family. It is the ultimate comfort food for me and my brother and sister."

Use a heavy oven mitt when handling a hot cast-iron skillet.

Some people inherit not only their grandparents' recipes but also the cast-iron pots and pans—Dutch ovens, skillets, cornbread pans—they used to prepare them. If you're lucky enough to acquire such an heirloom, don't despair if it seems worse for wear. Cast-iron cookware is resilient and can usually be rescued with a little elbow grease. (See restoration instructions at www. lodgemfg.com.) That rusty relic may become your favorite piece of kitchen equipment.

Crispy Cornbread

This is a flat cornbread, so it's naturally a little crisp. To make it extra crisp, flip it over in the pan when it's done and return it to the oven for a few minutes more. Pair it with a bowl of beans, chili, or beef stew, and you've got a complete meal.

1 cup yellow cornmeal
1 teaspoon baking powder
¼ teaspoon soda
½ teaspoon salt
1 egg, beaten
1 cup buttermilk
Vegetable oil
Butter

Mix dry ingredients. Stir in egg and buttermilk and mix well.

Lightly coat the bottom and sides of an 8-inch cast-iron skillet or baking pan with vegetable oil and heat until very hot. Pour off excess vegetable oil or add to mixture, if desired, and mix well. Pour mixture into hot cast-iron skillet or pan. Bake at 400°F about 20 minutes or until browned. Serve hot with butter. *Makes about 6 servings*

Contributed by Courtney Crawford Braddock
Lorene Scott Hulse's great-granddaughter
Tarrant County

When Courtney had to switch to a gluten-free diet several years ago, she found she really missed cornbread. Her grandmother remembered that the cornbread recipe Courtney's great-grandmother (Mama) had used didn't include flour, so she sent it to her to try. "I loved it," says Courtney. "Most cornbread mixes and recipes have at least a little flour in them, but not this one. It meant I could eat cornbread again."

Fresh buttermilk is best, but keep the powdered variety in the pantry to use when you don't have fresh on hand. Or fall back on the old standby: 1 tablespoon vinegar stirred into 1 cup milk is the equivalent of 1 cup buttermilk.

Lorene Scott Hulse (Mama)

1901–1999

Lamb and Lubbock Counties

Lorene Scott Hulse. Courtesy of Courtney Braddock.

Annie Dusek Kossa
1898–1972
Fayette County

Grandma Kossa's Homemade Bread (CZECH)

Baking bread is not a skill learned overnight; expect to experiment a few times before you get it right. The good news: When it comes to homemade bread, even the failures are delicious hot from the oven, sliced thick, and slathered with butter.

1 tablespoon sugar
2½ (2-ounce) compressed yeast cakes
1½ cups warm water
1 tablespoon melted Crisco
About 5 cups flour
Pinch of salt
Additional Crisco
Melted butter

Combine sugar and yeast with water in a large bowl and stir until dissolved. Add melted shortening, flour, and salt, mixing well. Turn dough out onto a well-floured surface and knead until smooth and elastic (about 5 minutes). Grease bowl well with Crisco and place kneaded dough in it, turning to grease top. Cover with a damp cloth and let rise in a warm area until doubled in bulk (usually no more than 30 minutes, depending on climate and humidity).

Punch dough down, turn out onto a floured surface, and knead four or five times. Replace dough in greased bowl, turning to grease top, cover, and let it rise a second time until doubled in bulk, about 30 minutes.

Divide dough in half and place each half in a 9 x 5-inch greased loaf pan. Grease tops of dough with Crisco and allow to rise about 30 minutes, or until doubled in bulk. Bake at 400°F for no more than 45 minutes (watch the color of the crust carefully). Remove bread from pans immediately; cool on wire rack. Brush tops of loaves with butter. *Makes 2 loaves*

Contributed by Cathy "CC" Moore Chaloupka
Annie Dusek Kossa's granddaughter
Fayette County

Chapter 2: Recipes

CC says this is a common recipe in many old Czech families. She estimates that at least two generations of the Kossa family made the bread before her grandmother did. The Kossa (originally "Koza," meaning goat herders) family has been in Texas since 1856 and helped found Dubina in southern Fayette County, the first Czech-Moravian community in Texas. "The bread was used daily in Czech-Moravian culture," says CC, "because the members were predominantly poor cotton farmers who didn't have a lot of money for food."

CC's mother, Amelia (Emily) Marie Margaret Danish Kossa Moore, also made this bread. "My dad and I would always finish the loaf before it got cool – fighting for the ends as well," says CC. "I've been making it for decades, but it's never as good as hers was." Today another baker is coming up in the ranks. CC's eight-year-old daughter, Katharina Marie Chaloupka, is already making her own pastries from scratch. She also speaks a little Czech. "My husband, David, and I intend to make sure she remembers her heritage," says CC.

Listed on the National Register of Historic Places, the Historic Dubina District includes Sts. Cyril and Methodius Catholic Church, one of four "painted churches" in Fayette County. With its central bell tower and exquisitely embellished sky-blue ceiling, the church still lies at the center of community life, and the church's annual parish picnic (the first Sunday in July) offers visitors plenty of opportunities to experience Czech culture. The picnic's headliner is fried chicken, but you'll also find Czech sausage and sauerkraut (served over mashed potatoes!), as well as pivo (beer) and kolaches. Polka dancing chases away the calories. Call 979–725–6714 for details.

For a guided tour of all four painted churches and other area tours – including one called "Kolaches, Kollections, Kuisine, and Kulture" – contact CC at Rural Texas Tourism, LLC at cc@cvctx.com or 979–561–6667. Having a fifth-generation Fayette County native as a guide adds a special dimension to tours.

Baking times and temperatures vary depending on your oven. The first time you make a bread recipe, watch carefully when the loaf begins to brown. You may want to make some adjustments the next time you bake it.

The opportunities to learn about Czech culture abound in Texas. Many Catholic churches throughout the state have an annual parish picnic (or two) similar to that of Sts. Cyril and Methodius Catholic Church in Dubina. In addition, there are multiple polka, kolache, and sausage festivals at which you can enjoy Czech cuisine.

The Texas Czech Heritage and Cultural Center in La Grange, an expansive complex that includes a museum, library, amphitheater, and "Czech village," offers a number of events, including a Heritage Fest & Muziky in October. The celebration features polka bands, dancing, heritage demonstrations, and plenty of Czech food. Call 888-785-4500 or 979-968-9399 or see www.czechtexas.org.

The Czech Center Museum Houston features exhibits and events devoted to showcasing aspects of traditional Czech culture, including food. Call 713-528-2060 or see www.czechcenter.org.

Hot Rolls

A 10-inch cast-iron skillet works perfectly for this recipe, but you can use a round cake pan as well.

1 (0.25-ounce) package Fleischmann's RapidRise Yeast
   or other instant active dry yeast
⅓ cup sugar, divided
1 cup lukewarm water
2 tablespoons vegetable oil
2¾ cups flour, divided
1 teaspoon salt
Additional vegetable oil

Mix yeast, 1½ tablespoons of the sugar, and water together in a small bowl; allow mixture to stand a few minutes, or until bubbles begin forming on top.

Stir vegetable oil and remaining sugar into yeast mixture; set aside.

Measure 2¼ cups of the flour into a large bowl and stir in salt. Form a well in the center and pour the liquid mixture into it. Stir until mixture forms a soft dough. Allow dough to rise about an hour, or until doubled in size.

Pour remaining ½ cup flour onto a sheet of waxed paper and place dough on top. Knead dough only until it can be handled. The dough should be very soft. Do not add too much flour. Form dough into 10 round rolls and place in a generously greased pan or skillet. Grease tops of rolls with vegetable oil. Allow rolls to rise about 30 minutes, or until doubled in size. Bake at 350°F for about 25 minutes or until rolls are browned. *Makes 10 rolls*

Contributed by Peggie Elizabeth Hogan Moseley
Maggie Verena Carroll Tucker's granddaughter
Jefferson County

Maggie Verena Carroll Tucker

1892–1963

Cherokee and Sabine Counties

Peggie has been baking these rolls for more than forty-five years, and she's made few changes during that time. The original recipe called for cake yeast, but she uses the RapidRise dry yeast instead. She also uses vegetable oil instead of the original melted shortening. She emphasizes that it's important to keep the dough very soft. "These are undoubtedly the lightest rolls that I have ever eaten," she says, "but too much flour will make them heavy."

Peggie suspects that her grandmother found the recipe in a newspaper or magazine. "She was an excellent cook, and she was always clipping recipes," she adds. "I make this recipe about four times a month, for family meals as well as for holidays and birthdays. [It] has been a family favorite for three generations. When we start a meal and have these rolls, someone always asks, 'Are these Grandma's rolls?'"

Helen Smiles Jones McKey

Born in 1923

Nueces, Matagorda, Wharton, Lavaca, Harris, Victoria, and Jackson Counties

Helen Smiles Jones McKey. Courtesy of Helen McKey.

Jailhouse Rolls

Plan to mix up the dough for these no-knead rolls a day ahead. If you like, save some dough so that you can have fresh rolls another time. (Keep the dough refrigerated and use it within a few days.)

1 (0.25-ounce) package active dry yeast
1½ cups lukewarm water
1 cup cooked, mashed potatoes (requires 2 to 3 potatoes)
1 cup butter or margarine, melted and cooled
3 eggs
1 cup sugar
1½ teaspoons salt
7 cups flour
Additional melted butter or margarine

Stir yeast into 1½ cups lukewarm water to dissolve and set aside. Combine mashed potatoes, butter, eggs, sugar, and salt in a large bowl and mix well. Blend in flour. Add yeast mixture and mix well. Place dough in a large, greased bowl, cover with a damp cloth, and place in the refrigerator overnight.

Chapter 2: Recipes

Turn dough out onto a floured surface and roll out to ½-inch thickness; cut with a biscuit cutter. Place rolls on 2 lightly greased baking sheets and brush tops with additional melted butter. Cover and let rise for about 3 hours. Bake at 450°F for 10 to 12 minutes, or until golden. *Makes about 4 dozen rolls*

Contributed by Kaitlyn "Kaitie" Marie Braddock
Helen Smiles Jones McKey's granddaughter
Brazoria County

Author's Note: My mother, Helen McKey, has made these rolls for family gatherings for years, delighting both children and adults. It's always fun to watch some of the daintiest eaters in the clan go back for third, fourth, fifth, and even sixth helpings. Last Christmas, two of my nieces, Kaitie Braddock and Jenny McKey (the latter lives in France), decided that Grandma deserved a break and made the rolls themselves, following her recipe. They were a success, and the Jailhouse Rolls tradition lives on.

However, the story doesn't end there. I recently discovered that Jailhouse Rolls have another tradition that has nothing to do with my family. I had always been curious about the origin of the recipe, especially its name, so when I began compiling recipes for this cookbook, I did some sleuthing. I knew the rolls didn't originate with Mother; she had always credited my late aunt Tennie (Authemia McKey), who had lived in Jefferson County, with giving her the recipe. I started with my aunt's immediate family members but had no luck; they had no idea where she had obtained it.

I turned to the Internet, where I saw many references to Jailhouse Rolls but with conflicting stories about their origin. However, all the stories related to Beaumont or Jefferson County, which spurred my interest. One of the Internet sources stated that she had found the recipe in the Beaumont newspaper, so I e-mailed the *Beaumont Enterprise* to see if anyone on staff had the scoop on this bread. No one did, but the newspaper published a brief article asking readers for help in nailing down the origin of Jailhouse Rolls. "When the story ran, we were blown up with calls and e-mails," says reporter Manuella Libardi. "Apparently, [those rolls] were a sensation."

Manuella followed up the next week with a lengthy feature titled "Meet the Woman behind Beaumont's Famous Jailhouse Rolls," complete with several photos of Juanita Ward, who cooked for Beaumont jails (city and county) for almost three decades before retiring in 1992. Manuella reported that Juanita created the recipe shortly after she began working for Willie Bauer, who was chief of police.

According to the September 1, 2014 article, Juanita made the rolls "only on special occasions, usually for grand juries during trials and sometimes for FBI agents. . . . When she had enough leftover dough from those occasions, she baked the rolls for the inmates." The rolls were a hit with jurors, judges, and law-enforcement officers, as well as inmates. Chief Bauer came up with the name "Jailhouse Rolls." After an event featuring the popular bread was televised locally, interest in the recipe mushroomed, and it was passed among cooks across the country. One of those cooks was my aunt, who eventually passed the recipe to my mother. Thanks to an enterprising reporter, I finally know the backstory of my family's Jailhouse Rolls tradition. I suspect that many other families enjoy the same tradition. We're all indebted to Juanita Ward, the cook responsible for Beaumont's legendary rolls.

Granny's Master Mix

This recipe is similar to the original Master Mix developed at Purdue University in 1948. A mixture of premeasured dry ingredients and fat, it keeps for six weeks without refrigeration; you can use it to make a number of breads and desserts in less time than it would take starting from scratch. Recipes for biscuits and muffins follow. (Look for Master Mix recipes for yellow cake/chocolate cake, coffee cake, drop cookies, and gingerbread in the Desserts section.)

5 pounds unsifted flour
2½ cups nonfat dry milk
¾ cup baking powder
3 tablespoons salt
2 tablespoons cream of tartar
½ cup sugar
2 pounds (about 4⅔ cups) vegetable shortening

Combine all ingredients except shortening and sift together in a large bowl. Cut shortening into dry ingredients using a pastry blender until the mixture looks like cornmeal. Place in a tightly covered container and store at room temperature. *Makes about 29 cups of Master Mix*

Contributed by Tasha Harper-Werner
Authemia "Tennie" Brown McKey's granddaughter
Tyler County

asha says she makes a batch of Master Mix about once a week. "It's so versatile," she explains. "You can have a pan of hot, fresh biscuits in under fifteen minutes any night of the week or a fresh scratch cake in a moment's notice. I use it constantly. Every one of my five kids loves the biscuits I make with it. I once used it to make one hundred biscuits, which I took to the local elementary school — along with venison cream gravy — as a teacher-appreciation gift."

A photographer who specializes in children's portraits, Tasha scanned the basic recipe, as well as all its variations, and created a graphic that she had printed onto a canvas. "I hung the canvas on a kitchen cabinet for decoration and easy reference," she adds.

Authemia "Tennie" Brown McKey (Granny)
1921–2010
Lavaca, Hardin, and Tyler Counties

Authemia "Tennie" Brown McKey. Courtesy of Tasha Harper-Werner.

Tasha remembers her granny using the Master Mix to make pancakes, coffee cake, and gingerbread. "Her favorite was the gingerbread," says Tasha, who makes almost all the variations. "My teenage daughters, Hannahjane and Madison, also bake with the mix, so that makes this a fourth-generation recipe."

You can substitute milk for water in all the Master Mix variations for extra richness.

This mix makes an easy gift when paired with a recipe card. Simply place the amount of Master Mix needed in a Mason jar or other container and attach the appropriate recipe. If you like, you can include a baking pan. Wrapping everything up in a colorful dish towel takes it to the next level.

Authemia "Tennie" Brown McKey (Granny)

1921–2010

Lavaca, Hardin, and Tyler Counties

Granny's Master Mix Biscuits

For extra-fluffy biscuits, use milk instead of water and add a couple spoonfuls of sour cream.

3 cups Granny's Master Mix (see Granny's Master Mix recipe)
¾ cup water

Blend ingredients together. Knead 10 strokes. Roll out dough and cut out biscuits (or make drop biscuits) and place on a greased baking sheet. Bake at 450°F for 10 minutes. *Makes 18 biscuits*

Contributed by Tasha Harper-Werner
Authemia "Tennie" Brown McKey's granddaughter
Tyler County

When making biscuits, a light touch is best—stir the mixture just until blended and knead it only a few times. Using a baking sheet as described results in crusty sides, especially if you place the biscuits at least an inch apart. If you want soft sides, place the biscuits close together in a shallow pan.

Granny's Master Mix Muffins

Authemia "Tennie" Brown McKey (Granny)

1921–2010

Lavaca, Hardin, and Tyler Counties

These muffins aren't very sweet by today's standards. If you like a sweet muffin, add an extra ¼ cup sugar.

3 cups Granny's Master Mix (see Granny's Master Mix recipe)
2 tablespoons sugar
1 cup water
1 egg

Combine dry ingredients. Mix water and egg together in a separate bowl and blend with dry ingredients. Spoon into a lightly greased (12-cup) muffin pan, filling ⅔ full. Bake at 425°F for 25 minutes. *Makes 1 dozen muffins*

Contributed by Tasha Harper-Werner
Authemia "Tennie" Brown McKey's granddaughter
Tyler County

Authemia "Tennie" Brown McKey with her husband, Dewey McKey, and their daughter, Pam. Courtesy of Tasha Harper-Werner.

Main Dishes

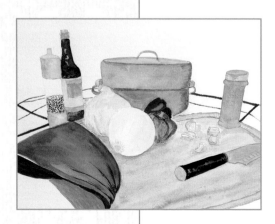

Chicken and Dumplings (POLISH)

For a healthier (but less authentic) dish, use boned and skinned chicken breasts instead of a whole chicken. For extra flavor, add finely chopped celery and carrots, minced garlic, and a little chicken bouillon.

Vegetable oil or bacon grease
1 whole chicken, cut into pieces
1 onion, chopped
Salt and pepper
Vegetable oil or bacon grease
1 cup flour
1 teaspoon salt
1 egg
3 tablespoons milk

Heat a little vegetable oil or bacon grease in a large Dutch oven or stockpot. Add chicken pieces, onion, and salt and pepper to taste. Sauté mixture until chicken has lost its raw appearance. Fill the pot with enough water to cover the chicken; cover and cook over low heat for 1½ to 2 hours, or until chicken is tender. (This recipe derives from a time when older hens and roosters were commonly used in soups and stews; a supermarket fryer requires only 45 minutes to 1 hour to cook.)

Remove chicken pieces, reserving broth. When chicken is cool, remove the meat, discarding skin and bones. When broth is cool, lift off as much fat as possible.

Sift flour and 1 teaspoon salt into a bowl. Mix egg and milk together and add to flour mixture; stir only until combined. Place dough on a floured surface and gently roll out to about ⅛-inch thickness. Cut dough into 2-inch squares. Let the dough rest and dry for 1 to 2 hours.

Bring chicken broth to a rolling boil. Taste and add salt if needed. Drop in dumplings one at a time, being careful not to crowd them (cook in batches), and cook about 10 minutes. Remove cooked dumplings with a slotted spoon and place in a bowl; keep warm. Repeat the process with

Agnes Mary Ploch Kosub
(*Stadeka*)
1883–1947
Bexar and Wilson Counties

Agnes Mary Ploch Kosub. Courtesy of Genny Kraus.

remaining dough. Return cooked chicken and dumplings to stockpot. If broth is too thin, thicken by slowly stirring in a smooth flour-water mixture. *Makes about 6 servings*

Contributed by Genevieve (Genny) Agnes Scheel Kraus
Agnes Mary Ploch Kosub's granddaughter
Bexar County

"*My husband and children love this dish,*" *says Genny.* "*I usually make it when the weather starts to turn cooler or on a cold winter day. On a day like that, there is nothing like a big bowl of chicken and dumplings. This is comfort food.*" *Genny says her grandmother, and later her mother, served the hearty entrée with the chicken pieces left whole rather than remove the skin and bones. Waste not, want not was their attitude.* "*If it was close to Thanksgiving, Mom would save and freeze the gizzards to use in turkey dressing,*" *she adds.* "*Mom would also save some of the chicken fat to flavor the other dishes she made.*

"*I like to cook it one day and serve it the next,*" *Genny continues.* "*The dumplings are even better tasting because they have sat in the wonderful flavored broth overnight.*"

Rolling out the dumplings revives special memories for Genny. "*When I see them drying on the drain board in the kitchen and surrounded by the dusting of flour and the rolling pin lying there, I remember my childhood and the many wonderful family times we had together with all of my aunts and uncles,*" *she says.* "*Our Kosub family was very close. We would celebrate the holidays together, go fishing, have picnics at Uncle Pete's tank, or just sit on the front porch at Papa's house and talk or listen to a baseball game on the radio.*

"*My grandmother and my mom did not write down their recipes. I am sure that my grandmother helped her mother with the cooking at home, and then she taught her daughters. So many of the meals required tons of prep (see Procuring the Chicken). I am sure no one thought of writing it down on paper. The children learn by doing it with their mom. My mother later on in life finally did write down some of her recipes. When I wanted to learn how to cook a dish, she had me watch and cook with her. When you would ask her about quantities, she would just say, 'Oh, it is very simple. You just put in a little of this and a little of that.'*"

Dumplings are hardly exclusive to Polish cuisine, but Polish dishes include diverse examples (rolled flat, drop, and filled), and Genny feels this recipe reflects

Procuring the Chicken

GENNY KRAUS

When I was a little girl in San Antonio, I remember going shopping with my mother to purchase chickens for Grandma and us. Everyone went to Porter's to buy their chickens. It was the neighborhood chicken house that sold fresh live chickens. Porter's would butcher your chicken for you for an additional fee, or you could take it home to kill and butcher it yourself. Taking the chicken home live was our normal routine. . . .

I personally hated going to Porter's. Just seeing all those clucking, white-feathered birds with those beady little eyes just staring at you was a very scary experience for me. Mom and I would walk through Porter's, and she would hold on to my little hand real tight and tell me, "Don't be afraid; they won't hurt you." She would look in each cage, checking out the birds, looking for just the right one. I am not sure what qualities she looked for in the chicken. I was afraid to ask. All I cared about was getting out of there. . . .

We lived next door to my mother's parents. Mom and I would butcher our chickens at Grandma's house. Her place was set up for all types of butchering. . . . Outside by Grandma's back porch, she had a table that had a white porcelain top trimmed in black. I can still see my grandmother and me standing there, plucking all of those chicken feathers. Grandma would tease me about my fear of chickens. But I would just listen and keep plucking because that was my job. . . .

I didn't know it at the time, but that is how you make wonderful family memories. . . . This chore was nothing unusual for its day. It was just a part of the everyday life routine. The end result of all that hard work produced a great-tasting chicken and dumplings for the family dinner table.

her Polish heritage. It's likely that her grandmother learned how to make it from Genny's great-grandmother Josephine Golla Ploch (1841–1921).

Josephine Ploch's biography illustrates the difficulties early Texas settlers faced. According to family records, her family emigrated from Poland in the 1850s and landed in Indianola, where an epidemic was raging. She lost all family members except two brothers. A Mexican family named Casanova took the children to San Antonio and cared for them. Josephine later worked as a housekeeper before meeting Casper Ploch, another Polish immigrant. The couple married in 1860 at San Antonio's San Fernando Cathedral. They had thirteen children, three of whom died as infants, and lived on a farm in La Vernia. Agnes Ploch Kosub was their twelfth child.

A pizza cutter makes cutting dough into dumplings or noodles fast and easy.

Chapter 2: Recipes

Kuni's Homemade Egg Noodles with Chicken (GERMAN)

Kunigunda "Kuni" Schirmer Rieken

1888–1954

Lubbock County

This recipe gets right to the point — the tender, delicious noodles. If you want to take a more traditional route, start by stewing a chicken, which will result in more than enough chicken broth and an ample amount of cooked chicken. Want to make the noodles one day and cook them later? You can store the dried noodles in an airtight plastic bag in the refrigerator for several days before cooking.

2 eggs
Water to fill half-eggshell twice
About 2¼ cups flour
3 (32-ounce) boxes or 7 (14-ounce) cans chicken broth
1½ to 2 cups cooked, chopped chicken (optional)

Break eggs into bowl, *saving best half-eggshell*. Using half-eggshell as your measuring device, add one-half shell of tap water (about 2 tablespoons) per egg. Mix water and eggs together. Stir in flour 1 cup at a time, mixing after each cup; add just enough flour until dough can be rolled out. *The amount of flour depends on the size of the egg.* Mixture will be very thick.

Roll dough into a ball and place it on a floured surface. Using a rolling pin, roll dough as thin as possible into a rectangle and place to dry on a dish towel laid over several layers of newspaper. Let dry for 4 to 5 hours (flip dough occasionally), or until edges of the dough feel dry. The rest of the dough should not be completely dry. If it gets too dry, the noodles will be tough.

Place chicken broth in a Dutch oven or other large pot and bring to a boil. Slice dough into thin strips and drop individually into boiling broth. (You can also roll the dough up into a long roll to slice and then unroll and drop individual strips into boiling broth.) Lower heat and simmer for 25 to 30 minutes, or until noodles reach desired tenderness. Stir in cooked chicken, if desired, and simmer briefly before serving.
Makes 4 generous cups

Kunigunda "Kuni" Schirmer Rieken with her husband, Reiner Rieken. Courtesy of Jeri Rieken-Speer.

Contributed by Jeri Lyn Rieken-Speer
Kunigunda "Kuni" Schirmer Rieken's granddaughter
Lubbock County

eri makes this dish once or twice a year, usually during Thanksgiving and Christmas holidays. "My whole family loves these noodles," she says, "especially my children. My grandmother Rieken – Kuni – died when I was four years old," continues Jeri. "She brought the recipe with her when she emigrated from Germany as a young girl. The story I was told is that she worked as an 'indentured servant' to pay for her passage. Kuni passed this recipe on to her daughter and to her sons' wives, including my mother, Ruth Greenhill Rieken. When I was a child, we had a rotation system among these relatives of going to a different house for Thanksgiving and Christmas. It didn't matter which house or what else was served, noodles were expected!

"I remember my mother and aunts making practically vats of these noodles to feed our German farm family (with lots of big men!). When they ran out of counter space to dry the dough, they'd put dish towels over the backs of dining chairs and hang the rectangles of dough over them. For holidays, Aunt Sis would make one of my cousins a separate potful of noodles, which he would easily consume. At least that way, the rest of us got some, too.

"Kuni made the noodles with chicken or turkey stock from cooking her own birds," Jeri adds. "I use mostly canned broth now. Also, I purchase eggs from the supermarket, and my grandmother had eggs from her own hens."

Another difference is that Jeri usually adds chopped, cooked chicken or roast beef to her noodles. "Sometimes I just open a large can of all-white chicken," she says. Interestingly, Kuni, as well as her daughter and daughters-in-law, rarely mixed noodles or any side dish with meat, though they might pull out a roast turkey, chicken, or ham from the refrigerator to serve with them when it was time for a meal. "Dad and his siblings referred to a casserole or any other dish that involved a mixture of foods as 'slumgullion,'" explains Jeri, "and they wanted no part of it. They preferred that each food be served separately."

Jeri's departure from tradition notwithstanding, Kuni's Homemade Egg Noodles is now a fourth-generation Texas recipe. "My daughter, Amy, has made them for friends and family, and my son, Justin, recently made them for his family," she explains. "I'm hoping one of my grandchildren will make it a fifth-generation recipe."

If making noodles solo sounds overwhelming, invite a few family members to come for the day and make a big batch together. Mix the dough and roll it out in the morning, have sandwiches and snacks for lunch, and then kick back in the afternoon while the dough dries. (At some point, tuck a couple of chickens and some vegetables into the oven to roast for supper.) That evening, slice the dough into strips, cook a steaming pot of flavorful noodles, and retrieve the roasted chicken and vegetables from the oven for a family feast. Spouses and others will likely show up about this time. Afterward, everyone goes home with extra bags of noodles to enjoy later.

The Sauer-Beckmann Farmstead (part of the Lyndon B. Johnson State Park & Historic Site) near Stonewall offers visitors a glimpse of the lives of a Texas-German farm family in the early part of the twentieth century. Wearing period clothing, interpreters perform farm and household chores, from milking and slopping the hogs to churning butter and making lye soap. Daily activities include cooking a meal on a wood-burning stove, with fruits and vegetables grown on the site. Seasonal activities include plowing the garden, butchering, and canning. Special events include a program on holiday cookie decorating and German Christmas traditions in November and a tree-lighting ceremony in December. For details about the site, ongoing programs, and special events, call 830–644–2252; or see http://tpwd.texas.gov/state-parks/lyndon-b-johnson.

Glenda Hulse Pope

Born in 1933

Lubbock, Dallas, and Lamb Counties

Glenda Hulse Pope. Courtesy of Courtney Braddock.

Poppy Seed Chicken

This is a good recipe to make ahead. Combine the ingredients as directed, refrigerate or freeze, and bake later.

1 pound boned and skinned chicken breast halves
Salt
1 (10¾-ounce) can cream of chicken soup
2 cups shredded Monterey Jack cheese
8 ounces sour cream
3 tablespoons poppy seeds, divided
½ cup butter, melted
1½ rolls (about 50) Ritz crackers, crushed

Season chicken breasts lightly with salt (other ingredients will also make the dish salty) and place in a medium saucepan. Cover chicken with water and bring to a boil. Reduce heat to low, partly cover, and simmer for about 20 minutes or until chicken is tender. Remove chicken and set aside, reserving broth for another use.

Combine soup, cheese, sour cream, and 1½ tablespoons of the poppy seeds in a bowl; set aside.

When chicken has cooled, cut into cubes and place in a greased 13 x 9-inch baking dish. Pour soup mixture over chicken.

Combine melted butter, crushed crackers, and remaining poppy seeds; sprinkle over soup mixture. Bake at 350°F for 30 minutes. *Makes 4 to 6 servings*

Contributed by Courtney Crawford Braddock
Glenda Hulse Pope's granddaughter
Tarrant County

Courtney says she makes Poppy Seed Chicken about once a month; it's a family favorite. She usually makes two pans, one regular and one gluten-free. For the latter, she uses gluten-free cream of chicken soup and Glutino (gluten-free) crackers. Courtney's three girls — all in elementary school — help make this dish, so it's fast becoming a fourth-generation recipe.

Turkey Spaghetti

Thelma Ulala West Shannon (Munnie)
1900–1980
Tarrant County

Leftovers star in this dish, so don't toss the turkey carcass after you carve the holiday bird. You'll need it — and 3 cups of bite-size cooked turkey — to make this satisfying entrée. (If you like, skip the first five ingredients in favor of packaged low-salt chicken broth and substitute cooked chicken for the turkey.) Note that this turkey spaghetti is soupier than most; it's more like a stew than a casserole.

2 large stalks celery
1 reserved and refrigerated turkey carcass with turkey remnants
1 carrot, coarsely chopped
1 additional small onion, coarsely chopped
Salt and pepper
1 (16-ounce) package spaghetti, broken into pieces
2 tablespoons butter
1 small onion, diced
1 clove garlic, minced
8 ounces mushrooms, sliced
1 (10-ounce) package frozen green peas
1 (4-ounce) jar pimientos, undrained
1 (16-ounce) can whole tomatoes, undrained and chopped
3 cups bite-size cooked turkey
Additional salt and pepper
About 1 cup shredded mild cheddar cheese

Dice celery, reserving leaves separately, and set aside.

Thelma Ulala West Shannon.
Courtesy of Anne Isham.

Place turkey carcass in a pot just large enough to hold it. Add celery leaves, carrots, and coarsely chopped onions, and just enough water to cover. Add salt and pepper to taste. (Note: If turkey was heavily brined, this will affect the saltiness of the broth.) Bring mixture to a boil, lower heat, cover, and simmer 1 to 2 hours, stirring occasionally.

Strain broth, discard bones and vegetables, and set aside turkey bits. Return broth to pot and taste; if too salty, stir in a little water. Bring broth to boil, add broken spaghetti, lower heat, and simmer until spaghetti is tender. Do not drain. Amount of broth should equal 1½ to 2 cups at this point; remove excess broth and save for another use.

In a separate pan, sauté diced onion in butter. Stir into broth-spaghetti mixture, along with diced celery, garlic, mushrooms, peas, pimientos, and tomatoes, and continue cooking until celery and mushrooms are tender. Stir in 3 cups cooked turkey, reserved turkey bits, and salt and pepper to taste. Serve with a slotted spoon onto plates or ladle into bowls; top each portion with shredded cheese. *Makes 12 to 15 servings*

Contributed by Anne Shannon Lewis Isham
Thelma Ulala West Shannon's granddaughter
Travis County

"I think Munnie made up Turkey Spaghetti to feed a large family on leftovers," says Anne. "She was a young housewife during the Depression and was fiendishly clever at making something wonderful from whatever was on hand. It was so popular that she later adapted it for large parties. One of my younger brothers called it 'Turkey Fergetti,' so we all call it that now."

Anne has been making this dish for more than forty-five years, usually after Thanksgiving, when she has leftover turkey. "I tried adding fresh corn," she says, "but the purists in the family complained. They like their Turkey Fergetti the traditional way."

Mrs. Kelly's Chicken and Rice

Ellen Sprott Kelly
1886–1965
Falls County

The contributor of this recipe warns: Do not even think of making this dish with margarine or milk; if you do, it will be awful. Yes, it's a rich dish; think comfort food.

4 whole chicken breasts
Salt and pepper
1 cup rice
1 pint cream
½ cup butter

Season chicken with salt and pepper. Place chicken in a Dutch oven; add enough water to cover chicken by 1 inch. Bring to a boil; cover, reduce heat, and simmer over medium heat about 45 minutes, or until meat is falling off the bones. Drain, reserving broth. Remove and discard skin. Let chicken cool. Strain broth.

Measure strained broth and add enough water to make 2½ cups liquid. Pour liquid into saucepan, heat to boiling, and add rice. Cover, reduce heat, and simmer 15 to 20 minutes, or until rice is tender.

Remove chicken from bones; discard bones. Cut chicken into bite-size pieces. Return chicken to Dutch oven and add cooked rice. Stir in cream. Add butter a little at a time so that the rice absorbs it. Cook over low heat a few minutes, or until flavors blend. Taste and add a little more pepper, if desired, to cut the richness slightly. Note that the chicken will stick easily and absorbs liquid very quickly. *Makes 6 to 8 servings*

Contributed by Karey Patterson Bresenhan
Ellen Sprott Kelly's granddaughter by marriage
Fayette County

*K*arey has made this recipe since 1963, when she married into the Bresenhan family. "Mrs. Kelly was a gifted cook and passed that talent down to her daughter Mary Kelly Bresenhan, who gave me the recipe," she says. "I make it

Ellen Sprott Kelly. Courtesy of Karey Bresenhan.

quite often because my husband and I both love it. It's comfort food to the max. It's a great dish to make ahead, since that allows time for the flavors to blend. And because it is so rich, you end up with leftovers, which taste even better than the dish did the first day!

"The original recipe called for a fryer. We don't see that designation often today. It also called for cutting up a chicken — who has time when you can buy it as pieces in the grocery store? So I use chicken breasts since my husband doesn't like dark meat." Another tip Karey has is to let the rice brown just slightly, especially when you reheat it. "Never, ever burn it," she says, "but a little browning makes it even better. The dish reheats wonderfully and can even be frozen successfully."

Karey doesn't know where the Chicken and Rice recipe originated, but she thinks it's probably representative of the cooking in Ellen Kelly's day. "Most Texas farm wives had chickens and a cow or two to produce butter and cream," she notes, "so they had all the basic ingredients."

Ellen Sprott Kelly with her husband, Charlie, and their daughters, Mary (left) and Evangeline. Courtesy of Karey Bresenhan.

Czech Picnic Stew (CZECH)

You'll need a stockpot or large Dutch oven to make this hearty concoction. It's usually served straight out of the pot onto buttered potatoes or mashed potatoes with Czech Sauerkraut on the side. Some people make it a triple-decker and top the potatoes with kraut before ladling on the stew. (Prepare potatoes and sauerkraut as the stew nears completion.)

Vegetable oil
3 pounds beef stew meat or cut-up beef roast
1 extra-large onion or 2 medium onions, cubed
3 garlic cloves, chopped
2½ teaspoons salt
2¼ teaspoons black pepper
¼ teaspoon chili powder
4 bay leaves
1 large potato, diced (red potatoes work best)
6 large potatoes, peeled, chopped, cooked, drained, and buttered
Czech Sauerkraut (see recipe in Vegetables and Sides section)

Sauté meat, onions, garlic, salt, pepper, and chili powder in a small amount of oil until meat turns gray. (Do not drain.) Add just enough water to cover meat mixture. Add bay leaves, bring to a boil, and reduce heat to just above simmering; cook about an hour or until meat is tender. Add more water as needed during cooking to keep water level just above meat mixture.

Stir in the diced potatoes and return to heat. The potatoes should cook down and serve to thicken the stew. Continue simmering another 30 minutes or until meat can be cut with a fork. Remove bay leaves. Place about ½ cup of the buttered potatoes on a plate and ladle stew on top. Serve with Czech Sauerkraut. *Makes about 6 servings*

Contributed by Otto Franklin Mozisek Jr.
Josef Mozisek's grandson
Victoria County

Josef Mozisek
1884–1943
Lavaca County

Josef Mozisek with his wife, Apolina Mozisek. Courtesy of Otto Mozisek Jr.

"*This stew has been made for almost every Czech picnic and wedding in South Texas for generations," says Otto. "It's a real tradition."*

Although Otto's grandfather died before he was born, he remembers his late father, Otto Mozisek Sr., making gallons of the popular dish for family weddings, fund-raisers, and the annual fall picnic at St. Joseph Catholic Church in Inez. "He always made it outside, over an open fire," says Otto. "The pot he cooked it in was too deep to use on a regular stove; he would have had to stand on a ladder to see into it. One Christmas, all of his children got together and bought him a new, twenty-gallon stockpot from a restaurant-supply store; he was surprised and pleased."

Otto's father was well known in the area for his stew. Even today, more than sixteen years after his father's death, Otto says it's not unusual for someone from the Inez area to come up to him and ask, "Wasn't it your dad who made that great stew?"

No one knows exactly what Otto's father put into his stew — he kept that a secret, tying up all his seasonings in a cheesecloth bag. But he taught several family members how to make the basic dish. "I make it, and two of my brothers and a brother-in-law make it," says Otto. "Each one of us does it a little differently."

This stew uses potatoes instead of flour or cornstarch for thickening. Try using carrots, squash, corn, and beans in the same way in other stews. Another way of thickening a stew is to cut up and cook the vegetables as you would normally, remove a few chunks once they're tender, mash or puree them, and then add the mixture back to the stew.

Oyster Stew

A watched pot never boils, and that's a good thing in the case of Oyster Stew. This savory concoction requires more than a half hour of stirring and simmering, but the results are worth it. Serve it as a light main dish or as a hearty appetizer.

2 cups fresh raw oysters, thoroughly washed
3 large bay leaves
Salt and pepper
¼ cup (½ stick) butter or margarine
6 cups warm milk
½ bunch green onions, sliced
3 peppercorns
3 whole allspice
Nutmeg

Sauté oysters, bay leaves, salt, and pepper in butter or margarine in a large Dutch oven or stockpot about 10 minutes or until oysters are completely cooked and curled. Add warm milk, green onions, peppercorns, and allspice. Simmer about 30 minutes, stirring frequently so milk doesn't scorch. *Do not boil.* Remove bay leaves, peppercorns, and allspice before serving. Lightly sprinkle nutmeg over top. *Makes 6 to 8 servings*

Contributed by Danny Koop
Hettie Louise Hoffman Wiede's grandson
Jackson County

*T*hanks to the availability of fresh oysters on the nearby Texas coast, the Koop family enjoys oysters in many forms during the winter months. "My dad used to harvest his own oysters in Matagorda Bay," says Danny. "Everyone in the family loves to eat my grandmother's Oyster Stew, usually as an appetizer before a full meal of fried oysters and shrimp. We make it for special family gatherings."

Hettie Louise Hoffman Wiede

1890–1982

Caldwell and Jackson Counties

Hettie Louise Hoffman Wiede. Courtesy of Danny Koop.

Juanita Cruz Soto (Momo)

1916–2007

Caldwell and Travis Counties

Momo's Caldo (MEXICAN)

This soup can be made with beef, as shown here, or chicken. (Cut a whole chicken into pieces — drumsticks, thighs, wings — and cook it with the vegetables, just as you do the beef. You'll need to adjust the initial cooking time, however. When the chicken is tender, you can fish out the bones and skin, if you like.) Either way — beef or chicken — it's best to make this dish the day before you plan to serve it so the flavors will have time to blend.

2 pounds beef stew meat
1½ pounds beef neck bones
1 cup sliced carrots
2 (8-ounce) cans tomato sauce
1 large zucchini, halved lengthwise and sliced
1 large yellow squash, halved lengthwise and sliced
½ small green cabbage, coarsely chopped
¾ cup chopped celery
¼ cup finely chopped onion
1½ cups uncooked long-grain rice
Salt and pepper to taste

Place all ingredients except rice, salt, and pepper in a large Dutch oven or stockpot. Add water to cover to a level about 3 inches from the top. Bring to a boil over medium to high heat. Lower heat, cover, and simmer 2 hours or until beef is tender.

*Juanita Cruz Soto.
Courtesy of Irma Galvan.*

Add rice and simmer an additional hour, stirring occasionally.

Add salt and pepper to taste. Remove from heat and allow to cool. Remove neck bones and skim off fat. *Makes about 14 servings*

Contributed by Irma Soto Galvan
Juanita Cruz Soto's granddaughter
Travis County

*I*rma says recipes were never written down in her family, so it took her awhile to perfect the taste of her grandmother's caldo (soup). She sometimes substitutes potatoes for rice and sometimes omits the cabbage, but generally, it's the same basic soup. She likes to make it in the cooler months and usually serves it with fresh cornbread.

"My grandmother learned to make this caldo around the age of eight by watching my great-grandmother," says Irma. "Momo was taken out of school just before entering the eighth grade to help her mother. She was the second of eight children — four girls and four boys. My great-grandfather farmed corn, cotton, sugar cane, and millet on land the family owned near Mendoza. The foods they grew not only fed the family but also fed the animals they raised, such as pigs, Longhorns, chickens, and geese. All of the children worked in the fields.

"I don't think of this soup as representing our Hispanic heritage as much as it does the life of a Texas farm family," Irma continues. "They didn't have a lot in those days, which makes me think about how little money the farmers made compared to all their hard work, and I appreciate this recipe even more."

Since Irma's grandmother learned how to make the caldo from her mother (Luciana Torrez Cruz, 1874–1912), Momo's Caldo is actually a fourth-generation Texas recipe.

You can lower the amount of fat in any soup or stew simply by making it the day before you plan to serve it and refrigerating it overnight. The next morning you can easily remove the solidified fat on top before reheating.

Sara Isassi Cásares
(*Mama Grande*)

1886–1974

Hidalgo County

Sara Isassi Cásares.
Courtesy of Sylvia Cásares.

Pork Tamales (MEXICAN)

Making tamales involves a lot of work. Even when the work is shared, it's best to spread the steps out over several days. This recipe is broken down into three stages. Take your time and follow the steps in each stage for a succulent finale.

STAGE 1 (DO UP TO A WEEK AHEAD OF TIME): PREPARE CHILE SAUCES FOR MASA AND PORK GUISADO.

Chile Sauce for Masa
5 cascabel chiles (a.k.a. guajillo chiles)
   washed with stems and seeds removed
2¼ cups water

Combine chiles and water in a medium saucepan. Bring to a boil over high heat. Reduce heat and simmer for 15 minutes. Set aside and cool for 10 minutes.

Place chiles and remaining liquid in container of an electric blender and process about 1 minute. Pour mixture through a fine sieve to remove solids: discard solids. Refrigerate liquid for later use in preparing masa dough.

Chile Sauce for Pork Guisado
13–17 cascabel chiles, washed with stems and seeds removed
4 árbol chiles, with stems removed
½ large yellow onion, cut into quarters
4½ cups water, divided
2 cloves garlic, peeled

Place all ingredients except ¼ cup water and garlic in a large stockpot. Bring to a boil over high heat. Reduce heat and simmer for 20 minutes. Set aside and cool for 10 minutes.

Place mixture in the container of an electric food processor or blender and process 30 to 45 seconds, or until mixture is smooth. Pour liquid through a fine sieve to remove solids; discard solids.

Chapter 2: Recipes

Blend garlic with remaining ¼ cup water and add to pureed chiles. Refrigerate for use in Pork Guisado.

STAGE 2 (DO THE DAY BEFORE): BROWN AND SEASON PORK, PREPARE PORK GUISADO, AND PREPARE CORN HUSKS.

Browned and Seasoned Pork for Pork Guisado
7½ pounds pork butt (should yield 4½ pounds after fat is trimmed)
5 cups water
½ large yellow onion, cut into quarters
6 garlic cloves, peeled and minced
1 tablespoon salt
¼ cup vegetable oil

Cube pork, trimming as much fat as possible. Place pork and other ingredients except vegetable oil in a large stockpot. Bring to a boil over high heat. Reduce heat and simmer for about 90 minutes, or until pork is very tender.

Remove pork from pot using a slotted spoon and set aside in a medium bowl. Refrigerate 3¼ cups of the remaining pork stock for later use in preparing masa dough.

Heat vegetable oil in a large sauté pan over medium heat until oil is hot. Add cooked pork a little at a time and sauté until pork is slightly golden. Cover and refrigerate Browned and Seasoned Pork for later use in Pork Guisado.

Pork Guisado
Chile Sauce for Pork Guisado (previously prepared)
Browned and Seasoned Pork (previously prepared)
2 garlic cloves, minced
1½ teaspoons ground cumin
1½ teaspoons Mexican oregano
1½ teaspoons ground black pepper
1 tablespoon salt

Combine Chile Sauce for Pork Guisado with Browned and Seasoned Pork in a large stockpot. Stir in remaining ingredients and simmer 15 minutes over medium heat to blend flavors. Remove from heat and cool 15 to 20 minutes.

Once the pork has cooled sufficiently, shred the pork pieces by hand or use a fork, if desired. (Hand shredding will result in the largest yield.) Refrigerate Pork Guisado until ready to assemble tamales.

Corn Husk Preparation
When purchasing corn husks for tamales, choose the ones that have the cleanest appearance. You don't want to see a lot of dark specks, holes, or corn silks in the bag.

1 bag corn husks
1 gallon warm water

Place corn husks and water in a container large enough to cover the husks with water. Place a heavy, waterproof object on top of husks to hold them down under the water. Soak husks at least 1 hour before assembling tamales.

STAGE 3 (DO ON THE FINAL DAY): PREPARE MASA, ASSEMBLE TAMALES, AND STEAM TAMALES.

Masa Preparation
14 cups instant corn flour
1 tablespoon plus 2 teaspoons baking powder
4 teaspoons salt
4 cups (or 2 pounds) fresh or commercially prepared lard
3¼ cups pork stock (set aside earlier)
1½ cups Chile Sauce for Masa (previously prepared)
4 cups water

Combine dry ingredients in an extra-large bowl. Mix well by hand. Set aside.

Combine lard, pork stock, Chile Sauce for Masa, and water in a large stockpot. Warm over low heat to melt the lard, using a whisk to blend all the ingredients. Gradually add the warm liquid to the dry mixture, about 3 cups at a time. Mix ingredients together and knead dough in bowl by hand until well blended and light. This will take about 10 minutes. Cover dough and set aside briefly until assembling tamales.

Tamale Assembly

You'll need several tablespoons or putty spreaders, a small bowl of water, and a container to place tamales in after they've been assembled. Gather tools and all prepared ingredients within reach: masa dough, soaked corn husks, and Pork Guisado.

Select a corn husk and narrow the width to the desired size. (The length is not important because the excess will be tucked under.) The husk will resemble a triangle — wide on top and narrow on the bottom. Try to keep the tamale size consistent so that the tamales will cook uniformly.

Place about ¼ cup of the masa dough in the inside top center of the corn husk. (The inside of the corn husk has a rougher texture than the outside.) With the back of a tablespoon or putty spreader, spread the dough evenly to near the edges of the husk. The masa dough should be spread only in the top 4 inches (approximately) of the husk; the remainder of the husk should remain bare. Occasionally dip the spreading tool in water to make the process easier.

Place approximately 2 tablespoons (1 ounce) of the Pork Guisado filling down the center of the spread masa dough, lengthwise.

Fold the tamale inward from the sides into thirds, one side of the husk at a time toward the center, so that the last fold overlaps the other. Bend the empty bottom tail part of the husk up over the fold. Place tamale with the tail tucked under in the container. Repeat until all masa dough and filling are used up.

Steaming Tamales

You'll need a tamale steamer or a 20-quart stockpot with a steamer rack at the base.

Place a coin in the bottom of the pot (you will see why later), replace the rack, and add enough water to the pot so that it reaches the rack. The tamales should remain above the water. Line the bottom of the steamer rack with a single layer of flattened corn husks.

Place the first layer of tamales on the flattened corn husks, tails tucked under, in a wagon wheel-spoke pattern. The open ends should be pointed toward the center. Place the next layer loosely between the "spokes" with the open ends resting and raised on the first layer and the closed ends either resting on the tamales below or on the flattened corn husks. Continue to loosely stack in this fashion until all the tamales are stacked. If done correctly, you should have a loosely packed tower or "tepee" design. Allow at least ¼ inch to ½ inch around the sides of the tamales in the "tepee." There should be enough room around each tamale to allow steam to circulate and cook all sides.

Sara Isassi Cásares with her husband, Nicolas Cásares. Courtesy of Sylvia Cásares.

Cover the tamales with another flattened layer of corn husks to contain the steam. Cover the stockpot and cook tamales over low heat for about 1½ hours. If you hear the coin rattling, add more water. After tamales have steamed, turn off heat (leave pot covered, on the burner) and allow to finish cooking for another 30 minutes. Do not open the lid during this time.

Test tamales for doneness: Completely cooked tamales should peel easily from the husk. If not done, continue steaming for another 15 minutes or more until you are certain they are done. *Makes 8 to 16 dozen tamales, depending on size made*

Contributed by Sylvia Cásares
Sara Isassi Cásares's granddaughter
Harris County

Restaurant owner, caterer, and cooking-school teacher Sylvia Cásares says many of her recipes originated with her grandmother (Mama Grande), including this recipe for Pork Tamales. Look for it on the menu of Sylvia's Enchilada Kitchen, which has three locations in Houston.

"Mama Grande had fourteen children, so she was always cooking," says Sylvia. "That was her life, feeding her family. When I was growing up in Brownsville, we made the fifty-mile trip to her home in Donna most Sundays, so I have a lot of memories of the food she made in her small kitchen — things like carne guisada, picadillo, and enchiladas. We'd make tamales as a family during the holidays and afterwards have a feast with charro beans, guacamole, salsa, and tamales. There's nothing better than freshly made tamales right out of the steamer."

When Sylvia began developing recipes for her restaurant, she spent many hours systematically trying to replicate the foods from the little kitchen in Donna. "My grandmother learned to cook from her mother, so she didn't have any written recipes," explains Sylvia. "But as humans, we have powerful memories of flavors, and if you have an idea of how something is supposed to taste and you play around with the ingredients, you can re-create the dish. That's what I did; I just kept adjusting the recipes until the flavors were right.

"I encourage the students in my cooking classes to do the same thing if they have a 'lost recipe,'" she continues. "I tell them to keep a notebook and record every attempt at making the dish. If something is missing, try adding more or less of a particular ingredient or substitute a new one. If you have the desire and patience, you can eventually resurrect the dish."

If you'd like in-depth lessons on making tamales, consider signing up for "Tamales 101," a hands-on class Sylvia usually offers each fall. Can't make it to Houston for the class? Order the DVD Tamales 101: A Primer on the Ancient Art of Tamale-Making *(Sylvia Cásares Copeland and Kim C. Foore, 2007) for $19.95 plus tax by calling 713–629–0730. For information about cooking classes and restaurant locations, see www.sylviasenchiladas.com.*

The Tamalada

Each December, many Mexican American families in Texas gather for a generations-old tradition that involves equal parts hard work and fun. Here Sylvia Cásares describes some of her *tamalada* memories.

"When I was a child, tamale making was always a family affair at my home," says Sylvia, who grew up in Brownsville. "With all the work required, a large group is routinely involved. The more, the merrier. It can be any combination of family, friends, and neighbors of various ages. . . . The party that inevitably ensues is traditionally called a tamalada. The large yield produced at a tamalada is usually shared by the participants, with each family taking a portion home to eat or give away as gifts."

Tamales played a large part in the family's Christmas traditions. "We always had a tamale dinner on Christmas Eve," says Sylvia. "Until New Year's Day, the tamales were available for three meals a day if we wanted them, and usually we did. We would have toasted tamales in the morning with hot chocolate, some more tamales at lunchtime, and then more again at dinner. Making the tamales was a lot of work, but then the family cooks were off the hook for the remainder of the Christmas season.

"On Christmas morning we would first open our presents and then all share in tamales with a big pot of Mexican hot chocolate, chiles, and whatever else had been prepared. It just wouldn't be Christmas without tamales!

"Even as an adult, I still returned with my children to Brownsville for the Christmas tamalada and traditional Christmas tamales. My mother would always send tamales home with us when we returned to Houston. We would put them in the freezer, and my kids would pull them out a little at a time, reheat them in the microwave, and eat them until they were gone. Tamales in July — what a treat!"

While tamaladas reflect Mexican American culture, people from other ethnic backgrounds are increasingly co-opting these colorful events and making them part of their own holiday traditions. If you love tamales and a good party, tamaladas are a perfect way to celebrate.

Pork Tamales recipe and "The Tamalada" adapted by permission in part from brochure included with DVD *Tamales 101: A Primer on the Ancient Art of Tamale-Making* (Sylvia Cásares Copeland and Kim C. Foore, 2007).

Author's Note: When I was looking for a tamale recipe, I was referred to Lonnie Limón, who is part of a large Mexican American family based in Austin. While talking to Lonnie, I learned that his girlfriend, Crystal Canú, who grew up in the Rio Grande Valley, was so interested in learning to make tamales that she was organizing a tamalada on her own. I was intrigued — here was a young Mexican American woman who had evidently missed out on the tamalada tradition and had decided to rectify the situation. The scenario had the makings of a good story. Lonnie put me in touch with Crystal, who did indeed organize a tamalada in September 2014. Kudos to Crystal for helping preserve this joyful, delicious tradition.

My First Tamalada

CRYSTAL CANTÚ

I wanted to learn how to make tamales to celebrate my diverse background and my love for food and cooking. I come from a family of mixed heritage and ethnicities. My mother is 100 percent Puerto Rican, while my father is of Mexican, Polish, and Native American descent.

Puerto Ricans eat *pasteles*, which are similar to tamales. The most notable difference is that the masa is made from vegetables like plantains and yucca (not corn). I've had the pleasure of making pasteles with my Puerto Rican family in southern Wisconsin at Thanksgiving for the last several years.

My father's family lives in the Rio Grande Valley — an area primarily populated by Hispanics and influenced by Mexican culture. In "the Valley," as it's lovingly referred to, tamales are as bountiful as the air we breathe and the water we drink. You can buy them at any grocery store or from your neighbor or any family friend—which for my family and many others eliminates the need for tamaladas. (Note: There's a very popular tamale store called Delia's with several locations in the Valley that people visit regularly. They make the best tamales!)

Given the abundance of tamales in the Valley, it's easy to see why I never had a chance to make them. But because I know how to make pasteles, I thought it was important to have the same experience celebrating my Mexican heritage. Several of my girlfriends—who are also Mexican American—never learned to make them, either, so I thought it would be fun for us to learn together.

I knew that Lonnie's grandmother's best friend, Mary Rodella, made some of the best tamales in Austin. So I approached her and asked if she would teach us. She agreed, so one Saturday morning last September, three friends and I met at Mary's home. Lonnie's grandmother, mother, and aunt were also in attendance to help mentor us in tamale making, so there were a total of eight women making tamales together. It was a wonderful experience that lasted *all day*!

In addition to learning the art of making tamales, my friends and I enjoyed the camaraderie associated with sitting together and performing what I realized was a pretty monotonous series of tasks: making and spreading the masa, rolling the tamales, steaming the tamales, et cetera. We cracked jokes, drank wine, and took breaks to enjoy the fruits of our labor. Those were some pretty delicious breaks! All together, we made between forty and fifty dozen beef and chicken/cheese tamales. Both kinds were delicious, but I have to say I loved the chicken/cheese. Each of us left with five to six dozen tamales.

Would I host another tamalada? Absolutely, with Mary's help. While I now understand the process, I think I'd need to experience another four or five tamaladas before I could host one on my own. Similar to pasteles, tamales involve a lot of steps, but with the support of a team, all the work gets done and everyone has a lot of fun.

**Ima McKey Fenner
(Big Mama)**
1895–1983
Lavaca County

Plantation Supper

8 ounces egg noodles
1 pound ground beef
½ cup chopped onion
4 to 6 ounces mushrooms, sliced (optional)
1 (10¾-ounce) can cream of mushroom soup
¾ cup milk
1 (8-ounce) package cream cheese
1 (16-ounce) can whole corn, drained, or 1 cup frozen corn
¼ cup diced pimientos
½ teaspoon salt
Dash of pepper

Cook noodles in boiling water; drain well and set aside.

Brown meat, onions, and mushrooms (if using) in a large skillet; remove mixture from pan, drain well, and set aside.

Drain skillet; add soup and cook over low heat until soup thins. Stir in milk and then add cooked noodles, meat mixture, and remainder of ingredients. Continue cooking until mixture is thoroughly heated and blended. *Makes about 8 servings*

Contributed by Cynthia "Cindy" Robinson English
Ima McKey Fenner's granddaughter
Nueces County

Cindy says she's been making her grandmother's Plantation Supper for more than forty years. "It's a wonderfully versatile recipe," she says, "so you can go lots of directions with it. I added the fresh mushrooms, and I usually use frozen corn now." Cindy's mom made this dish often when Cindy was growing up, and it was a regular when she was raising her own kids. "My 'kids' still request it when they're here," she says.

Dirty Rice (CAJUN)

This dish is plenty spicy as is, but if you want to add a little extra heat, stir in a sprinkling of crushed red pepper.

Noelie Marie Hebert Gilbert
1909–1988
Jefferson County

1 tablespoon vegetable oil
1 pound ground beef
½ pound ground pork sausage
1 small onion, chopped
1 cup chopped celery
1 teaspoon chopped garlic
½ green pepper, chopped
1 tablespoon Kitchen Bouquet
2 (10¾-ounce) cans chicken or beef broth
1½ to 2 cups cooked rice
1 (8-ounce) box Zatarain's Dirty Rice Mix
1 to 2 handfuls (2 to 4 tablespoons) chopped green onions
    (tops only)
"Slap Ya Mama" Cajun Seasoning

Noelie Marie Hebert Gilbert with her husband, Whitney Gilbert. Courtesy of Peggy Scarborough.

Sauté ground beef and pork sausage in vegetable oil in a Dutch oven or other large pot. Do not drain. Stir in onion, celery, garlic, and green pepper and continue cooking. Add Kitchen Bouquet, broth, cooked rice, and Zatarain's Dirty Rice Mix (empty contents of box into mixture); stir well. Bring mixture to a boil and then reduce heat. Stir several times, cover, and simmer over low heat about 25 minutes. Remove from heat and stir in green onions and a sprinkling of Cajun seasoning. Let stand for about 5 minutes and then serve. *Makes 10–15 servings*

Contributed by Peggy Sterling Scarborough
Noelie Marie Hebert Gilbert's granddaughter
Williamson County

Peggy's family actually traces this recipe back to her great-grandmother Marie Denis Hebert (Nan) (1877–1969), who lived in Rayne, Louisiana, before moving to Beaumont. "Rice was used as a filler to extend meals," says Peggy. "Cajuns used any and all combinations of food to stretch a meal for their families. My grandmother told me that once my great-grandfather wanted Nan to change up the recipe for variety, so she added smothered eggplant and came up with Eggplant Dressing.

"Each time I make Dirty Rice," adds Peggy, "the aroma stirs memories of growing up in a Cajun kitchen, just like my own granddaughters' experience in my kitchen." Peggy makes Dirty Rice for family gatherings, potlucks, and barbecues, as well as for special requests. Over the years, she added the Kitchen Bouquet (to make the dish darker), the Zatarain's mix, and Cajun Seasoning. "As a Cajun cook, I usually just eyeball the amounts," she says. "Rarely do I follow the exact measurements. It's all good in the end."

When you see "handfuls" and other imprecise measurements in a stew or side dish recipe, this usually signals "Don't sweat it; use a little more or a little less of this ingredient, depending on how much you like the flavor." It's a different matter, however, in regard to baking. For a guide to interpreting obscure measurements (often found in heirloom recipes), see the resources section.

Nanny's Tomato Gravy and Venison

Using a can of diced tomatoes and green chiles rather than diced tomatoes makes this dish plenty hot for most palates, so you may want to omit the jalapeños. You can also turn down the heat by opting for salt and pepper instead of the Creole seasoning.

Jerusha "Jo" Love Clark Schnitz (Nanny)

1885–1981

Gonzales, Wilson, and Guadalupe Counties

Bacon fat or shortening
About 2½ cups flour, divided
3 pounds venison, sliced ½-inch thick
Tony Chachere's Creole Seasoning or salt and pepper
1 large onion, quartered and sliced
1 medium bell pepper, quartered and sliced
2 or more cloves garlic, minced
1 (10-ounce) can diced tomatoes or diced tomatoes
    and green chiles
2 (10-ounce) cans water
1 tablespoon whole comino seeds
1 to 2 jalapeños (optional)
salt and pepper

Jerusha "Jo" Love Clark Schnitz (center) with her husband, Herman Schnitz, and her sister Beasley Clark. Courtesy of Jean Schnitz.

Place sufficient bacon fat or shortening to fry meat in a large (at least 14-inch) skillet and begin heating skillet.

Place about 2 cups of the flour in a shallow container (one that has a lid) and add about a third of the meat in a single layer. Season surface of meat with Creole seasoning or salt and pepper. Put lid on container and shake well to coat meat.

Fry meat on high heat to brown, but don't cook through. While first batch of meat is frying, prepare second batch of meat in the same way with the remaining flour in container. Repeat until all the meat is browned well. Remove meat as it browns and set aside. Discard any unused flour.

Pour off all but ¼ cup fat. Add onion, bell pepper, and garlic and sauté over low heat until vegetables are softened. Scrape up the crunchy bits at the bottom of the skillet and don't drain fat. Stir in about ½ cup flour and add water as needed to make a thick paste. Add canned tomatoes, cans of water, comino seeds, and jalapeños, if desired. Stir well and bring to a boil. Add water as necessary to make a light gravy.

Return meat to skillet. Simmer uncovered for at least an hour or until meat is tender. Add water as necessary to adjust gravy consistency, but mixture should end up fairly thick. Taste gravy and add salt and pepper as desired. *Makes 6 to 8 servings*

Contributed by David Schnitz
Jerusha "Jo" Love Clark Schnitz's grandson
Jim Wells County

*D*avid admits to adapting his grandmother's recipe a bit. For example, Jo Schnitz would have used tomatoes that she canned herself. David has also made several "heat" modifications to suit his taste, but it's true to the original in most respects. "Nanny's Tomato Gravy works well with almost any kind of meat — beef, chicken, pork, and game," he says. During dove season, he often uses two dozen dove breasts in place of the venison.

"This dish is good served as the main meal with excess gravy over biscuits, bread, potatoes, or most anything," says David. "It's also excellent as a breakfast meal with leftovers served on heated flour tortillas. You have to cut the meat up a little for this, of course. It reminds me of carne guisada tacos."

David's mother, Jean Schnitz, says that her mother-in-law made this dish often for her nine children. "This included seven big boys who could consume mountains of gravy and mashed potatoes," she adds. "I can only imagine the quantity required for a single meal."

An inveterate hunter, David enjoys making this concoction in a Dutch oven at deer camp. "You prepare it the same way, to the point when you add the meat back to the skillet," he says. "Then you get a pretty good fire going, with the Dutch oven on a grill above the fire. Let the fire burn down to good, hot coals and then leave it and go hunting. It will simmer itself down to the correct tenderness. The traditional Dutch-oven method — putting the coals under the Dutch oven and on top of the lid — will require constant attention, so put it on a grill over good, hot coals or leave a non-hunter with the tending duties."

Brisket with Chuckwagon Hollandaise

There are many ways to smoke a brisket, and just as many strong opinions. However, most self-respecting Texans agree on one thing: They draw the line at mopping a brisket with a tomato-based concoction. Using it as a plate sauce . . . well, that's a different matter.

Trim, season, and smoke an 8-pound brisket (purchased packer style, with fat layer intact) as desired. When the brisket is nearly done, prepare the sauce.

Chuckwagon Hollandaise
1 cup Heinz Ketchup
1 cup water
⅓ cup Lea & Perrins Worcestershire Sauce
Juice of half a lemon
A long curl of lemon rind, shaved off with a potato peeler
½ cup butter

Combine ketchup and 1 cup water in a small saucepan. Stir in Worcestershire sauce, lemon juice, and lemon peel and heat to simmering. Remove from heat and stir in butter as it melts.

Treat the mixture with respect: Keep it warm, but don't let it boil after the butter goes in. (It is basically a Hollandaise sauce, with so much butter that boiling turns it into a unappetizing, gooey mess. If that happens, you can restore it by whisking in a little bit of the sauce with a tablespoon of mayonnaise, and then whisking in the rest by dribbles as it regains the emulsion. However, it is much better just to not let this happen.) Pour sauce into a gravy boat or similar container and ladle onto barbecue plates as desired. *Makes about 3 cups*

Contributed by Meredith McClain
Rita Cook McClain's granddaughter
Lubbock County

Rita Cook McClain
1882–1961
Williamson County

Rita Cook McClain.
Courtesy of Meredith McClain.

*A*s the head of food service at the first women's dormitory at Southwestern University in Georgetown, Rita Cook McClain was an excellent cook. However, she wasn't above doing a little sleuthing to obtain a good recipe. Meredith received her grandmother's recipe for Chuckwagon Hollandaise from her older brother, Martin McClain of Detroit, Michigan, who played a key role in procuring the secret recipe. Here Martin relates the backstory:

"Bob Gaines was a colored man who lived in Georgetown from the 1940s to the 1960s. He did every large public barbecue in Georgetown during those years, for the Sheriff's Posse, the Country Cub, family reunions, et cetera. The ladies of the town tried to imitate his barbecue sauce, but he never gave out the recipe and they never got it right. He was doing a large barbecue at the Georgetown Country Club when I was about eight years old, and my grandmother McClain sent me on to 'help' him and also note closely what went into the sauce. His recipe, from direct observation, involved six bottles of ketchup, two bottles of Worcestershire sauce, six lemons, two whole lemon rinds, and two pounds of the secret ingredient, namely, fresh butter."

Both Meredith and Martin have made smaller batches of the sauce for decades, but Meredith felt obligated to ask her brother for permission before submitting the recipe. He agreed, noting, "Unless you make your living with it, every recipe should be public property. I never told [the recipe] to anybody while Bob Gaines was alive, but now that he has gone to that long pit in the sky, it should be made public."

Rita Cook McClain with her husband, George Albert McClain, and their sons, George McClain (top left) and Will Kelly McClain. Courtesy of Meredith McClain.

While this recipe probably didn't originate on a chuckwagon, it brings to mind the ranch setting that plays such a large role in the Texas mystique. For a firsthand look at a working cattle ranch portrayed through four generations of one family history, visit George Ranch Historical Park in Richmond. The twenty-three thousand–acre spread features interpreters in period dress at four historic homes, as well as cowboys and cattle demonstrations. In addition to numerous living-history events that focus on Texas heritage, the park has a Historic Food Program that includes three categories: a monthly Chuckwagon Breakfast, seasonal Fireside Supper Cooking Classes, and Saturday Historic Lunches.

The Saturday lunches feature a choice of seven historical meals that rotate through the park every week and reflect the different ranching eras and the statuses of various groups on the ranch. For example, a meal at the 1890s Sharecropper's Cabin might feature Deep-Fried Catfish and Buttermilk Pie, while a meal at the 1890s Davis Mansion might feature Roast Beef and Yorkshire Pudding. Each meal includes a culinary history lesson from the ranch chef in which he explains why particular foods were chosen and how they were influenced by various cultures. For more information about the park and its events, call 281–343–0218 or see www.georgeranch.org.

Minnie Frances McKey Smith Spittler (Nanny)

1921–2000

Brown, El Paso, and Lavaca Counties

Nanny's Slow-Cooker Pot Roast

Meal preparation doesn't get much easier than this. Let the roast cook all day, add crusty rolls and a salad, and you've got dinner on the table in minutes.

8 to 12 red potatoes, peeled and cut into chunks
1 pound whole carrots (about 7) or baby carrots, sliced crosswise
1 yellow onion, quartered or chopped
3 or 4 whole allspice
2 whole bay leaves
2 or 3 fresh garlic cloves, peeled and chopped
1 cup beef broth
1 (3- to 4-pound) chuck or shoulder roast
Salt and pepper

Place potatoes, carrots, onion, allspice, bay leaves, and garlic in a 6- to 8-quart slow cooker. Add beef broth and mix vegetables and seasonings together.

Season roast with salt and pepper and place it fatty side down on top of the vegetables. Cover and cook on low setting 8 to 10 hours, or until roast falls apart and vegetables are tender. Transfer roast and vegetables to a platter, reserving broth; discard allspice and bay leaves. Pour broth into a gravy boat or similar container and serve with roast. *Makes about 8 servings*

Contributed by Shannon Smith Stilwell
Minnie Frances McKey Smith Spittler's granddaughter
Harris County

*M*innie Spittler had a number of hobbies, including playing the guitar, hunting, crocheting, and painting. She was also known for her cooking and once won a prize for her pineapple upside-down cake.

Shannon learned how to make this easy pot roast from her grandmother more than thirty years ago. It's easy on the budget, too. "Get a cheap roast and cook it long enough," says Shannon, "and it will be super-tender." The dish is a family

Chapter 2: Recipes

favorite, so she serves it about once a month. "If you like a thicker gravy, you can make one with the juices and a little flour," she says, " but we like it as is."

It's fitting that Shannon ended up with one of her grandmother's recipe books, which she treasures both for the recipes and the memories they evoke. "I remember Nanny preparing each family member's favorite sweet treat for their birthdays," says Shannon. "She always made Gooey Cake [a yellow cake topped with crushed pineapple, vanilla pudding, and Cool Whip] for me, and it's still my number-one comfort dessert, whereas her pot roast is my favorite comfort meal."

Minnie Frances McKey Smith Spittler. Courtesy of Helen McKey.

Sicilian Pizza (SICILIAN)

This is a thick-crust pizza, typically made on a large, rectangular cookie sheet or baking sheet. Unlike Northern Italian pizza, it does not have a tomato-sauce base but relies on lots of olive oil to provide flavor and moisture. A note about anchovies: Buy them in a jar; avoid the tinned varieties because they tend to be mushy.

1 (16-ounce) package Pillsbury Hot Roll Mix
Extra-virgin olive oil
6 to 8 whole, firm anchovies
½ cup chopped chives
3 tablespoons fresh oregano
½ to ¾ cup freshly grated Parmesan cheese

Rose Mortellaro Parmesan (right) and her sister-in-law Camille Parmesan (the contributor's godmother). Courtesy of Camille Parmesan.

Follow directions on hot roll mix for pizza crust, letting the dough rise until double in size two different times (allow an hour for rising each time). Turn dough out onto lightly floured board and pull gently until you have an oval shape. Then place dough on a large, rectangular baking pan that is at least ¾-inch deep. Continue to gently push dough down and into corners. Create a higher edge to help hold pizza shape.

Sprinkle olive oil lightly over entire pizza. Tear anchovies into about 6 or 7 small pieces each (reserve the remainder for another use). Gently press pieces into the dough, taking care not to lose the rise. Sprinkle herbs and cheese evenly over top. Sprinkle again with olive oil, taking care to coat the edges fairly evenly. Remember that the olive oil is the "sauce," so be generous!

Bake pizza at 350°F for 30 to 40 minutes. It's ready when edges are brown but main portion of pizza is a pale gold. Don't overcook; if it's brown all over, it will be dry. *Makes about 16 servings*

Contributed by Camille Parmesan
Rose Mortellaro Parmesan's granddaughter
Travis County

*W*ith a name like Parmesan, is it any wonder that this contributor has a recipe for pizza, albeit an unusual one? "My grandmother was born in Rockport sometime in the 1890s and grew up on farms in what is now Houston," says Camille. "The family farmed 'truck crops' (tomatoes, various squashes, et cetera) and also made their own wine. Her parents and her older siblings were born in Sicily. . . . They came from a little town . . . up in the mountains (Alia). This pizza is definitely from that area. It's very different from 'Italian pizza' (which my grandmother called 'Northern pizza') because it doesn't have a tomato sauce. And it doesn't have a white/cream sauce like many French pizzas have."

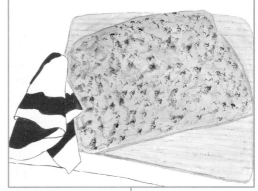

Camille has been making the pizza since she was about ten years old. She now uses the boxed hot-roll mix instead of making the bread from scratch as her grandmother did. "She'd make pizza on her bread day," she explains. "She'd make two to three loaves of homemade white bread and use some of the dough for a pizza.

"I recently tried it with bakery focaccia as the base bread, and that worked well," she adds. "Ready-made focaccias tend to be flavored, so just be careful you get a flavor that will complement the anchovies. Sometimes I substitute fresh salted anchovies for the bottled ones — a good Italian deli will often have them. However, I find they're too salty to use as is, so I wash off some of the salt. I also like Herbes de Provence a bit better than the fresh oregano, but that's very nontraditional. Some people I've given the recipe to like to add grated mozzarella as the last ingredient, but that's also very nontraditional."

Camille makes Sicilian Pizza about once a year, sometimes for family get-togethers, sometimes for friends. "I have a big family," she says. "Grandma and Grandpa each had some twelve siblings. I have five sisters, their kids add up to seven nieces/nephews, and now we're getting the next generation of babies. This pizza is so unusual that several of us use it as the dish to take to friends, work potlucks, et cetera. It's always a big hit, though I did have a friend take one bite, moan, and spit it out, shouting "There are hairs in this!' The 'hairs' were, of course, the anchovy bones. Guess it's not for everyone!"

Small jars of whole anchovies can be difficult to find, so you may have to buy a larger jar than you actually need for this recipe. The good news is that leftover anchovies add another dimension to recipes from tapenades to Caesar salad.

**Lillian Piazza Cappello
(Mema)**

1917–2004

Harris County

*Lillian Piazza Cappello.
Courtesy of Bob Ruggiero Jr.*

Ham Pie (Pizzagaina) (ITALIAN)

This is a firm, peppery pie that's often served around Easter in Italian American communities. Like many holiday favorites, it's not a low-calorie dish. It's also not easy to make. To speed up the process, ask the person behind the deli counter to cut all the meats into ¼-inch slices; this makes it much easier to cube the meat later. If you can't find basket cheese, substitute additional mozzarella. And if the cost of prosciuttino is prohibitive, substitute prosciutto; just scrape off most of the pepper (otherwise the pie will be too peppery) and cut off the fat.

6 ounces Krakus ham (a Polish ham with little fat), sliced ¼-inch thick
6 ounces prosciuttino (a lean Italian ham), sliced ¼-inch thick
6 ounces soppressata (a dry Italian salami), sliced ¼-inch thick
6 ounces abruzzesa sausage, sliced ¼-inch thick
4 ounces pepperoni, sliced ¼-inch thick
1 (1-pound) fresh basket cheese (a.k.a. Easter cheese or formaggio fresca)
8 ounces (solid) mozzarella
10 extra-large eggs
8 ounces ricotta
2 cups flour
⅔ teaspoon baking powder
⅓ teaspoon salt
⅓ teaspoon coarsely ground pepper
3 tablespoons Crisco
½ cup ice water
1 additional extra-large egg, well beaten

Remove and discard any edges of fat from the two hams, as well as any casings from the three sausages. Cut all meats, basket cheese, and mozzarella into small cubes. Set aside.

Beat the 10 eggs together and stir in ricotta. Add cubed meats and other cheeses and mix well. Refrigerate until crust is ready.

Combine flour, baking powder, salt, and pepper. Cut in Crisco. Add ice water and mix well. The dough will be sticky. Divide the dough in half and roll out 2 crusts. Place the bottom crust in a greased and floured 13 x 9-inch casserole dish. Pour in meat-cheese mixture. Place the remaining crust on top and crimp the edges of the crusts together. Prick top crust with fork five times. Brush top crust with the beaten egg. Bake at 350°F for 1 hour and 45 minutes, or when moisture stops seeping through top crust. *Makes 12 to 15 servings*

Contributed by Bob Ruggiero Jr.
Lillian Piazza Cappello's grandson
Harris County

A public relations professional and arts writer by trade, Bob has fond memories of his grandmother's Italian cooking. He has tried his hand at making several of her dishes, including Ham Pie, which he prepares once a year for Easter in his Mema's honor. His other favorites include Spinach-Sausage Pie (see next recipe) and Hot Antipasto (see Vegetables and Sides section).

Italy Comes to Texas

BOB RUGGIERO JR.

My maternal grandmother, Lillian Piazza Cappello, was born in 1917 in Bridgeport, Connecticut. As a child, she immigrated back to Italy with her mother and sister for several years, before returning to the United States for good. My own family came to Houston in 1977. But I—at the age of seven—was initially confounded by the native food choices I found in the Bayou City at restaurants and on the school lunch menu. Burritos? Sloppy Joes? Barbecue brisket? Frito pie?

I was instantly nostalgic for the Italian cuisine I had been nourished by and known so well up to that point. And over the ensuing decades, every trip I made back to Connecticut had two areas of prime interest for me: family first, and food second. As Lillian (or, as I only ever called her, "Mema") was a very traditional Italian woman, she could most often be found in the kitchen. She worked hard at creating her tomato-sauce-based culinary masterpieces, whose smell would waft into every room of her house.

After my grandfather died in the early eighties, my parents begged, begged her for years to come live with us in Texas. But the excuses were always the same: "I'll be a bother. I'll be in the way. I have my friends and my church here. You don't need an old woman around." She would periodically visit us, though—and instantly take over the kitchen.

In 2002, after the passing of my own father, I pleaded with her on the phone to come to Texas. My mother needed her. I and my own new family and my brother needed her. Ah! Now she was needed! That was different. She came to Texas in 2002 and lived with my mother until she passed in 2004. But she would consistently tell us that she'd discovered how much she loved Texas—and not having to live around snow all those years. And how she wished she had come earlier. Many afternoons she would sit in a lawn chair in my mother's front yard just enjoying the warm Texas weather while listening to her Andrea Bocelli CDs.

And while she was not able to cook like she used to by that point, she would often "supervise" my mother making the family recipes in the kitchen—while occasionally butting in to stir a pot, slice some garlic, or grate some cheese. So she could be useful. When I was attending college at the University of Texas at Austin in the late eighties, I often received care packages from my Mema. You know, because they might not have toothpaste or shampoo or anginett (Italian lemon cookies) out here in the Wild West. (OK, she may have had a point on that last one.)

One day, I saw on a television show someone saying that a great way to have a family keepsake would be to ask your grandmother to write down her favorite recipes—in her own hand—for you to keep. What a great idea! I called Mema the very next morning, and within a week, I had another care package (including toothpaste, of course). Those handwritten recipe cards—along with more I inherited from my mother—are some of my most treasured possessions. I hope you enjoy a little taste of Connecticut Italian–gone–Lone Star State here as well. *Buon appetito*!

Lillian Piazza Cappello (Mema)

1917–2004

Harris County

Spinach-Sausage Pie (ITALIAN)

Think of this pie as a quiche and serve it with a salad and fruit. It also works well as part of a buffet in which there are several main-dish choices.

1 pound Italian sausage, with skin removed, and crumbled
2 (10-ounce) packages frozen chopped spinach
6 eggs
Salt and pepper
8 ounces sharp cheddar cheese, grated
1 (14.1-ounce) package refrigerated pie crusts (2 crusts), thawed,
    or 2 (10-inch) homemade pie crusts

Sauté sausage in a frying pan; drain oil and set aside.

Cook spinach slightly; squeeze until dry and set aside.

Break eggs into a medium bowl, reserving 1 egg yolk. Set egg yolk aside and beat remaining eggs. Add sausage, spinach, salt and pepper to taste, and cheese and mix well.

Unroll 1 pie crust and place in greased 10-inch pie plate. Pour mixture into crust. Unroll remaining crust and place over mixture. Crimp edges of crust together. Prick top crust four times with fork. Beat reserved egg yolk and brush over top crust. Bake at 350°F for 1 hour, or until crust is lightly browned. *Makes 6 to 8 servings*

Contributed by Bob Ruggiero Jr.
Lillian Piazza Cappello's grandson
Harris County

*B*ob was only seven years old when his immediate family moved from Connecticut to Texas (see Ham Pie recipe), but he remembers always having Sunday dinners with his extended Italian family when they still lived in the New Haven area. "Of course, because there were so many of us, we were crammed not only at the main table but at various other surfaces. Including the kids' table!" he says. "That was one of the things I missed the most when we moved, those dinners with a cacophony of noise, laughter, impassioned polemics, and —— most of all —— the sights and smells of the food."

Lillian Piazza Cappello. Courtesy of Bob Ruggiero Jr.

Vegetables and Sides

Grandmother's Creamy-Sour Potato Salad (SCOTCH-IRISH)

Alpha Mae McLendon Amerine Stone

1889–1981

Milam and Dallas Counties

Timing is important when making this salad. Once the potatoes are cooked, it's important to work quickly. You should make the sauce first, and be sure to have the pickles and onions chopped and the eggs boiled and peeled ahead of time, too. If you use commercial pickles, consider omitting the salt since they're often saltier than homemade.

1½ cups mayonnaise
¾ cup apple cider vinegar
1 tablespoon sugar
3 tablespoons prepared mustard
Dash of salt
Dash of pepper
5 pounds red potatoes, peeled and quartered
2 medium sour pickles, chopped
1 medium onion, chopped
3 boiled eggs, peeled

Mix first six ingredients together (the sauce) and refrigerate.

Boil potatoes until fork-tender. Immediately drain and then mash potatoes thoroughly (use the same pot). Quickly stir in half of the refrigerated sauce while potatoes are still hot. Gradually add enough of the remaining sauce until mixture resembles a thick cake batter. (Discard any remaining sauce.) Stir in pickles and onions and pour mixture into a large bowl. Grate boiled eggs over the top.

Refrigerate salad overnight, or at least 6 to 7 hours until thoroughly cooled. Salad will thicken as it cools. *Makes 8 large servings*

Contributed by Janet "Jan" Pritchett Litvin
Alpha Mae McLendon Amerine Stone's granddaughter
Dallas County

Alpha Mae McLendon Amerine Stone. Courtesy of Jan Litvin.

*J*an Litvin makes a lot of potato salad. She even cans her own sour pickles each July mainly for use in this recipe "because commercial pickles have too much salt." She has made the salad for every major holiday – Thanksgiving, Christmas, Easter, Fourth of July – for more than thirty-five years.

"When I make it for family celebrations, I use ten pounds of potatoes, which makes two huge bowlfuls for eighteen to twenty people," she says. "When we have more than that, I use up to twenty pounds of potatoes. There is never any left as it's our favorite holiday dish. I frequently get calls from my nieces and nephews to make sure that I am going to bring the potato salad. We usually have cranberry sauce with the meal, but no one ever eats much of it; this salad takes its place.

"Grandmother used to tell me that [when she was young], they would make this dish the day before a particular winter event, put it in a mesh bag, and then hang it outside the window to keep it cold because there was no refrigeration."

Although Jan received this recipe from her grandmother, it originated much earlier. "Grandmother continuously told us that the recipe had been in the McLendon family for nine generations," says Jan, "all the way back to the late 1600s in [what became] Anson County, North Carolina, where our ancestor Dennis McLendon was a judge." The first immigrant in the family to come to America, Dennis received his appointment from King Charles. According to Jan, the recipe originated with Dennis's family and has been passed down through the generations.

"Grandmother always talked about the importance of knowing where we came from to know where we are going," says Jan. "She spent some fifty years researching family history. Her lifelong desire was to become a member of the Daughters of the American Revolution (DAR), but she was unable to prove that our ancestor Ezekiel McLendon (1742–1802) had served in the Revolutionary War." After Alpha's death, Jan took up the cause and was able to secure a paper that stated that Ezekiel was a "runner" for the Continental Army. "In other words," says Jan, "he gathered foodstuffs and 'ran' them to the troops." Today Jan and her sister, Pat Sargent, are proud members of the DAR.

Jan spent a lot of time with her grandparents while growing up. "It was never boring," she says, "because Grandmother was always busy. She was a marvelous seamstress and professional tailor. She did French weaving for the finest stores in Dallas, including Neiman Marcus. She was also a wonderful cook and canned most everything she grew in her one-acre garden. My grandfather built her a U-shaped closet next to the kitchen. The shelves were ten to twelve inches high and two jars deep. It held hundreds of canned goods, including her canned peaches, which were divine. My favorites, though, were the tomatoes and pickles."

Alpha no doubt used the pickles when she made the legendary potato salad, which brings us back to the nine-generations-old recipe. "Because of my grandmother's determination to keep it secret, it's never been published until now," says Jan.

Alpha Mae McLendon Amerine Stone with her husband, Ben Stone, and two of their seven children, Joe (standing) and William. Courtesy of Jan Litvin.

Mildred Faye Jones Tipton

Born in 1925

Matagorda, Wharton, Harris, and Jackson Counties

Mildred Faye Jones Tipton.
Courtesy of Helen McKey.

Potato Soup

For more milk flavor, use nonfat dry milk mixed twice as strong as the package directions suggest. This gives the soup more flavor without adding more liquid.

1 quart chicken stock
6 large potatoes, peeled and cut into small chunks
½ large onion, diced
1 cup grated American or Cheddar cheese or 1 cup Velveeta, cut into chunks
1 cup milk (regular or reconstituted instant nonfat dry milk)
1 (10-ounce) can Ro*Tel Tomatoes & Green Chilies (or less if desired)
1 teaspoon celery seed
Salt and pepper

Cook potatoes and onion in chicken stock, covered, until tender; do not drain. Add cheese and allow to melt.

Stir in milk, tomatoes and green chilies, celery seed, salt, and pepper to taste. Heat thoroughly and serve hot. *Makes about 6 servings*

Contributed by Anna Volkmer Zahn
Mildred Faye Jones Tipton's granddaughter
Wharton County

*A*nna says she's been helping her grandma make this soup since she was eight years old. "It's a favorite of mine," she explains. "When I was in elementary school, I began 'faking sick,' knowing that I would get to spend the day with Grandma. We would make this soup, as well as chicken noodle soup (with homemade noodles), and peanut butter cookies. We played my favorite dice game, Farkel. (Somehow, I always won.) When we heard my mom's car pull up, I would run to the couch and act sick. Grandma always convinced my mom that I needed to stay home 'one more day!' When I was still at home, Grandma and I made this soup together. Later, when I would come home from college on the weekends, Grandma would have a container of Potato Soup ready to send back with me on Sunday afternoon."

Another tradition the two shared when Anna was growing up was making sugar cookies together, especially at Christmas. "Sometimes I'll go over to her house now, and she will have the cookies made but need help icing them," she says. Another special memory involves pancakes. "When I got my driver's license," says Anna, "I would go to Grandma's every morning for breakfast. There would always be her delicious homemade pancakes. I would be running late, and Grandma's smoke alarms would be going off. I sure miss those days, and the pancakes!"

Keep instant nonfat dry milk on hand for culinary emergencies; reconstituted, it works as well as milk in most recipes. However, unless you expect to use it often, forgo the large boxes and opt for small packages that make as little as a quart of milk.

**Artie Metia
Collier Greenhill
(Nanny)**

1893–1978

**Lubbock and Bell
Counties**

*Artie Metia Collier Greenhill.
Courtesy of Jeri Rieken-Speer.*

Nanny's Scalloped Potatoes

*Side dish or main dish? You can omit the ham altogether or add more to make the
dish meatier.*

2 large potatoes, peeled and sliced very thin, divided
1 large onion, sliced into very thin rounds, divided
4 to 5 tablespoons flour, divided
Salt and pepper
Garlic salt (optional)
½ cup butter or margarine, sliced into thin pats, divided
4 to 8 thin slices of ham, left whole (optional)
4 to 8 slices of American cheese, grated (or 2 to 3 cups grated cheese)
1 to 2 cups milk
Additional grated American cheese for topping (optional)
Dash or two of paprika
Pinch of dried parsley flakes

Place a layer of potatoes in a lightly greased, 3- to 4-quart casserole (or
two 1½- to 2-quart casseroles), followed by a layer of onions. Sprinkle
with 1 to 1½ tablespoons flour—enough to lightly cover the top. Sprinkle
with salt and pepper to taste (and garlic salt, if desired). Dot with pats
of butter. Cover with a layer of ham and a layer of cheese. Repeat until
all potatoes are used, making sure that potatoes are the top layer. Pour
enough milk over the top to cover the layers. Bake at 350°F for 1 to 1½
hours, or until potatoes are tender.

Remove dish, top with additional grated cheese, if desired, and sprinkle
with paprika and parsley. Return dish to oven and bake a few minutes
more, or until cheese melts. *Makes 6 to 8 servings*

Contributed by Jeri Lyn Rieken-Speer
Artie Metia Collier Greenhill's granddaughter
Lubbock County

"*My* grandmother was originally from Kentucky and had deep Southern roots," says Jeri. "She wore gloves to drive and never went outdoors without a hat or scarf. She was also a strong, independent woman who ran the family farm when she became a widow at age twenty-eight. She did this while raising two children, taking care of 'Grandpa' (who lived with the family), and working at the courthouse in Lubbock. She was a strong influence in my life and taught me a lot."

Jeri doesn't know the origin of Nanny's Scalloped Potatoes, but she thinks the recipe was passed down to her grandmother from her mother (Ruth Helen Lawrence Collier), whose family was English. Regardless, it is a crowd-pleaser with both Jeri's Greenhill relatives and those in her dad's German family. "Nanny and my mother (Ruth Greenhill Rieken) made this dish as far back as I can remember," says Jeri. "They baked a much larger quantity of it than I do, using an oval, blue-and-white-flecked enamel baking pan. They served it as both a side dish and a main dish.

"Mother was known for this dish and was often asked to bring it to church and family parties. When we were planning our last extended Rieken family get-together in 1993, some of my dad's relatives requested that she bring Nanny's Scalloped Potatoes. However, Mother had already been diagnosed with Alzheimer's by then, and she didn't know if she could do it. So she and I and my grown children, Amy and Justin, all made it together, and it seemed to go over fine.

"I've been making the dish myself since I was seventeen," says Jeri. "These days, I make it once or twice a year — usually for Thanksgiving or Christmas. The leftovers — if there are any — taste even better reheated."

To make the most of a stockpile of dried herbs and spices, store them according to frequency of use. Store those you use regularly in a cool, dry place away from a heat source like a range or dishwasher. For those you use infrequently, seal the lids securely and store them in the freezer.

Helen Smiles Jones McKey (Grandma Helen)

Born in 1923

Matagorda, Wharton, Lavaca, Harris, Victoria, and Jackson Counties

Helen Smiles Jones McKey. Courtesy of Helen McKey.

Candied Sweet Potatoes

Fresh sweet potatoes taste the best, but you can use two 16-ounce cans of sweet potatoes, if you like. Just drain the juice, reserve ¼ cup, and substitute it for the water in the recipe.

2 pounds sweet potatoes (4 large or 6 medium)
¼ cup butter
½ cup sugar
½ cup firmly packed light brown sugar
¼ cup water
½ cup chopped pecans or walnuts (optional)
1 (16-ounce) bag marshmallows (large or mini)

Wash sweet potatoes, dry well, and bake at 375°F for 1 hour or until done. Cool.

Peel sweet potatoes, cut into large chunks, and place in a greased, medium-sized baking dish.

Melt butter in a thick-bottomed pan and add sugars and ¼ cup water. Bring mixture to a boil and heat until sugars dissolve. If using nuts, stir into mixture. Pour over sweet potatoes. Bake at 400°F about 20 minutes.

Remove baking dish from oven and top with marshmallows. Return to oven and bake for a few minutes until marshmallows are golden brown.
Makes 8 to 10 servings

Contributed by Courtney Crawford Braddock
Helen Smiles Jones McKey's granddaughter by marriage
Tarrant County

"*C*andied Sweet Potatoes always remind me of Thanksgiving," says Courtney, maybe because this casserole is standard fare on Grandma Helen's holiday table, where Courtney first encountered it more than a decade ago. Nuts make the dish more festive, but in recent years, Courtney has omitted them since one of her children has a nut allergy. With marshmallows on top, it's still plenty festive.

Baked sweet potatoes are good all by themselves, hot from the oven and slathered with butter as the basis of a meal, or cold, straight from the fridge as a snack.

Lucy Wu's Fried Rice (CHINESE)

Lucia "Lucy" Ching-On Lee Wu

1917–1987

Harris and Tarrant Counties

If you have leftover rice on hand, this dish is a natural. In fact, the cooked rice needs to be at least a half-day old; otherwise, it's too sticky. (Two or three days old is even better.) Plan to cook the meat and sausage ahead of time, too. The rest of the dish goes together quickly.

¼ cup vegetable oil, divided
2 garlic cloves, peeled and pressed
4 to 6 thin slices of peeled fresh ginger, divided
2 tablespoons chopped green onions or scallions
1 teaspoon dried shrimp
½ (10-ounce) package frozen green peas, defrosted
2 eggs, beaten
3 cups cooked long-grain rice, 1 to 3 days old
¼ teaspoon garlic salt
¾ cup chopped, cooked meat (any kind with very little fat)
½ cup chopped, cooked Chinese pork sausage
Salt and pepper

Place 2 tablespoons of the vegetable oil in a 12-inch skillet or wok, swirl oil to coat the bottom and sides of the pan, and heat until oil is hot. Using a spatula, fry garlic and 2 to 3 slices of the ginger until brown. Remove from oil and reserve in a serving bowl. Fry green onions and shrimp briefly; remove from oil and add to bowl. Fry peas until soft; remove from oil and add to bowl. Fry beaten eggs, breaking up into bits, and add to bowl.

Wash and dry skillet. Place remaining vegetable oil in pan and heat until oil is hot. Fry remaining ginger until brown; remove from oil and add to bowl. Fry rice and then turn heat to low. For 1 minute, turn the rice over and over with a spatula to fluff it. Stir in garlic salt. Add remaining ingredients and contents of bowl to skillet. Combine everything and turn mixture over and over again for 30 seconds. Adjust salt and pepper to taste and serve. *Makes 4 to 5 servings*

Contributed by Lucy Brianna Wu Weberlein
Lucia "Lucy" Ching-On Lee Wu's granddaughter
Travis County

Lucia "Lucy" Ching-On Lee Wu. Courtesy of Jane Wu.

*L*ucia Wu died before her granddaughter was born, so Lucy never met her grandmother (and namesake), but she enjoys making Fried Rice for family and friends.

Lucia and her husband, Shang Zhih, and their three young children emigrated from Hong Kong to the United States in 1956. Like many 1950s Chinese immigrants, they'd left the People's Republic of China for Hong Kong a few years earlier to escape living under Communist leader Mao's regime. They were sponsored by one of Shang Zhih's brothers and his wife, who lived in Fort Worth, and owned an Asian imports shop near Texas Christian University.

The couple eventually moved to Houston, where they owned a grocery store in the East End and raised four children. Lucy's mother, Jane Wu, remembers her mother making Fried Rice often during those years. "She made it as a side dish," says Jane, "utilizing leftovers and ingredients at hand.

Chapter 2: Recipes

"After my parents sold the store and my father retired, my mom worked at Sakowitz [a large department store]," says Jane. "She was independent-minded and preferred to continue working. After she took Fried Rice to a employee potluck, her co-workers requested the recipe. My mom didn't write down recipes, so one of my sisters helped her organize it in written form, and it was published in the company newsletter. That's fortunate, because it's the only written recipe we have from her."

You don't have to have a wok to make stir-fry dishes, but it's definitely the best tool for the job. Another useful tool is a wok spatula or stir-fry spatula, a broad, slightly curved spatula that makes it easy to move food around the sides of the pan quickly.

Stir-frying may have its roots in Asian cuisines, but the French principle of *mise en place* (set in place) plays an important role. With the fast pace of cooking involved, it's essential to cut, measure, and mix most of the ingredients ahead of time and then place them nearby, ready to go.

The Texas State Museum of Asian Cultures & Education Center in Corpus Christi celebrated its fortieth anniversary in 2014. It offers art exhibits, educational programs, and a number of annual events, including a Lunar New Year celebration (in January or February). Events often feature traditional Asian fare. Call 361–881–8827 or see www.asianculturesmuseum.org.

The UTSA Institute of Texan Cultures holds a one-day Asian Festival each January or February (depending on the date of the Lunar New Year), which features food from Japanese, Korean, Thai, Laotian, Philippine, and other Asian cuisines, as well as multicultural cooking demonstrations. Other offerings include traditional Asian dance and music, cultural performances, and children's activities. Call 210–458–2300 or see www.texancultures.com.

Other Asian festivals and events take place in Austin, Houston, Dallas, and Plano.

*Lorene Scott Hulse. Courtesy
of Courtney Braddock.*

Black-eyed Peas

*To soak or not to soak dried black-eyed peas? The official word is that it's not
necessary unless you have peas that are old. However, since you don't know the
provenance of the peas you buy in the grocery store, you might want to soak them
six hours or overnight before you start cooking. (This recipe was tested both ways
with good results each time.) If time isn't an issue, follow the same procedure
described here but cook the peas on low in a slow cooker for 6 to 8 hours. Don't
overcook the peas, or they will become mushy.*

1 (16-ounce) package (2 cups) dried black-eyed peas
2 to 4 slices bacon, cut into small pieces
Salt and pepper

Sort peas by hand to remove tiny stones or damaged or broken peas.
Place peas and bacon in a Dutch oven or other large pot; add enough
water to cover peas by at least 1 inch. Bring to a boil; cover, reduce heat,
and simmer over medium heat about an hour, or until peas are tender.
Season with salt and pepper. Serve with cornbread. *Makes 10 to 12
servings*

Contributed by Courtney Crawford Braddock
Lorene Scott Hulse's great-granddaughter
Tarrant County

*lack-eyed peas have a long tradition in Courtney's family. "We always
had them for New Year's Day, of course," she says, "and both my great-
grandmother and my grandmother made them often. I think that black-eyed peas
and cornbread made an inexpensive meal back then." Courtney's grandmother
Glenda Hulse Pope, who passed along her mother's recipe to Courtney, shares a
family story:*

*"There is a funny story with the peas. . . . Mother always had lunch prepared
on Sunday morning before we left for church. This particular Sunday, she had
put the peas in the pressure cooker, and during church, she couldn't remember
if she had turned it off. She got my attention and asked me to go home and see
if she had indeed turned off the fire under the peas. When I entered the kitchen,*

there were little black, hard peas all over the floor, and the pressure cooker had melted completely down to the lid. If it had exploded, we would have had a big hole in the ceiling. Thankfully, that story ended well — all we had was a big cleanup! That [episode] didn't stop Mother from using pressure cookers, however. She replaced several."

These days Courtney doesn't use a pressure cooker but prepares her black-eyed peas in a slow cooker. When she makes the dish for her family, she adds onions and her husband's favorite seasoning — jalapeños. Some things haven't changed, though — her family still passes the cornbread when they have black-eyed peas. It's a combination she says represents comfort food to her.

To add more flavor to black-eyed peas, cook them in a combination of water and chicken or beef stock. Try adding leftover ham or a ham hock instead of bacon. Adding onion, minced garlic, garlic chives, paprika, or rosemary also enhances the flavor.

Purple Hull Peas
(AFRICAN AMERICAN)

The ham hock adds wonderful flavor to the peas. Some people discard it before serving; others enjoy eating the meaty bits along with the peas.

1 smoked ham hock
2 quarts (fresh or frozen) shelled purple hull peas (if using fresh peas,
    you'll need about 4 pounds in the shell)
Pinch of sugar
Salt
Pepper
Paprika

Keep a teakettle of hot, near-boiling water on the stovetop.

Place smoked ham hock in large pot and add enough water to bring water level to about ½ inch above ham hock. Cook, covered, on medium-high heat for 1 to 2 hours, or until tender.

Addie Jane Lewis Odom (Big Mama)
1893–1987
Newton County

Addie Jane Lewis Odom. Courtesy of Harold Odom Jr.

Add water as needed from teakettle to bring water level to ½ inch above ham hock, and bring to a boil. Reduce heat, add peas, and cover. Let peas simmer until they are just tender (about 1 hour), checking every 15 to 20 minutes to make sure the water level is approximately ½ inch above the peas. If more water is needed, add it from the teakettle.

Once the peas are tender, add sugar, and then season with salt, pepper, and paprika to taste (start with ½ teaspoon each). Continue to let the peas simmer on low heat about 30 minutes, or until the water level is even with the peas. *Makes 12 to 16 servings*

Contributed by Lareatha Honette "Nette" Clay
Addie Jane Lewis Odom's granddaughter
Dallas County

A former commissioner of the Texas Historical Commission, Lareatha has always had a deep respect for her African American heritage. She remembers growing up eating purple hull peas, a lot of purple hull peas. "Although they're a summer crop, we'd usually 'put them up' in the freezer so that we could have them year-round," she says. "Now I mostly make them whenever I am around family. That's because I only know how to make a huge pot, and as a single person, that seems wasteful. They're a favorite of almost everyone in my family — my mother, sister, brothers, and nephews.

"My grandmother and her sisters cooked using the 'a little of this, a little of that' method, so unfortunately, there are no written recipes." Lareatha sometimes substitutes smoked turkey necks for the ham hock and likes to add baby okra to the mixture. She attributes this last preference to her exposure to "Louisiana-cooking influences" while growing up in Beaumont. Other than that, she says this recipe represents the way her family has cooked purple hull peas for generations.

"My grandmother always kept a teakettle of water on the stove and added hot water to the peas from there. While the hot water from a faucet in a modern kitchen would probably be hot enough, I just keep a teakettle of simmering water on the stove when I'm cooking these peas (or any other peas or beans)."

As a veteran pea picker, Lareatha has several stories to share about picking peas. "My grandparents grew purple hull peas on their farm in Newton County, and every summer my mother would take us [my sister, brothers, and me] there and we'd spend a whole day (at least it seemed that long to me) picking peas.

We'd take them back home to Beaumont and dump them on the floor in a back room adjacent to the kitchen. The next few days (maybe a week – again, I was young, so it may have seemed longer than is actually was) we'd spend all day shelling them until our fingertips were purple. Then we'd 'put them up,' which involved rinsing or 'blanching' them with hot water and putting them in plastic bags for the freezer. One year, after we'd finished shelling them, we were so tired that my mother decided to leave them out overnight and put them up the next day. The next morning, many of the peas had begun to sprout, so we spent that morning pulling out the sprouts before we could get them ready for freezing. Needless to say, we pushed through any desire to 'rest' during our pea-shelling and preserving activities in subsequent years.

"In those days, some farmers would allow people to come into their fields, pay a fee, and pick produce. [The practice continues today, albeit in a limited fashion.] That way, the person picking the vegetables could get the produce for a lower price than he or she would pay if the farmer harvested the vegetables. I learned that my grandparents had such arrangements one day in the late 1960s when my grandmother told us, 'Some people are coming over to pick some peas. If they ask you to help them, say No.'

"Later that day, a woman with a couple of teenagers came by, and sure enough, said to my sister, brothers, and me, 'Any of you nigras want to help me pick peas? I'll give you a nickel a bushel.' Thinking about how much work it would take to get a bushel of peas and how a nickel didn't seem worth it, but mostly knowing there was no way we'd defy my grandmother, we said, 'No.' Looking back, I wonder if that was my grandmother's small way of participating in the civil rights movement, which was at its height during that time. It was common to expect black children/teens/adults to work at the whim of white people back then, and my grandmother had decided that her grandchildren would not be a part of that system/culture on that day.

"By the time I was a young adult, my grandparents had stopped large-scale farming and only planted enough peas, corn, greens, beans, potatoes, and a few other items for themselves and family members. So my grandfather (A. T. Odom) regularly joined us in the field during purple hull pea season to pick our peas. He liked to tell lots of stories and jokes as we worked. Unfortunately, he stuttered, so it was hard to understand everything he said, but he'd get so tickled at his own stories and begin to laugh so hard that we'd *all have a good laugh, even though about half the time, we didn't know what the joke was about."*

Lareatha's grandparents' farm was in Shankleville, a freedmen's community in Newton County with a proud history (see Big Mama Addie Odom's Tea Cakes recipe in the Desserts section). In 1988, Lareatha helped found the Shankleville Historical Society, which works to preserve Shankleville's heritage and that of similar freedmen's communities in Texas. In 2014, Lareatha and other members of the society organized the annual Texas Purple Hull Pea Festival, which takes place in late June on the grounds of the Addie L. and A. T. Odom Homestead. The festival features contests (pea picking, pea shelling, and more), cooking demonstrations, and symposia on the cultural significance of purple hull peas and other signature Deep East Texas and Southeast Texas foods. For more information about the Shankleville Historical Society and a link to the Texas Purple Hull Pea Festival, see www.shankleville.org.

When cooking a pot of peas or beans and additional water is needed, make sure to add hot water; otherwise, the legumes will split.

Wendish Noodles (WENDISH)

Two things to know upfront about making noodles: If you use yard eggs (as do the volunteer cooks at the Texas Wendish Heritage Museum), you can usually eliminate the water. Try to avoid making noodles when it's damp outside; the weather affects how fast they'll dry.

3 eggs
Water to fill half-eggshell 3 times (about 6 tablespoons)
3 cups flour plus additional amount for rolling out dough
¼ teaspoon salt
2 quarts chicken broth
2 tablespoons butter
Chopped parsley (optional)

Break eggs into a large bowl, saving the most intact half-eggshell. Beat eggs and water together. Add 3 cups flour and salt to form stiff dough. Roll out dough into a rectangle about ⅛-inch thick on a well-floured

Anna Mattijehtz Mitschke (Mutta)

Circa 1870–1961

Lee County

Anna Mattijehtz Mitschke. Courtesy of Hattie Schautschick.

Chapter 2: Recipes

cutting board or countertop. Allow dough to dry about 10 minutes, turning occasionally.

When dough is dry but still pliable, cut into long sections about 3 inches wide. Take 3-inch sections and cut into thin strips about ⅛-inch wide. Cut noodle strips into preferred length for cooking. Place cut noodles on a dish towel and fluff noodles so air can circulate around them. Allow cut noodles to dry thoroughly, at least overnight, or longer if necessary. If noodles won't be cooked right away, store them in a sealed plastic bag in either the pantry or freezer for up to six months.

When ready to cook noodles, place chicken broth in a large pot and begin cooking over high heat. When broth is boiling, stir in butter, parsley, and dried noodles. Cover and cook noodles over medium heat for 10 minutes, or until tender. *Be careful not to overcook.* Remove pot from heat, leaving lid on, and let sit another 10 to 15 minutes. Do not drain. *Makes 1 pound of noodles or 20 servings*

Contributed by Hattie Mitschke Schautschick
Anna Mattijehtz Mitschke's granddaughter
Lee County

A lifelong resident of Serbin, a small, close-knit community in Lee County that her Wendish ancestors established more than a century ago, Hattie has been making these noodles as long as she can remember. "I learned how by making them with my mother [Louise Mertink Mitschke] and grandmother," she says. "As a young child, I helped cut the noodles after the dough had dried. My daughter Zelda started learning the same way."

Hattie's grandmother was born in Germany and came to America in the late 1800s. Hattie notes that the noodles recipe "was handed down from the original group of more than five hundred Wends who emigrated from Prussia [once an area in Germany] in 1854 . . . and settled Serbin."

Noodles are an important part of Wendish culture. "The first solid food for most Wendish babies has been — and still is — these homemade noodles," says Hattie. Older residents consume their share, too. Even today, Wendish families serve them for lunch every Sunday, as well as for weddings, anniversary celebrations, and other special occasions.

It turns out that non-Wends love the noodles, too. Hattie heads a team of volunteers who meet twice a week to make noodles to sell on behalf of the Texas Wendish Heritage Museum in Serbin. (Among the team members is Hattie's daughter Zelda Richards.) The dried noodles are sold at the museum and at several small groceries and bakeries in surrounding towns. The team's considerable efforts — they make up to 275 pounds each week — help fund museum activities, all of which are aimed at preserving Wendish culture. The only Wendish museum in the United States, it includes a central building that houses displays interpreting the history of the Wends, an office, gift shop, library, and archives; a converted schoolhouse; two log buildings; and outdoor farm-equipment exhibits.

The museum complex and the picnic grounds of the adjacent St. Paul Lutheran Church provide the setting for the annual Wendish Fest, which is held the fourth Sunday in September and draws several thousand people. Participants learn about Wendish history and culture and enjoy live music, washer pitching and other traditional games, children's activities, noodle making and other culinary demonstrations, traditional crafts demonstrations, exhibits, and an abundance of delicious Wendish food. For more information about the museum or the festival, call 979–366–2441 or see www.texaswendish.org.

Anna Mattijehtz Mitschke (seated), her daughter Clara Mitschke Synatsch, and her son Johnny Mitschke. Courtesy of Hattie Schautschick.

Nannie's Cornbread Dressing with Giblet Gravy
(AFRICAN AMERICAN)

Annie Owens Dunbar (Nannie)

1918–1973

Fannin County

Annie Owens Dunbar. Courtesy of Beverly D. Hamilton.

This recipe calls for both turkey giblets and turkey drippings, so plan to bake the requisite turkey before you start. You'll also need to make the Buttermilk Cornbread and Toasted Bread Crumbs beforehand. Another planning note: If you make the first part of the Giblet Gravy recipe – the broth – before making the dressing, you can use some of it to replace the chicken or vegetable broth in the dressing. (There will still be enough turkey broth for the gravy.) For moister dressing, spoon an additional ½ cup broth over the dressing before the last 30 minutes of baking.

1 cup melted butter, divided
1 large onion, chopped
3 stalks celery, chopped
1 green pepper, chopped
1½ teaspoons minced garlic
4 cups coarsely crumbled Buttermilk Cornbread
    (recipe follows)
1½ cups Toasted Bread Crumbs (recipe follows)
2 teaspoons poultry seasoning
1½ teaspoons dried thyme
1½ teaspoons dried sage
2 teaspoons salt
1 teaspoon pepper
3 eggs, beaten
1½ cups chicken broth or vegetable broth
Giblet Gravy (recipe follows)

Heat ½ cup of the butter in a small skillet and sauté onion, celery, green pepper, and garlic for 5 minutes, or until vegetables are tender. Remove from heat and cool.

Transfer vegetables to a large bowl. Add crumbled cornbread, bread crumbs, and seasonings. Toss to mix well. Add beaten eggs, remaining ½ cup melted butter, and broth and toss well. Spoon dressing lightly into a buttered 13 x 9-inch baking dish; *do not pack*. Bake at 350°F, covered, for 30 minutes. Then uncover and bake about 30 minutes longer, or until browned. Serve with turkey and Giblet Gravy. *Makes 10 to 12 servings*

Buttermilk Cornbread
2 cups flour
2 cups cornmeal
2 tablespoons baking powder
1 teaspoon baking soda
1½ teaspoons salt
2 eggs, lightly beaten
2 cups buttermilk
½ cup melted butter

Combine flour, cornmeal, baking powder, baking soda, and salt in a mixing bowl. Mix with a wire whisk until well blended. Whisk in eggs and buttermilk until well mixed. Pour melted butter into a 10-inch cast-iron skillet and place in a 400°F oven for a few minutes, or until butter is bubbly. Remove skillet from oven and stir butter into batter. Pour batter into skillet, return to oven, and bake 20 to 25 minutes, or until golden brown.

Cool cornbread completely and break into large pieces. Let stand, uncovered, overnight, or store in a sealed plastic bag up to 3 days. *Makes enough cornbread for Nannie's Cornbread Dressing*

Toasted Bread Crumbs
Place 12 slices stale French bread in the bowl of a food processor and pulse a few times to make fine bread crumbs. Spread bread crumbs in a shallow baking pan and bake at 325°F for 15 minutes, or until dry, stirring halfway through cooking time to prevent overbrowning. (Crumbs will reduce in volume after toasting.) *Makes about 1½ cups*

Giblet Gravy

1 package turkey giblets (the paper-wrapped package inside the turkey)
½ cup chopped celery
1 cup chopped onion
5 black peppercorns
3 to 4 stems parsley, chopped
2 quarts water
Freshly baked turkey with turkey drippings
½ cup flour
Salt and pepper

Combine giblets, vegetables, peppercorns, parsley, and 2 quarts of water in a large saucepan and bring to a boil. Reduce heat and simmer 2 hours. Remove peppercorns from broth and discard. Remove meat from broth, reserving broth. Dice meat. Set aside both broth and meat.

Remove baked turkey from roasting pan and pour off drippings. Measure ¼ cup drippings and set aside; discard remaining drippings or save for another use. Stir 2 cups broth into roasting pan (save remaining broth for another use). Place roasting pan on stovetop burner and cook over low heat a few minutes, stirring and scraping bottom of the pan to loosen browned bits.

Heat reserved ¼ cup drippings in a saucepan. Whisk in flour. Cook over medium heat 3 to 5 minutes, stirring constantly, until mixture is lightly browned. Add broth and browned bits from roasting pan in small batches, cooking and stirring until mixture thickens. Add reserved giblets to saucepan and season to taste with salt and pepper. Cook a few minutes longer to warm giblets. For a thinner gravy, add additional broth as needed. *Makes about 2½ cups*

Contributed by Toni Hamilton Tipton-Martin
Annie Owens Dunbar's granddaughter
Travis County

*C*ulinary journalist Toni Tipton-Martin has been making Nannie's Cornbread Dressing for more than two decades. She says it's a longtime Thanksgiving favorite in her family, although each generation has updated the recipe since her grandmother made it.

"Nannie soaked two slices of white bread in milk mixed with egg and added that to bind the mixture," says Toni. "She also sprinkled in a pinch of baking powder just before putting the dressing into the pan, to make it extra fluffy.

"After Nannie passed away at an early age from cancer, my mom started making changes in her diet. She stopped adding the bread because she was not eating white processed flour, substituted whole-wheat flour for the white flour in the cornbread, and changed chicken broth to vegetable broth. Today Mom uses millet flour and aluminum-free baking powder and makes a separate pan of dressing to suit her vegetarian lifestyle. She bakes the seasonings and sautéed vegetables into the cornbread so that the flavors meld. My version circles back to Nannie's original: I use the buttermilk cornbread recipe from my first book, A Taste of Heritage: New African American Cuisine [*John Wiley and Sons, 1998*] and make my own fresh bread crumbs from stale French bread."

Toni hasn't always been a whiz at making dressing. "The first time I made Thanksgiving dinner in my own kitchen, without Mom's help, was my first year as food editor at the Cleveland Plain Dealer," says Toni. "I was cooking for my new husband's family, and they were expecting something spectacular from me as a professional 'chef.' I followed Nannie's recipe, substituting fresh herbs and packing the mixture neatly into the pan. It was a horrible, tasteless brick. I hid in the mudroom, crying on the telephone with my mom, who helped me face my hungry in-laws waiting in the dining room. I did eventually master the recipe over the years (it's important not to pack the dressing into the pan), making it a signature dish for a holiday demo at Whole Foods' Culinary Center in Austin, but now my sister-in-law has taken over making the dressing for holiday gatherings, adapting her version with tastes imparted by her father, a trained chef who was born and raised in New Orleans."

Toni thinks it's likely that the original recipe for Nannie's Cornbread Dressing came from another chef — her great-grandmother Ann Young Owens (Big Momma), who was head of catering at the Wilshire Ebell Theatre in Los Angeles during the 1950s. "This dish represents classic Southern cooking, which African Americans and whites share responsibility for creating," she says.

This premise is at the heart of Toni's current project: a traveling exhibit, blog, and 2015 book, The Jemima Code: Two Centuries of African American Cookbooks (*University of Texas Press, 2015*), which celebrates the important *legacy of African American cooks and their cookbooks. The book earned her a 2014 John Egerton Prize from Southern Foodways Alliance.*

The coauthor of three other books, Toni was the first African American food editor of a major daily newspaper (the Cleveland Plain Dealer)*. She has also worked as the nutrition writer for the* Los Angeles Times *and as a contributing editor of* Heart & Soul *magazine. She is cofounder and former president of Southern Foodways Alliance. She also cofounded Foodways Texas (see resources section) in 2010 and has served as president of the board.*

Aunt Earle's Cushaw

Cushaw is a large, crookneck winter squash with green-and-white stripes. It's an heirloom vegetable, so you're not likely to find it in a grocery store. Look for it at farmers' markets in the fall.

1 (6- to 8-pound) cushaw, peeled and cut into small cubes
2 cups brown sugar
3 tablespoons melted butter

Combine squash and enough water to cover in a large saucepan and cook, uncovered, about 30 minutes, or until tender. Drain water and spread a layer of squash in the bottom of a 9 x 9-inch casserole dish.

Combine brown sugar and melted butter. Spread half the mixture over the first layer of squash. Add a second layer of squash and spread the remaining brown sugar–butter mixture over the top. Bake at 375°F for 20 minutes, or until top is crispy brown. *Makes 8 to 10 servings*

Contributed by Kathryn Nell Roberts
Anna Earle Armstrong McCreight's great-niece
Williamson County

Anna Earle Armstrong McCreight (Aunt Earle)

1891–1977

Gregg County

Anna Earle Armstrong McCreight. Courtesy of Kathryn Nell Roberts.

Kathryn says that the first time she ever had cushaw was at her aunt Earle's home in Longview. "Thereafter I was always delighted to see it delivered to the table," she adds. "Even my siblings, who were not fond of squash, enjoyed this version. Aunt Earle always served this delicious dish at holiday dinners in the formal dining room. "Memories of those holiday dinners remain fresh in Kathryn's mind. "Aunt Earle and her longtime, devoted housekeeper, Odessa Johnson, would wear aprons over their fine dresses while working in the kitchen, preparing the dishes to go with the turkey or ham," she says. "On Thanksgiving, Aunt Earle used her Thanksgiving English bone china with designs of turkeys and farms and red covered bridges. At Christmastime, she used her collection of antique hand-painted china." (For more about Kathryn's great-aunt, see Aunt Earle's Pound Cake recipe in the Desserts section.)

Cushaw is also known as "kershaw," "Tennessee sweet potato squash," and "kershaw pumpkin." Some Southern cooks swear by it as a substitute for pumpkin in pumpkin pie. If you're lucky enough to find it at a farmers' market, try it and see if you agree. It's also wonderful roasted with a little olive oil.

Tales of Aunt Earle

KATHRYN NELL ROBERTS

Aunt Earle was my paternal grandmother's sister. The Armstrong girls grew up on the John Kittle Armstrong farm in Gladewater. They learned to tat, embroider, needlepoint, quilt, and make hats. They also developed good business sense. My grandmother Nell went to work making hats for a milliner. Earle embroidered elegant handkerchiefs for Nieman Marcus. Even then, she had a rule that she lived by: She saved fifty cents of every dollar that passed through her hands.

In 1917, Earle married prominent railroad attorney Erasmuth Young of Longview (the same year my grandmother Nell married my grandfather John C. Roberts). They built a large, Victorian home in Longview and took in boarders. A gentleman boarder working as an oil prospector buying up royalties recognized Earle's good business sense, and they became great friends. Walter Priddy taught Earle to invest her money, and they made an agreement that he would pay rent in warrants—a security that entitles the holder to purchase stock at a fixed price. This proved to be a lucrative arrangement, as the warrants represented the successful company that Mr. Priddy later founded—the Sabine Royalty Corporation, known today as the Sabine Royalty Trust.

Earle was an active member of the First Baptist Church of Longview and regularly entertained her bridge club and other groups at her home. After becoming widowed, she traveled across Texas to visit friends and family. Because her late husband had been an attorney for the largest railroads in the United States, she had a lifetime pass and traveled everywhere for free. She was known to take the train from Northeast Texas to the Hot Wells Mineral Resort in San Antonio and also stayed at the Baker Hotel in Mineral Wells with a church group.

While on one such trip, fellow church member George McCreight asked for her hand in marriage and she accepted. They married in 1943. My grandparents, who had settled in Denton, would regularly trek over to Longview for a visit and enjoy fine meals from Earle's kitchen. Mr. 'Mac' founded the First State Bank in Longview, was on the board of directors for Lone Star Steel Company, and was an investor in numerous enterprises. He eventually became the mayor of Longview. They shared the good life for many years. After Mr. Mac died in 1966, Earle continued to live in Longview and enjoy her friends and community.

**Augusta Margeta
Kneupper Heitkamp**
(*Gross Oma*)

1860–1945

Comal County

Baked Squash

*With lemon zest, this casserole tastes surprisingly like lemon meringue pie.
Yellow squash usually doesn't have to be peeled, but if you have any older squash
with thick skins, peel those and discard any large seeds.*

2 eggs, separated
1 cup whole milk
2 tablespoons cornstarch
3 cups cooked, drained, and mashed yellow squash
   (requires 6 to 8 medium squash)
½ cup sugar, divided
½ teaspoon salt
1 teaspoon lemon zest or 1 teaspoon vanilla and 1 teaspoon cinnamon

*Augusta Margeta Kneupper
Heitkamp (right) and her daughter
Bertha Heitkamp Rosenberg.
Courtesy of Dee Henneke.*

100

Chapter 2: Recipes

Beat egg yolks and combine with milk and cornstarch in a mixing bowl. Add squash, ¼ cup of the sugar, salt, and lemon zest (or vanilla and cinnamon) and mix well. Place mixture in a greased 9 x 9-inch casserole dish and bake at 375°F for about 40 minutes. Remove from oven and set aside.

Beat egg whites at high speed with an electric mixer until foamy. Add remaining ¼ cup sugar, a little at a time, while continuing to beat for 2 to 4 minutes, or until stiff peaks form and sugar dissolves. Spread meringue over top of squash mixture and bake at 325°F about 15 minutes, or until meringue browns. *Makes about 8 servings*

Contributed by Nadine "Dee" Vernell Rosenberg Henneke
Augusta Margeta Kneupper Heitkamp's great-granddaughter
DeWitt County

"*Baked Squash is my favorite heirloom recipe, and it's the oldest one of all," says Dee. "People comment that it tastes too good to be a vegetable, that it should be a dessert. I've made it for almost sixty years. My girls make it, too, so it is a five-generation recipe."*

Dee's ancestors were German, but she doesn't know the origin of the recipe. "I make it whenever I have yellow squash," she says. "Some years the garden produces abundantly — then I make it more often. I think the recipe most likely originated one summer when my great-grandmother was faced with a large quantity of yellow squash from her garden."

Ruby S. Patterson
1897–1979
Dallas, Cameron, and Harris Counties

Aunt Ruby's Baked Cabbage

Using Ritz crackers makes this dish a little richer. You can also substitute two (1-ounce) bags of potato chips for either type of cracker. (If using potato chip crumbs, omit the butter.) Aunt Ruby likely made white sauce the traditional way, but Microwave White Sauce is an almost-scorch-proof alternative.

2 sleeves of Ritz or saltine crackers (about 70 or 80 crackers, respectively)
2 to 3 tablespoons butter, melted
Microwave White Sauce (recipe follows) or 1 cup white sauce (any recipe)
1 cup shredded Cheddar cheese
1 head cabbage, coarsely shredded or julienned

Crush crackers into crumbs and stir into melted butter until crumbs are well coated with butter. Set aside.

Combine 1 cup white sauce and cheese in a saucepan and cook over low heat until cheese melts, stirring constantly (or microwave on High in a microwave-safe dish until cheese melts). Set aside.

Simmer cabbage in salted water for about 10 minutes, or until tender. Drain. Add cheese sauce and mix well. Place mixture in a greased 1-quart casserole. Top generously with buttered crumbs and bake at 350°F for about 30 minutes, or until golden brown. *Makes 6 to 8 servings*

Microwave White Sauce
2 tablespoons butter or margarine
2 tablespoons flour
About ½ teaspoon salt
$\frac{1}{16}$ teaspoon pepper (use white pepper if you don't want black specks)
1 cup milk

102 *Chapter 2: Recipes*

Melt butter in a microwave-safe dish in microwave, being careful not to brown it. Add flour, salt, pepper, and milk and mix well. Cook in microwave on High until sauce has thickened, about 3 minutes, stopping and stirring the mixture several times. Sauce will be done when medium-thick and doesn't taste of uncooked flour. *Makes 1 cup*

Contributed by Julie Catherine Puentes Schrab
Ruby S. Patterson's "adopted" great-niece
Travis County

*F*amily relationships can be complicated to explain to outsiders. "Aunt Ruby is my stepmother's cousin's aunt by marriage," says Julie. "But my stepmother [Nancy O'Bryant Puentes] thought of her as an aunt when she was growing up, so we all claimed her as a communal 'Aunt Ruby.' I don't think she minded, as she had no children of her own.*

"Aunt Ruby was known for her beautiful clothes and costume jewelry, her perfectly groomed hair, and beautifully manicured nails with red polish. She always wore high heels (size 4) because she was tiny. That's why this photo of her with a fish close to half her size, with her hair tied up by a scarf, and barefoot, is so funny to the family. She and her husband, Garland Patterson, always went to 'the lakes' in Minnesota each summer, where the photo was taken. Following the death of her husband, she went to work at Palais Royal in Houston and enjoyed being around all the pretty things."

No one in the family knows where or how Ruby acquired the Baked Cabbage recipe. "But we do know she was proud of the dish and known for it," says Julie. "It's a great way to serve cabbage that everyone seems to like. Even people who normally don't like cabbage like it."

Ruby S. Patterson. Courtesy of Karey Bresenhan.

**Lillian Piazza Cappello
(Mema)**

1917–2004

Harris County

Hot Antipasto (ITALIAN)

Unlike cold antipasto, which consists of vegetables, cheeses, and meats arranged on a bed of lettuce, this dish is mixed together like a stew. It's traditionally served on small plates before the main course, but it also works as a side dish.

1 pound red or Yukon gold potatoes, unpeeled, cut into chunks,
    boiled, and drained
1 (12-ounce) jar red sweet roasted peppers, drained and sliced thin
2 cans artichoke hearts, drained and quartered
2 (8-ounce) cans whole mushrooms, drained
1 (6-ounce) can whole black olives (pitted), drained and divided
Salt and pepper
Garlic powder
1 cup olive oil
1 cup flavored bread crumbs
2 tablespoons butter, cut into small pieces

*Lillian Piazza Cappello.
Courtesy of Bob Ruggiero Jr.*

Combine first 3 ingredients in a buttered 13 x 9-inch pan.

Slice each mushroom into three pieces and add to potato mixture. Slice each olive in half. Set aside half the olives and add remaining olives to potato mixture. Add seasonings to taste. Pour olive oil over top of mixture, sprinkle with bread crumbs, and dot with butter. Distribute remaining olives over top of dish. Bake at 350°F for 30 minutes.
Makes 6 servings

Contributed by Bob Ruggiero Jr.
Lillian Piazza Cappello's grandson
Harris County

*B*ob *lived in Connecticut in the midst of a large, extended Italian family before moving to Texas. (His grandmother followed five years later; see Ham Pie in the Main Dishes section). "When all the family gathered for dinner, the Hot Antipasto was ladled out onto small plates and served before the main meal, which might include as many as eight different offerings," he says. "As a child, I found my grandmother's and great-aunt's serving dishes interesting," he says. "Each had little sections or compartments that held different food items. Sampling each one made it fun, and the variety of items made eating interesting."*

The olive oil stars in this dish, so use the best quality you can find. Not sure which brand is best? Buy several bottles and taste-test with small chunks of rustic bread. If you cook with olive oil on a regular basis, the experiment is a good investment.

Josef Mozisek. Courtesy of Otto Mozisek Jr.

Czech Sauerkraut (CZECH)

This side dish is usually served with Czech Picnic Stew (see recipe in the Main Dishes section), but it's often paired with sausage, fried chicken, and other meats, too.

2 slices bacon, diced
Flour
1 (14.4-ounce) can sauerkraut, undrained
Water
Salt and pepper

Fry bacon pieces. Stir in enough flour to make a thick gravy and cook over low heat until flour is browned. Stir in sauerkraut. Add water as needed; however, mixture should be thick. Taste (mixture will be salty from the bacon) and add salt and pepper as desired. *Makes 6 servings if served with Czech Picnic Stew (see Main Dishes section) or 4 servings if served as a side dish*

Contributed by Otto Franklin Mozisek Jr.
Josef Mozisek's grandson
Victoria County

Otto's grandfather used homemade sauerkraut in this dish, as did Otto's father when he first began making it. "When I was growing up in the 1950s, we still made our own sauerkraut," says Otto, "as well as our own deer and pork sausage from deer we hunted and hogs we raised. There were six of us kids, plus my parents, and we lived eight miles outside of Inez. We smoked the sausage ourselves along with bacon and other parts of the hog. We also raised chickens — sometimes we butchered one hundred at a time for the freezer — and had a two-acre garden. Almost everything we ate, we either raised or hunted."

Chapter 2: Recipes

Spoonbread

More like a pudding than a bread, this well-loved Southern side dish complements many a menu.

1 cup yellow cornmeal
1 teaspoon salt
1 teaspoon sugar
2 tablespoons butter
1 cup buttermilk
4 eggs, well beaten

Measure cornmeal into a medium bowl. Stir in ½ cup cold water and set aside.

Bring 2 cups of water to a boil. Add salt, sugar, and wet cornmeal, stirring constantly, and cook 1 minute. Add butter, buttermilk, and then eggs and beat until smooth. Pour mixture into a buttered 1½-quart casserole and bake at 400°F about 40 minutes, or until a toothpick inserted in the center comes out clean. *Makes 6 to 8 servings*

Contributed by Meredith McClain
Rita Cook McClain's granddaughter
Lubbock County

"My brother Martin and I dearly love this recipe from our grandmother," says Meredith. *"It's such a simple item, but delicious and elegant. Grandmother served it in a glass container straight from the oven, which she placed in an aluminum holder that had fancy sides and little feet. I once prepared it for Ann Clark, Austin chef, cooking teacher, and my dear friend from graduate-school days; unfortunately, as I was moving it from the oven, the glass dish broke. Darn! Better luck to everyone else!"*

Rita Cook McClain
1882–1961
Williamson County

Rita Cook McClain.
Courtesy of Meredith McClain.

Desserts

Cakes

Cookies

Pies and Cobblers

Puddings

Other Desserts

Cakes

Chocolate-Cinnamon Cake

A prime example of a Texas sheet cake, this recipe is easy to make and serves a large group. For the best results, make the icing during the last few minutes that the cake is baking and be ready to pour it onto the cake as soon as it comes out of the oven. This allows the icing to soak into the cake, resulting in a moist, fudgy texture.

2 cups flour
2 cups sugar
1 teaspoon cinnamon
½ cup (1 stick) butter
¼ cup cocoa
1 cup water
½ cup buttermilk
2 eggs, slightly beaten
1 teaspoon vanilla
Chocolate Icing (recipe follows)

Sift flour, sugar, and cinnamon together in a large mixing bowl; set aside.

Combine butter, cocoa, and 1 cup water in a saucepan and bring to a boil. Pour over dry ingredients and stir until smooth. Add buttermilk, beaten eggs, and vanilla and mix well. Pour batter into a greased and floured 18 x 12-inch jelly roll or sheet cake pan. Bake at 350°F for 20 to 25 minutes, or until a toothpick inserted in the center comes out clean. Leave cake in pan and pour Chocolate Icing over warm cake; spread icing to edges.
Makes 24 servings

Bessie Hackney Shanafelt (Nana)

1902–1976

Jones, Haskell, Hardeman, and Guadalupe Counties

Bessie Hackney Shanafelt. Courtesy of Kathleen Martin.

Chocolate Icing

½ cup (1 stick) butter
¼ cup cocoa
¼ cup plus 2 tablespoons milk
1 pound powdered sugar, sifted (4¾ cups sifted powdered sugar)
1 cup chopped pecans

Combine, butter, cocoa, and milk in a saucepan. Bring to a boil and then remove from heat. Stir in powdered sugar and pecans. Beat well before spreading on cake. *Makes enough icing for Chocolate-Cinnamon Cake*

Contributed by Kathleen Shanafelt Martin
Bessie Hackney Shanafelt's granddaughter
Jackson County

"*Nana could really stretch a dollar and make the food she cooked go a long way,*" *says Kathleen. "She'd take leftover pie-crust dough, spread it with butter, sprinkle it with sugar and cinnamon, and then roll it up and cut it into slices, which she'd bake in the oven until it was crispy. Yum . . . so good. She would also fry baloney and use that as a main course. . . . But nobody at her house was ever hungry! She always had dishes with little dabs of leftovers in the fridge and a half-piece of leftover bacon on top of the stove. Nana never wasted anything.*

"*She was an amazing cook. My sisters remember her making homemade egg noodles and laying them over the backs of the kitchen chairs to dry. She'd use these to make a big pot of chicken and noodles. And she would always serve this yummy, rich chocolate cake when all the family came to visit her. The Martin family loves it, too. We're all chocoholics!*"

References to "Texas sheet cake" abound even in non-Texas cookbooks, but there's no evidence that this dessert originated in the Lone Star State. It's popular throughout the United States. Did the name arise because the flat, rectangular cake seemed "as big as Texas"? Or because the icing features pecans (commonly associated with Texas)? And then there's the "sheath" vs. "sheet" issue—is "sheath cake" a common mispronunciation, or did the term derive from the way the frosting "sheathes" the warm cake as it's poured on top? No matter how you describe this cake, Texans are happy to claim it as their own.

Estelle Reese Morton
1898–1974
Wharton County

Estelle Morton's Chocolate Cake

Although this recipe calls for the cake to be iced in the pan, there's more than enough icing to cover the sides of the cake, too. To serve it this way, cool the cake in the pan on a wire rack for 10 minutes, invert it onto a large, rectangular dish, and spread icing over the entire cake.

1½ cups flour
1 cup sugar
3 tablespoons cocoa
1 teaspoon baking powder
1 teaspoon baking soda
1 teaspoon cinnamon
½ teaspoon salt
1 egg
1 cup buttermilk
½ cup vegetable oil
1 teaspoon vanilla
Chocolate Icing (recipe follows)

Mix dry ingredients together in a large bowl.

Combine egg and next three ingredients in a separate bowl and blend well. Add to dry ingredients and mix well. Pour mixture into a greased and floured 13 x 9-inch pan. Bake at 350°F for about 25 minutes. Leave cake in pan and spread icing onto warm cake. *Makes one 13-x 9-inch cake*

Chocolate Icing
1 cup sugar
¼ cup cocoa
6 tablespoons butter
¼ cup evaporated milk
1 teaspoon vanilla

Chapter 2: Recipes

Combine all ingredients except vanilla in a saucepan. Cook over medium heat, stirring constantly, until mixture comes to a hard boil. Boil for 1 minute; stir in vanilla. Cool icing for a few minutes. (Icing is thin, with the consistency of a glaze.) *Makes enough icing for one 13 x 9-inch cake*

Contributed by Vada Marie Morton Wolter
Estelle Reese Morton's granddaughter
Wharton County

"Grandma usually took this cake to church socials," says Vada. "Everyone always wanted some of 'Estelle's chocolate cake.' They sometimes got it with their meal when they went through the serving line rather than going back for dessert later and taking a chance on missing out." Vada herself has been making the cake "about fifty years!" and has never made any changes in her grandma's recipe. It's one of her family's favorite desserts, so she bakes it about once a month.

Estelle Reese Morton with her husband, Allen Morton. Courtesy of Vada Wolter.

Rita Cook McClain
1882–1961
Williamson County

Rita Cook McClain.
Courtesy of Meredith McClain.

Fresh Coconut Cake

When working with fresh coconut, the first step is to somehow extract the coconut meat from the shell. Here's Rita McClain's solution: "Send one child, seven to eleven years old, out to the sidewalk with a coconut, a hammer, and a big nail. He drives the nail into the three eyes of the coconut, shakes out the water, and drinks it. Then he pounds the coconut repeatedly (to loosen the meat) until it breaks. He pounds it some more until there are about eight chunks. These are brought into the kitchen, where the meat is pried out with a knife, separated from its brown skin, and grated into a moist, snowy heap."

1 cup (2 sticks) unsalted butter, softened
2 cups sugar
5 large eggs, separated
2 teaspoons lemon zest
3 tablespoons fresh lemon juice (you'll need about 3 lemons total)
2 teaspoons vanilla
2½ cups cake flour (don't use self-rising flour)
2 teaspoons baking powder
1 teaspoon salt
1 cup sour cream
Lemon Filling (recipe follows)
Fluffy Frosting (recipe follows)
Meat of 1 coconut, grated (2 to 4 cups)

Beat butter at medium speed with an electric mixer until creamy. Add sugar and beat 5 minutes, or until light and fluffy. Add egg yolks, one at a time, beating after each addition. Add lemon zest, lemon juice, and vanilla and beat well.

Blend together cake flour, baking powder, and salt in a separate bowl. Add flour mixture (in fourths) to egg mixture alternately with sour cream (in thirds), beating at low speed with an electric mixer.

Chapter 2: Recipes

Wash and dry beaters. Beat egg whites in a clean, dry bowl until stiff peaks form. Fold egg whites into batter and pour batter into 2 buttered and floured 9-inch cake pans. Bake at 350°F about 30 minutes, or until a toothpick inserted in the center comes out clean. Let cake cool in pans on a wire rack for 10 minutes; remove from pans and cool completely on wire rack.

Spread Lemon Filling between layers; spread Fluffy Frosting on top and sides of cake. Pat coconut onto top and sides of cake. *Makes one 2-layer cake*

Lemon Filling
1 cup sugar
Zest of 1 lemon
3 tablespoons cornstarch
¼ teaspoon salt
2 large egg yolks (reserve whites for Fluffy Frosting)
½ cup fresh lemon juice
2 tablespoons unsalted butter

Whirl sugar and lemon zest in the bowl of a food processor until lemon zest is chopped into tiny pieces. Combine lemon-sugar mixture with cornstarch and salt in a saucepan and blend well. Whisk in egg yolks and lemon juice. Bring mixture to a boil over medium heat; boil 1 minute. Remove from heat and whisk in butter until melted and smooth. Cover surface directly with plastic wrap; let cool to room temperature. *Makes enough filling for Fresh Coconut Cake*

Fluffy Frosting
3 large egg whites (2 reserved egg whites from Lemon Filling plus 1
    more; reserve egg yolk from last egg for another use)
¾ cup sugar
¼ teaspoon cream of tartar
3 tablespoons water
¼ teaspoon vanilla
¼ teaspoon almond extract

Fill bottom of a double boiler with water and heat until simmering.

Combine egg whites, sugar, cream of tartar, and 3 tablespoons water in the top pan of the double boiler. Beat 1 minute at high speed with a handheld electric mixer. Place mixture over simmering water, making sure that top pan of double boiler doesn't touch the water. Beat at high speed until stiff, shiny peaks form (about 7 minutes). Remove top pan from double boiler. Add vanilla and almond extract and beat 5 minutes longer, or until frosting is cool. *Makes enough frosting for Fresh Coconut Cake*

Contributed by Meredith McClain
Rita Cook McClain's granddaughter
Lubbock County

"Grandmother McClain usually served this cake when the Georgetown Ladies Luncheon Club met at her house. My older brother, Martin McClain, who lives in Detroit, remembers it well," says Meredith, "because he was the child required to extract the coconut meat. I honestly think he became a chemist because of his early cooking adventures with our grandmother." (See Brisket with Chuckwagon Hollandaise in the Main Dishes section.)

Meredith shares this note from her brother, who has researched their ancestry: "Rita Cook was born on a farm near Lebanon, Tennessee, where the Cooks raised hogs, corn, and tobacco. Colonel Cook used to sell a lot of his corn to bearded men who came down from the Tennessee hills for it in the early summer, when the corn was green and sweet and fermented nicely. He never asked them what they did with so much corn. The smoked ham and sausage they made right there on the farm were legendary. When we were children, Grandmother used to receive a Christmas ham from her brother, Joe, who ran the farm. But by 1950, the hams had become too valuable to give away like that."

Rita married and had two sons. After her husband died of tuberculosis, she accepted the job of running the kitchen at Cumberland University in Lebanon. Meredith explains how this decision led the young widow to move to Texas. "When the president of Southwestern University in Georgetown attended a conference at Cumberland in about 1928, he was impressed with the food he was served and asked to meet the person in charge of the kitchen. He told my grandmother that he could offer her the best, most modern kitchen in the

Southwest if she would take the train to visit Georgetown and accept a job as head of food service at the new women's dormitory at Southwestern.

"That's exactly what Grandmother did," continues Meredith. "She moved into the 'luxury' apartment in the brand-new Laura Kuykendall Hall and started the food service there. When the Depression hit, Southwestern University gave faculty members 'food vouchers' so they could eat in the women's dormitory dining hall."

Today, both Meredith and her brother enjoy making several of their grandmother's recipes. She says, "We love to serve them on special occasions to show off the culinary history of our family."

Grandma Zeman's Oatmeal Cake

This cake can be made in either an 11 x 8-inch or a 13 x 9-inch pan. If using the smaller pan, allow a little more time for baking.

1 cup regular oats
1¼ cups boiling water
1 cup sugar
1 cup firmly packed light brown sugar
½ cup shortening
2 eggs
1 teaspoon vanilla
1⅓ cups flour
1 teaspoon cinnamon
½ teaspoon salt
1 teaspoon baking soda
Topping (recipe follows)

Place oats in a small bowl and pour boiling water over them; let stand while mixing other ingredients.

Cream both sugars and shortening in a large bowl. Add eggs and vanilla and mix well.

Caroline Barak Zeman
1902–2000
Fort Bend County

Caroline Barak Zeman.
Courtesy of Jean Paul.

Sift together flour, cinnamon, salt, and baking soda. Stir into egg-sugar mixture and mix well. Add oatmeal and mix well. Spread batter into a greased and floured 11 x 8-inch pan (or 13 x 9-inch pan) and bake at 350°F for 30 minutes, or until a toothpick inserted in the center comes out clean.

Spread Topping over cake while cake is still warm. Place cake under broiler briefly until lightly browned. *Makes one 11 x 8-inch or one 13 x 9-inch cake*

Topping
6 tablespoons butter
1 tablespoon evaporated milk
¾ cup firmly packed light brown sugar
1 cup shredded coconut
1 cup chopped pecans

Mix butter and milk together in a saucepan and cook over low heat, stirring occasionally, until butter melts. Add brown sugar and bring the mixture to a boil over medium heat. Boil for 1 minute. Remove from heat and add coconut and pecans. *Makes enough topping for one 11 x 8-inch or one 13 x 9-inch cake*

Contributed by Jean Evelyn Matula Paul
Caroline Barak Zeman's granddaughter
Brazoria County

"*Grandma Zeman was a farmer's wife,*" *says Jean.* "*She and my grandpa [Willie Zeman] lived in Guy in Fort Bend County, where they grew cotton and corn, raised cattle, and always had a large garden. Grandma worked alongside Grandpa in the fields and canned vegetables from their garden and fruit from their trees. Somehow, she also managed to cook and maintain the home. It was always so clean you could eat off the floors.*"

"*I remember Grandma Zeman making this cake when I was a small child. She almost always made it for family get-togethers. If she didn't make it, we would ask where the cake was.*"

"I've been making it myself for more than forty years," adds Jean. "The only change I've made in the recipe is that I use Baker's Joy instead of greasing and flouring the pan. It's a favorite of mine and my sister's, so I usually make it at least once a year, usually for Thanksgiving and Christmas."

If a cake pan looks a little full when you put it in the oven, place a cookie sheet on the rack below it. This may save you some cleanup later.

The $300 Red Cake

The origin of this popular cake (also known as Red Velvet Cake) is associated with various urban legends, including the one passed down through Hilda Spencer's family. While its origin can't be substantiated, it's most definitely red.

½ cup shortening
1½ cups sugar
2 eggs
1 teaspoon vanilla
1 ounce red food coloring
2 teaspoons cocoa
1 cup buttermilk
2¼ cups flour
1 teaspoon baking soda
1 tablespoon vinegar
Red Cake Frosting (recipe follows)

Cream shortening and sugar in a large bowl. Add eggs and mix well to make a paste. Add vanilla, food coloring, cocoa, buttermilk, and flour. Beat with an electric mixer until blended. Stir in baking soda and vinegar. Pour batter into 2 greased and floured 8-inch round or square pans. Bake at 350°F for 30 minutes, or until a toothpick inserted in the center comes out clean. Cool cakes in pans 10 minutes; remove from pans and cool completely on wire racks.

Hilda "Jack" Ross Spencer
1911–1985
Refugio and Harris Counties

Hilda "Jack" Ross Spencer. Courtesy of Joy Huebel.

Split each layer in half horizontally with a string. Frost all four layers with Red Cake Frosting, stacking one layer on top of the other. Spread remaining frosting over top and sides of cake. *Makes one 4-layer cake*

Red Cake Frosting
1 cup milk
3 tablespoons flour
¾ cup plus 2 tablespoons butter
1 cup sugar
1 teaspoon vanilla

Combine milk and flour in a small saucepan. Cook mixture over low heat until it thickens, stirring constantly. Let cool completely.

Using an electric mixer, beat butter and sugar until the mixture is fluffy. Add flour-milk mixture slowly to creamed mixture and mix well. Stir in vanilla. *Makes enough frosting for The $300 Red Cake*

Contributed by Sarah Joy Emerson Huebel
Hilda "Jack" Ross Spencer's granddaughter
Travis County

"*When I was growing up, our family would visit my grandmother's house in La Porte, and we would all run to the kitchen to see if she had Red Cake,*" says Joy. "*If she did, it was not long until it was all gone. The recipe was passed down through my mother's side of the family, as well as the story behind the name — that someone had tasted the cake at a restaurant and asked for the recipe. The restaurant manager sent the recipe, along with a bill for three hundred dollars.*"

"*My grandmother often made this cake (including frosting it) ahead of time and would put it in the freezer. By the time everyone arrived, the cake would be defrosted and ready to eat.*"

Joy has been making the cake herself for more than thirty years. "*Everyone in the family loves it,*" she says. "*I usually make it for Christmas or Valentine's Day.*"

It's important to follow the instructions regarding slicing the cake layers in half. With four thin layers, the frosting can soak all the way through, which results in a moister cake.

Vanilla, Butter, and Nut Pound Cake (POLISH)

Brigid Snoga Gwosdz
1908–1999
Karnes and Jackson Counties

The distinctive vanilla-butternut flavoring used in this recipe can be difficult to find; look for it at most Kroger stores. The contributor favors McCormick Imitation Vanilla, Butter & Nut Flavor, which you can order online from Amazon. King Arthur Flour offers a similar product, Vanilla Butternut Flavor, on its website. You can also substitute regular vanilla extract; however the cake won't have the same taste or rich, yellow color as it does with the original flavoring.

¾ cup (1½ sticks) butter
½ cup Crisco
3 cups sugar
¼ teaspoon salt
5 large eggs
3 cups flour
1 (5-ounce) can evaporated milk (add water to make 1 cup)
1½ tablespoons Vanilla, Butter, & Nut Flavoring
Powdered sugar
Fresh strawberries (optional)

Do not preheat oven. Cream butter, Crisco, sugar, and salt in a large bowl. Add eggs one at a time, beating after each one. Add flour and milk alternately, beginning and ending with flour. Fold in flavoring by hand. Pour batter into a greased and floured 10-inch tube pan. *Place pan in a cold oven and then set temperature for 325°F.* Bake 1 hour and 45 minutes, or until top is golden brown (as seen through oven door). *Do not open oven door until time is up.* Then check for doneness by inserting a toothpick in the center of the cake; it should come out clean.

Remove cake from the oven and let pan cool on wire rack for 10 minutes. Run a knife around the edge of the cake to loosen it and then remove it from the pan and cool completely. When cool, dust with powdered sugar, using a paper doily as a stencil. Garnish with fresh strawberries, if desired. *Makes one 10-inch cake*

Brigid Snoga Gwosdz.
Courtesy of Cheryl Hertz.

Contributed by Cheryl Ann Hertz
Brigid Snoga Gwosdz's granddaughter
Victoria County

This pound cake recipe has made the rounds in Cheryl's family. She thinks it originated with her paternal grandmother, who lived in the Northeast, but her grandma Gwosdz also made the cake, as did Cheryl's late mother (Patricia Hertz). Today, Cheryl's sister, Cyndi, and her aunt Carolyn make the cake, as well as Cheryl and her sixteen-year-old son, Taylor McChesney.

"I make it about six times a year for family functions and work-related things," says Cheryl. "I always make it for Easter. The recipe probably came from Poland, because both of my grandmothers were Polish." [There are numerous references on the Internet to "Polish pound cake'" and "Polish church pound cake," both of which have similar ingredients and begin baking in a cold oven.]

"I started making the cake when I was twelve," continues Cheryl. "I was always asking 'Why start in a cold oven?' On occasion I would preheat the oven and then wonder why the cake didn't turn out right. I also wanted to open the oven door. Grandma would say, 'You have to follow the directions or the cake will be a flop.' And she was right.

"Mom said that Grandma served this cake at card parties in the mid-1980s," continues Cheryl. "Grandma probably bought the Vanilla, Butter, & Nut Flavor from a Watkins door-to-door salesman. We now get ours through relatives in Pennsylvania, but some larger grocery stores in Texas carry it. When Mom made it, she would sometimes add a little almond extract to give the cake additional 'nutty' flavor.

"My son, Taylor, helped my mom a lot in the kitchen when she was alive [Patricia Hertz died in 2011 after a long bout with breast cancer], and he often requested they make this cake. He called her 'Baba,' which is 'Grandma' in Polish. Even when she was so sick from chemo or other treatments, Baba never told her grandson no. Seeing the anticipation on Taylor's face as my mom poured the batter into the pan and he waited to lick the beaters was priceless, and watching them make the cake together was a true joy."

Grandmama Scudder's Pound Cake

1 cup shortening
1⅔ cups sugar
6 eggs
1 teaspoon vanilla
2 cups cake flour, sifted once
Whipped cream and strawberries (optional)

Cream shortening and sugar. Add eggs (Grandmama always cracked each egg in a saucer and added it only after she was sure it was "good") and beat well. Blend in vanilla. Stir in cake flour. Pour batter into a greased and floured loaf pan and bake at 350°F for slightly longer than an hour, or until toothpick inserted in center comes out clean. Pour 2 cups water (room temperature) into an ovenproof pan and place it on the rack beside the cake while it is baking to keep it moist.

Cool cake slightly and remove from pan. Slice and serve warm or cold, plain or with whipped cream and strawberries. *Makes 1 loaf*

Contributed by Jean Granberry Schnitz
Dora Belle Lee Scudder's granddaughter
Bexar County

"*G*r13andmama was not known in my family as a great cook," says Jean, "but when she was in her seventies and eighties (in the 1950s and 1960s), her specialty was this Pound Cake. She loved to tell that when there was an event at the church or elsewhere when people were asked to bring food, someone would specifically request that she bring her Pound Cake. You will note that her recipe is heavy on eggs. She said she developed this recipe because Grandpapa grew chickens, so they always had to figure out ways to use all those eggs. Grandmama always told that Grandpapa ate seven eggs for breakfast every morning of the world — and he lived to be eighty-five. He* did *eventually develop what they called 'hardening of the arteries,' but it took him longer than you might believe if you consider his daily cholesterol intake.*"

Dora Belle Lee Scudder (Grandmama)

1874–1970

Comanche, Palo Pinto, Baylor, Hale, Lubbock, Harris, Taylor, Victoria, Jim Wells, Willacy, Cameron, and Bee Counties

Dora Belle Lee Scudder. Courtesy of Jean Schnitz.

Some of Jean's relatives have traced her grandmother's ancestry all the way back to England and Ireland, but Jean doesn't know where or how her grandmother obtained the recipe. She thinks it likely dates to the early 1900s, "when she had a young family and they were living in Seymour or Plainview." She adds that her grandmother said she "developed" it. "Perhaps she adapted a similar recipe," says Jean.

Jean herself has made this cake since the 1950s. "I make it whenever I need to take a covered dish somewhere," she says. "And I make it during strawberry season because it sure is good with fresh strawberries – or dewberries – on top."

Another family tradition links Jean and her grandmother – that of playing the hammered dulcimer. Jean's great-grandfather C. A. Lee was a "music master" and taught all nine of his children, including Dora Lee, to play the dulcimer, as well as several other musical instruments. "My grandparents lived with us during most of my growing-up years," says Jean. "Grandmama and Grandpapa (who played the fiddle) played together almost every night. Grandpapa didn't do 'public appearances,' but Grandmama loved to play the dulcimer for programs at clubs and churches and 'you-name-it.'" Jean's grandmother began teaching her to play when she was around seven or eight years old, and she eventually learned dozens of traditional tunes from her, many with Irish roots.

Dora Belle Lee Scudder with her husband, Ira Scudder. Courtesy of Jean Granberry Schnitz.

Chapter 2: Recipes

Today Jean has the hammered dulcimer that C. A. Lee purchased before the Civil War and the family brought with them when they came to Texas from Missouri in 1878. "It's been played ever since," says Jean. "In 1967, Grandmama left it with me with a request that I 'take it places and play it for people.' I played at the Texas Folklife Festival in San Antonio for thirty-one years, plus hundreds of other places. I practice every week with a dulcimer group, and I still play for programs of all kinds."

A former president of the Texas Folklore Society and a prolific author, Jean has written extensively about many aspects of her childhood. To learn more about her hammered dulcimer heritage, look for Corners of Texas, edited by Francis Edward Abernethy (University of North Texas Press, 1993), which includes Jean's article "Hammered Dulcimers and Folk Songs: The Musical Heritage of the C. A. Lee Family." Jean published another article, "Take It Places and Play for People," in the fall 2009 issue of Dulcimer Player News.

The University of Texas at San Antonio Institute of Texan Cultures (ITC) in San Antonio offers displays representing twenty-six of the more than one hundred ethnic groups and cultures in Texas, a range of temporary exhibits, and educational programs, as well as a library that features rare books, photographic collections, and oral histories. In addition, the ITC hosts two large annual events: the Texas Folklife Festival in June and the Asian Festival in January or February, depending on the date of Lunar New Year. (For details about the latter, see Lucy Wu's Fried Rice recipe in the Vegetables and Sides section.)

The biggest cultural celebration in the state, the Texas Folklife Festival has taken place annually since 1972. Participants from more than forty cultural groups gather each June on the ITC grounds in San Antonio, and showcase the state's rich heritage with musical performances, other entertainment, traditional crafts demonstrations, and a wide variety of ethnic foods. Call 210–458–2300 or see www.texancultures.com.

Grandmama's Thrifty Ways

JEAN GRANBERRY SCHNITZ

Grandmama was well known in my family for her habit of not wasting anything or making something out of nothing. When Mama would make peach jam or jelly, Grandmama would take the peelings and cook them. Then she would press them through cheesecloth and make another jar or two of jelly. All chicken and/or turkey bones were boiled to make stock for soup.

Then there was the time we lived in the Rio Grande Valley, when there was such a bumper crop of cabbage that the market just completely fell and no one was harvesting cabbage anymore. The fields were full of cabbage, and farmers were telling people to take all they could use. One day I came home from high school in the 1940s and the house smelled rotten. There was sauerkraut in every container in the house— including, so help me, the bathtub. We had to bathe outside with a hose for a while until Grandmama's sauerkraut (which was actually very good) was ready to be canned.

Another story was that Grandmama was so frugal that she hated to waste anything at all. So at night she would put a pot of cornmeal mush on the coal oil stove so that the heat of the pilot light would not be wasted. My aunt said she was not thrilled to eat cornmeal mush every morning for breakfast (with the eggs, I guess), but it sure didn't waste the heat from the pilot light. Mama and Aunt Esther said it was actually not bad when smothered with freshly made butter and plenty of sugar and honey and swimming with fresh, heavy cream.

Aunt Earle's Pound Cake

Take butter and eggs out of the refrigerator 2 to 3 hours beforehand; they need to be at room temperature in order for the cake to be light and fluffy. Try using almond or lemon extract instead of vanilla for a subtle flavor difference. Top the cake with fresh berries or drizzle it with a lemon glaze (fresh lemon juice mixed with powdered sugar).

1 cup (2 sticks) butter or margarine at room temperature
2 cups sugar
6 eggs at room temperature
1 tablespoon vanilla
1 teaspoon lemon juice
2 cups flour

Beat butter and sugar together until creamy. Add eggs one at a time, beating after each addition. Add vanilla and lemon juice, and mix well. Add flour and mix until blended. Pour batter into a greased and floured 10-inch tube pan. Bake at 325°F for about 1 hour, or until cake is light golden brown on top and springs back when touched with finger.

Cool in pan on a wire rack 10 to 15 minutes. Slide a flat knife around sides of the pan; remove cake from pan and cool completely on a wire rack. *Makes one 10-inch cake*

Contributed by Kathryn Nell Roberts
Anna Earle Armstrong McCreight's great-niece
Williamson County

*K*athryn's great-aunt, who went by "Earle," had no children but left a legacy nonetheless. She was an accomplished cook, entertained often, and enjoyed making her acclaimed Pound Cake for nieces and nephews.

 Today, Kathryn makes the same cake about twelve times a year, sometimes pairing it with fresh strawberries and other times, blueberries. "Sometimes I use it for July 4, by covering it with Cool Whip and adding strawberries on one side and blueberries on the other," says Kathryn. "I've also done a lemon glaze and drizzled it over the warm cake as soon as it comes out of the pan. My friends

Anna Earle Armstrong McCreight (Aunt Earle)
1891–1977
Gregg County

Anna Earle Armstrong McCreight. Courtesy of Kathryn Nell Roberts.

and family often request that I make this cake. Aunt Earle served this cake at her regular bridge games and whenever she entertained friends at her lovely home. And it was always present whenever any of her nieces or nephews came to visit her in Longview.

"When I was in college in San Antonio, I regularly visited Aunt Earle on long weekends. I'd make the long drive across Texas to be with her and my parents, whose primary home was in Virginia at the time. We always gathered at Aunt Earle's house — my dad was like a son to her, and they were very close. After greeting everyone, I'd head to the kitchen, where I'd find a delicious, light blond pound cake under the metal cake cover on top of a glass cake plate, awaiting dinnertime. I'd always go peek at the cake. I now have that metal cake cover and cake plate. It represents my great-aunt's anticipation of my arrival and her loving thoughtfulness." (For more of Kathryn's memories of her great-aunt, see Aunt Earle's Cushaw in the Vegetables and Sides section.)

Authemia "Tennie" Brown McKey (Granny)

1921–2010

Lavaca, Hardin, and Tyler Counties

Granny's Master Mix Cake

This recipe makes a basic yellow cake. For a chocolate cake, add ½ cup cocoa and blend with the sugar and Granny's Master Mix.

3 cups Granny's Master Mix
   (see Granny's Master Mix recipe in Breads section)
½ cup sugar
2 eggs
1 cup water
1 teaspoon vanilla
Frosting (your choice)

Blend Master Mix with sugar in a large bowl.

Mix eggs and 1 cup water together in a separate bowl. Add half of this mixture to Master Mix–sugar mixture and beat 2 minutes. Add remaining egg-water mixture and vanilla and beat another 2 minutes. Pour batter into two 8-inch greased and floured pans. Bake at 375°F for 25 minutes, or until a toothpick inserted in center comes out clean. Cool in pans 10 minutes; remove layers from pans and cool completely on wire racks. Spread frosting between layers and on top and sides of cake. *Makes one 2-layer cake*

Contributed by Tasha Harper-Werner
Authemia "Tennie" Brown McKey's granddaughter
Tyler County

Granny's Master Mix Coffee Cake

3 cups Granny's Master Mix
   (see Granny's Master Mix recipe in Breads section)
½ cup white sugar
1 egg
⅔ cup water
½ cup brown sugar
½ teaspoon cinnamon
3 tablespoons butter
½ cup chopped nuts or raisins (optional)

Combine Master Mix, white sugar, egg, and ⅔ cup water and mix well. Pour batter into a greased and floured 8 x 8-inch pan.

Blend brown sugar, cinnamon, and butter together. Mix in nuts or raisins, if desired. Sprinkle over top of batter. Bake at 400°F for 25 minutes, or until a toothpick inserted in center comes out clean. *Makes 1 coffee cake*

Contributed by Tasha Harper-Werner
Authemia "Tennie" Brown McKey's granddaughter
Tyler County

To read some of Tasha's memories of her grandmother, see Granny's Master Mix recipe.

Authemia "Tennie" Brown McKey (Granny)

1921–2010

Lavaca, Hardin, and Tyler Counties

Authemia "Tennie" Brown McKey with her husband, Dewey McKey, and their daughter, Pam. Courtesy of Tasha Harper-Werner.

Baird Dorothea Jackson Wheat (Granny)

1898–1971

Austin and Coleman Counties

Baird Dorothea Jackson Wheat. Courtesy of Julia Moseley.

Granny Wheat's Fresh Apple Cake

3 cups flour
1½ teaspoons baking soda
1 teaspoon salt
½ teaspoon nutmeg
½ teaspoon cinnamon
2 eggs
1¼ cups vegetable oil
2 cups sugar
2 teaspoons vanilla
3 cups peeled and diced apples (3 medium or 2 large apples)
1 cup coarsely chopped pecans

Sift together flour, baking soda, salt, nutmeg, and cinnamon and blend well. Set aside.

Combine eggs, vegetable oil, sugar, and vanilla in a large bowl and beat well. Stir in flour mixture and mix well. Fold in apples and pecans. Pour batter into a greased and floured 10-inch tube pan and bake at 350°F for 1 hour and 15 minutes, or until toothpick inserted in center comes out clean. Cool cake for 5 minutes before removing from pan. *Makes one 10-inch cake*

Contributed by Julia Ann Huddleston Moseley
Baird Dorothea Jackson Wheat's granddaughter
Parker County

Chapter 2: Recipes

ulia claims deep Texas roots on both sides of her family. Her paternal great-great-grandparents came to Texas from Alabama in 1837. And on her mother's side, her great-great-grandfather Friederich Adam Hoffman and his two brothers emigrated from Germany and landed in New York in 1836; he arrived in Texas as early as 1838. He married Catrin Dorothea Graf in 1853. (Catrin had emigrated with her family from Germany and landed in Galveston in 1851.) Their daughter was Granny Wheat's mother. "Granny adored her grandmother Hoffman and was named for her," says Julia. "I gave my daughter Marie that same middle name — Dorothea."

Julia's not sure if Fresh Apple Cake represents Granny Wheat's German ancestry, but it likely does, "since her grandmother Hoffman greatly influenced her cooking." Regardless, it has become a tradition in her family. "I've been making it for more than forty-five years," she says, "and my husband made it once. When the Moseley family came to see the first grandson, born in 1969, my husband made the cake — accidentally using baking powder rather than baking soda — and then insisted that it was better that way," says Julia. "We still laugh about it. My daughter (Marie Dorothea Moseley Medina) makes this cake, too, so it's at least a fourth-generation recipe."

Preparing the apples is the most time-consuming step in making this cake. Many cooks swear by this method: Turn an apple on its side and cut a thin slice off each end with a sharp knife. Use a vegetable peeler to slice off vertical strips of the peel. Stand the "naked" apple on one end and slice through the apple as close to the core as possible. Repeat three times, and discard the core. Then, turn each quarter-apple on its flat side and slice and dice as desired. If the apples aren't going to be incorporated into the dish immediately, dip them in a mixture of lemon juice and water to prevent browning.

Cookies

**Rosa "Rose"
Catalina Carona
(MawMaw)**

1912–1996

**Jasper and
Jefferson Counties**

*Rosa "Rose" Catalina Carona.
Courtesy of Gwen Carona.*

Cuccidati (Sicilian Fig Cookies) (SICILIAN)

1 cup (2 sticks) margarine, softened
1½ cups sugar
2 eggs, beaten
5 cups flour (more if needed)
1 heaping tablespoon baking powder
Pinch of salt
2 teaspoons vanilla extract
2 teaspoons almond extract
Milk (if needed)
Fig Filling (recipe follows)
Icing (recipe follows)

Cream margarine and sugar together in a large bowl of an electric mixer. Add eggs and beat well.

Sift together flour, baking powder, and salt on waxed paper. Add to egg mixture and mix on low speed. Add vanilla and almond extracts to dough and mix well. Add a small amount of milk if more moisture is needed. Cut dough into 4 pieces and knead each on a floured board until smooth. Wrap each portion in plastic wrap and place in refrigerator until needed.

Prepare Fig Filling and Icing (see recipes below) and set aside.

Working with one portion of dough at a time, divide each portion into 6 pieces. Roll out each piece on a floured board into a 9 x 3-inch rectangle. Roll some of the Fig Filling into a cigar shape 9 inches long and place in center of dough rectangle. Fold the dough over the filling lengthwise. Pinch ends together and cut the 9-inch roll into 3 equal lengths. Take each 3-inch section and roll back and forth on the waxed paper to smooth the cookie. Bend into a half-moon shape and cut 2 slits in the top. Place cookies 1½ inches apart on a cookie sheet lined with parchment paper. Bake at 375°F for 15 minutes, or until cookies are golden. Remove cookies to a wire rack and cool slightly.

Glaze warm cookies with Icing and cool completely. (Note: Some Cuccidati are usually left unglazed for serving with coffee.) *Makes about 6 dozen*

Fig Filling
1 (10-ounce) package dried figs
½ cup orange marmalade
1 (8-ounce) jar fig preserves
¼ cup sugar
1½ tablespoons cinnamon
Pinch of black pepper
⅜ cup raisins
½ cup finely chopped pecans
¾ cup mixed candied fruit

Remove stems from figs (use scissors and dip tips into a glass of hot water when they become sticky). Place figs and remainder of ingredients in the bowl of a food processor and pulse until well mixed. *Makes enough filling for about 6 dozen Cuccidati*

Icing
1½ cups sifted powdered sugar
1½ teaspoons margarine, softened
1 teaspoon vanilla extract
1 to 2 tablespoons milk
Food coloring (yellow, blue, pink, and green)

Combine powdered sugar and margarine. Stir in vanilla. Add enough milk to make a thin glaze and mix well. Divide glaze into 4 portions and add a few drops of food coloring to each portion; blend well. *Makes enough glaze for about 6 dozen Cuccidati*

Contributed by Nicholas Carona, Rachel Carona Fishback,
   and Jennifer Carona Phelan
Rosa "Rose" Catalina Carona's great-grandchildren
Travis, Travis, and Jefferson Counties, respectively

*R*ose passed the Cuccidati recipe down to her daughter-in-law Gwen Provost Carona, who in turn taught several of her grandchildren to make the traditional cookie. "Rose learned the recipe from her mother-in-law, Virginia Dolce Carona, who was born in Bisacquino, Sicily," says Gwen. "Rose herself lived most of her life in Port Arthur and loved cooking for family and friends. When I married into the family, she shared this recipe with me. Rose actually didn't use recipes for cooking — just for baking. Her Cuccidati were among my children's favorite cookies.

"I started teaching my grandchildren to cook and bake in their early teens," says Gwen. "I enjoyed passing down the traditions of the past. They've mastered many other Sicilian recipes that I have taught them and are fine cooks. They have developed rich traditions to pass down to their own families."

For many years, Gwen helped prepare hundreds of Cuccidati each March for the St. Joseph's Altar at her church, St. Anthony's Basilica in Beaumont. "Cuccidati are among the many sweet delicacies at a St. Joseph's Altar," Gwen explains. "The altar's origin dates to medieval times during a famine in Sicily. The Sicilians asked St. Joseph to ask God to end the famine and drought. Their prayers were answered, and in gratitude, they erected altars, or tables, every March 19 to thank him for his help.

"The tradition continues today. Reasons for having St. Joseph's Altars vary: gratitude for healing the sick, having a happy family life, having success in studies or business, or the safe return of a loved one from war. Here, in Southeast Texas, they are more often held at Catholic churches that have large Sicilian American congregations. The food is lovingly prepared by the ladies of the parishes and shared with the poor in the community.

"Four of my granddaughters started helping me and the ladies of the church make Cuccidati while they were in high school and would come home to help after they were in college. [The two granddaughters not listed as contributors now live out of state.] When Nicholas visited, we'd make them together for special occasions. It's a recipe best made in a group. One person makes the sweet dough, another grinds the figs and makes the filling, another places the filling on the dough, the artist of the group shapes the cookies, and still another operates the ovens. It's hard to imagine that my mother-in-law made Cuccidati by herself for years."

Gwen's family members no longer gather on a regular basis to make Cuccidati, but the seed has been planted, so to speak. "My daughter Brenda [Carona Cascio] has fig trees and makes the fig preserves for the family like her grandmother Rose did," says Gwen. "Rose's great-granddaughter Rachel also makes fig preserves." With the main ingredient of Cuccidati so plentiful, the tradition promises to live on.

Pizzelle
(Traditional Italian Wedding Cookies)
(ITALIAN)

Gwen Provost Carona (Nana)

Born in 1936

Dallas, Harris, and Jefferson Counties

Italian weddings almost always feature these thin, waffle-textured cookies. In Italian homes, they're a standard for other special occasions and holidays, too. They're easy to make (with a little practice), but you'll need a pizzelle press to bake them. For the prettiest pizzelle, use a press without nonstick baking plates; it makes thinner, more delicate cookies.

6 eggs
1½ cups sugar
1 cup (2 sticks) margarine, melted and cooled (*do not use vegetable oil*)
2 tablespoons vanilla
2 tablespoons almond extract
3½ cups flour
4 teaspoons baking powder
Powdered sugar for dusting (about ¾ cup)

Gwen Provost Carona. Courtesy of Gwen Carona.

Beat eggs in a large bowl. Add sugar gradually and beat until smooth. Add cooled margarine, vanilla, and almond extract and mix well.

Sift flour and baking powder together on waxed paper. Add to egg mixture and blend until smooth. Dough will be sticky enough to drop from a spoon. *Never put the dough in the refrigerator.*

Preheat the pizzelle press according to manufacturer's directions and spray it with Pam. Drop about a tablespoon of batter onto the center of each grid pattern. Close lid of pizzelle press and bake approximately 40 to 50 seconds. Lift lid, remove pizzelle with a fork or spatula, and place it on the waxed paper to cool. Continue baking pizzelle until all the batter is used.

When pizzelle are completely cool, spread them out on waxed paper and use a sifter to dust them with powdered sugar. Gently tap pizzelle to shake off excess sugar and place in zip-top bags in groups of 10. *Makes about 5 dozen*

Note: To make mini-pizzelle for tea parties and other occasions, place a smaller amount of batter on the pizzelle press. Pizzelle can also be rolled to resemble cannoli. Take pizzelle hot off the press and roll over cannoli dowels (wooden cylinders of various sizes) and allow to cool. Fill with vanilla or chocolate custard and dust with powdered sugar.

Contributed by Nicholas Carona, Rachel Carona Fishback,
    and Jennifer Carona Phelan
Gwen Provost Carona's grandchildren
Travis, Travis, and Jefferson Counties, respectively

Gwen Carona's ancestry is actually French, Irish, and a mix of other nationalities; she began making pizzelle and other Italian delicacies after she married into a Sicilian family. "I bought my first pizzelle press in New York City," she says. "I made so many Pizzelle — more than one thousand some years — that the heating coil failed on the first machine." Although the lacy, delicate cookies are traditionally flavored with anise, Gwen's children and grandchildren didn't like this flavor, so her recipe calls for vanilla and almond extracts instead.

Nicholas Carona, now a college student, began making Pizzelle with his grandmother when he was eleven years old. When he was in middle school, one of his teachers asked students to make a recipe representing their heritage to share with the class. Already an experienced pizzelle maker by then, Nicholas borrowed his grandmother's pizzelle press, took it to school, and made the cookies on the spot, to the delight of his classmates and teacher.

Several other grandchildren are part of the Pizzelle tradition. For many years, the four granddaughters who lived nearby helped Gwen make Pizzelle each March for the St. Joseph's Altar at Saint Anthony's Cathedral Basilica in Beaumont. (For details about St. Joseph's Altars, see the Cuccidati recipe.)

A few Christmases ago, Gwen gave each of her five granddaughters a pizzelle press and passed along her own pizzelle press to Nicholas. The young pizzelle makers have grown up, some have married, and some have moved out of state. However, Nicholas and his cousins Rachel Carona Fishback and Jennifer Carona Phelan continue to make Pizzelle in Texas.

When making Pizzelle, it's a good idea to cover your work surface with a cloth and then cover that with waxed paper. Use a tablespoon of batter for your first attempts—to determine the size you want. (Pizzelle are usually about 4 inches in diameter.) If you want a larger cookie, use a heaping tablespoon of batter.

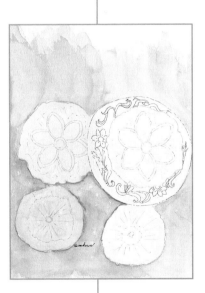

Myrtle Augusta Loomis Patterson (Gran)

1882–1959

Marion and Upshur Counties

Gran's Childress Cookies

1 cup (2 sticks) butter
2½ cups firmly packed brown sugar
2 eggs
4 cups flour
2½ teaspoons baking soda
¼ teaspoon salt
½ to 1 cup chopped pecans
36 (about 2 ounces) additional pecan halves

Cream butter and brown sugar in a large bowl. Add eggs and beat well.

Sift together flour, baking soda, and salt. Add along with chopped pecans to egg-butter mixture and mix well. Drop by teaspoonfuls onto a greased cookie sheet. Press a pecan half into center of each cookie. Bake at 350°F for 10 to 12 minutes. Remove to wire racks to cool. *Makes about 8 dozen*

Contributed by Karey Patterson Bresenhan
Myrtle Augusta Loomis Patterson's granddaughter
Fayette County

ℋ ow did Gran's Childress Cookies get their name? Karey thinks her grandmother probably got the recipe from a friend who lived in Childress (Texas). "She made them often when I was growing up," says Karey. "I loved these cookies so much as a child that I hunted for the recipe for decades," she adds. "After my mother died in 2002, it finally resurfaced — in Gran's own handwriting, right there in Mama's recipe box! I believe Mama simply forgot she had it, because she certainly knew I was trying to find it. I had hunted for it for so long that the mysterious Childress Cookies almost became a family legend."

Myrtle Patterson cooked quite a bit throughout her life. "Gran ran a boardinghouse in Gilmer during the 1930s oil boom, when oil-field workers in nearby Kilgore often had to drive for miles to find a bed," explains Karey. "She and Grandpop moved into their big sleeping porch, so she could make the rest of their house into bedrooms, where she slept the men in shifts. Gran cooked all day to feed 'her boys.' In return, they called her 'Ma' and loved her dearly.

Chapter 2: Recipes

"Even after the boom went bust, she never moved back into the rest of her house, but instead rented out rooms. However, there was no cooking and sleeping in shifts then.

"Gran had two sons of her own — my uncle Garland and Daddy — and made a 'trousseau' of twelve quilts for each of them. I grew up sleeping under Gran's quilts (and under Mama's, too, since she also brought a trousseau of thirteen quilts into her marriage). Snuggling down at night and then waking up in the morning under the beautiful colors and patterns created indelible memories for me." (See Granny's Miracle Cobbler recipe for more about the food and quilting traditions in Karey's family.)

Myrtle Augusta Loomis Patterson. Courtesy of Karey Bresenhan.

**Rosa Karow Henneke
(Maw-Maw)**

**1894–1973
DeWitt County**

Maw-Maw's Icebox Cookies

Also known as refrigerator cookies or slice-and-bake cookies, icebox cookies have long been popular because you can mix them up one day and bake them later. Some recipes say the dough keeps in the refrigerator for several weeks; however, a safer bet is several days. If you're not ready to bake the cookies then, store the dough in the freezer for up to a month.

1 cup (2 sticks) melted butter or margarine
2 cups firmly packed brown sugar
2 eggs
1 teaspoon vanilla
4 cups flour
½ teaspoon salt
½ teaspoon baking soda
1 teaspoon cream of tartar
1 cup chopped pecans

Combine melted butter, brown sugar, eggs, and vanilla in a large bowl and mix well.

Blend flour, salt, baking soda, and cream of tartar together. Add to first mixture and mix well. Stir in pecans. Dough will be very stiff; if too sticky to handle, place dough in refrigerator for a few minutes. Shape dough into 2 rolls (12 inches long and 1½ to 2 inches in diameter) and wrap each roll in waxed paper; refrigerate at least 4 hours or overnight. (Rolls can be kept in refrigerator for several days or in the freezer for up to a month.)

Slice cookies a little less than ½-inch thick and place on ungreased cookie sheet. Bake at 350°F for about 10 minutes, or until slightly browned. Remove to wire racks to cool. *Makes about 7 dozen*

Contributed by Elizabeth "Liz" Henneke Boenig
Rosa Karow Henneke's granddaughter
Brazos County

"*These cookies were my father's favorite cookies,*" *says Liz.* "*After his mother, Maw-Maw, died in 1973, my other grandmother, Grandmom, began making them for the family. Both grandmothers had pecan trees in their yards. Maw-Maw's Icebox Cookies were always kept in a round cookie tin. Since the cookies are smooth, round, and firm, they're easy to transport. I'd often receive a bag of them after visiting Grandmom and eat a lot of them on the drive home! This is the perfect dunking cookie for coffee or milk. Maw-Maw showed me my favorite way to enjoy them, though — top them with a spoonful of vanilla ice cream and eat!*"

Liz remembers a time when her family was visiting her grandmom (Minnie Rosenberg) after she had started making the cookies. She says, "*My father took a bite of one and said, 'Something is wrong with the cookies.' Grandmom replied with a sheepish grin, 'I forgot the soda.' My father said, 'You can't eat these cookies for sixty years and not notice when something is missing.'*"

Liz makes the cookies often today. "*Everyone loves the buttery, sugary, nutty taste,*" *she says.* "*And since both of my grandmothers are deceased now, when I make these cookies, I feel connected to them. It didn't matter if I was five years old or fifty years old, every time I visited my grandmothers, they always had icebox cookies for me to eat!*"

Rosa Karow Henneke with her husband, Henry Henneke. Courtesy of Dee Henneke.

Granny Wheat's Oatmeal-Coconut Cookies

1 cup (2 sticks) butter or margarine
1 cup sugar
1 cup firmly packed brown sugar
2 eggs
2 cups sifted flour
½ teaspoon salt
1 teaspoon baking soda
1 teaspoon baking powder
2 cups uncooked oats
1 cup flaked coconut
1 cup chopped pecans or walnuts
1 teaspoon vanilla

Cream butter or margarine in a large bowl. Add sugars and beat well. Add eggs and mix well.

Sift flour, salt, baking soda, and baking powder. Add to first mixture and mix well. Add oats, coconut, nuts, and vanilla in that order, mixing well after each addition. Drop by teaspoonfuls about 2 inches apart on ungreased cookie sheet. Bake at 350°F for 8 to 10 minutes. Cool 1 minute on cookie sheet. Remove to wire racks to cool thoroughly. *Makes 6 to 7 dozen*

Contributed by Julia Ann Huddleston Moseley
Baird Dorothea Jackson Wheat's granddaughter
Parker County

Baird Dorothea Jackson Wheat with her husband, Willie Wheat. Courtesy of Julia Moseley.

Chapter 2: Recipes

"When my sisters and I were young, we often went to the farm to visit our grandparents in Coleman County for the weekend. We'd pick Dad up at work in Fort Worth, so they could always guess what time we'd arrive. There were always hot cookies, and Granddad would make a fruit punch, usually a mixture of lemonade and grape juice, and anything else he wanted. Granny didn't have much strength. She had a form of multiple sclerosis, so cookies that could be made earlier were better for her. She could pull them out and bake them without it tiring her too much. Granddad always helped her, so he developed into a pretty good cook.

Even with her health problems, Granny raised chickens so she'd have her own eggs. They had cows, too, so she churned her own butter. I helped churn when I was there in the summer. (For more about Granny Wheat's legacy, see the Fresh Apple Cake recipe.)

Granny Wheat's Icebox Cookies

Baird Dorothea Jackson Wheat (Granny)

1898–1971

Austin and Coleman Counties

1 cup (2 sticks) butter or margarine
1½ cups firmly packed brown sugar
½ cup sugar
3 eggs
1 teaspoon vanilla
3 cups sifted flour
1 teaspoon baking soda
½ teaspoon salt
½ teaspoon cinnamon
1 cup chopped pecans

Cream butter or margarine and sugars in a large mixing bowl. Add eggs and vanilla and mix well.

Sift flour, baking soda, salt, and cinnamon together. Add to first mixture and mix well. Stir in pecans. Form into a log 1½ to 2 inches in diameter; wrap in plastic wrap, and chill overnight.

Cut chilled dough into ¼-inch slices and place on a lightly greased cookie sheet. Bake at 350°F for 10 minutes. Remove to wire racks to cool. *Makes 5 to 7 dozen*

Contributed by Julia Ann Huddleston Moseley
Baird Dorothea Jackson Wheat's granddaughter
Parker County

To read some of Julia's memories of her grandmother, see Granny Wheat's Oatmeal-Coconut Cookies and Granny Wheat's Fresh Apple Cake recipes.

Dorothy McCarter Martin (GMommy)

1920–2010

Calhoun, Hamilton, Navarro, and Victoria Counties

Dorothy McCarter Martin. Courtesy of Kathleen Martin.

GMommy's Oatmeal Cookies

1 cup (2 sticks) butter
1 cup sugar
2 eggs
2 cups sifted flour
½ teaspoon salt
½ teaspoon baking soda
1 teaspoon cinnamon
2 cups uncooked oats
1 cup chopped pecans
1 cup raisins

Cream butter and sugar in a large bowl. Add eggs and mix well. Add flour, salt, baking soda, and cinnamon and mix well. Stir in oats, pecans, and raisins. Drop small amounts of dough (teaspoonfuls) onto a lightly greased cookie sheet. (This makes for a very flat, thin, crisp cookie.) Bake at 350°F for about 15 minutes. Cool slightly; remove to wire racks to cool. *Makes 7 to 8 dozen*

Contributed by Margaret Martin Beabout
Dorothy McCarter Martin's granddaughter
Calhoun County

"*G*Mommy was a home economics teacher for more than thirty-five years, teaching in two different small towns in Central Texas," says Margaret. "She was of the 'old school,' where she taught everything from cooking, sewing, household cleaning, housekeeping finances, crafting decorations for holidays, table and social etiquette, and anything else you could imagine. Only my grandmother would teach her students how to polish silver! GMommy was always introducing us [my mother, sister, and me] to her former students when we were out shopping. All her students seemed to respect and admire her.

"She would often have new recipes when we came to visit, but she made this one regularly. It's a special oatmeal cookie because it is so crisp and crunchy with all the pecans and oats. (For Christmas, she would put red and green candied cherries on top.) GMommy liked to bake these cookies ahead and freeze them in Collins Street Bakery fruitcake tins. She'd bring one tin out for us to snack on while we played Skip-Bo and have three or four more tins in the freezer. We would snitch the frozen cookies out of the tins and rearrange them, hoping she wouldn't catch us."

Melt-in-Your-Mouth Sugar Cookies

If you don't have an heirloom berry bowl in your cupboard you can use to make a flower design on these cookies, you'll have to improvise. Look for an interesting design on the bottom of a glass or vase. A cookie stamp works, too.

1 cup sugar
1 cup sifted powdered sugar
1 cup Crisco vegetable oil
1 cup Crisco shortening
2 eggs
1 teaspoon vanilla
4 cups flour
1 teaspoon baking soda
1 teaspoon salt
1 teaspoon cream of tartar

Combine sugars, vegetable oil, and shortening in a large bowl and mix well. Add eggs and vanilla and mix well; set aside.

Averil Babb McCarter (Adie)
1895–1982
Jackson, Calhoun, Hamilton, and Navarro Counties

Averil Babb McCarter. Courtesy of Kathleen Martin.

Sift flour, baking soda, salt, and cream of tartar together and add gradually to first mixture, mixing well. Form into 1-inch balls and place on a lightly greased cookie sheet. Press top of each cookie with the bottom of a small cut-glass bowl or a cookie stamp. Bake at 350°F for about 12 minutes. Cool on wire racks. *Makes about 8 dozen*

Contributed by Kate Martin Howell
Averil Babb McCarter's great-granddaughter
Jackson County

"*These cookies are a Martin-family favorite,*" says Kate. "*They're light and airy and will melt in your mouth. The recipe originated with my great-grandmother Adie. She was born in Illinois but often visited the family ranch near the Texas Gulf Coast. After her husband died in 1951, Adie would spend the spring and summer with her sisters in Illinois and then come to Texas before Thanksgiving and live with her daughter Dorothy's family in Central Texas.*

"*Adie passed the recipe down to my grandmother Dorothy McCarter Martin — the Martin grandkids call her GMommy — and she's the one who always made these cookies for us. So we call them GMommy's Sugar Cookies. When GMommy made them, she would always press the bottom of one of Adie's crystal berry bowls on top of each cookie to make a flower design. She would serve them with homemade vanilla ice cream for dessert.*

"*When my sister, Margaret, got married in 2006, she had thirty dozen of these cookies made for her reception in honor of GMommy. The woman who made them used one of the berry bowls to make GMommy's same flower design on each one of the cookies. They were gone so fast, my mother never got one! Today, my sister and I each have one of the berry bowls, my brother has one, and my mother has one. When we make these cookies, we use one of Adie's bowls to make them just like GMommy did.*"

Tamale Cookies

Filled with cinnamon, sugar, and pecans, these little cookies really do look like miniature tamales. Sprinkling a little more sugar on them before they bake makes them sparkle. If you like, you can mix in a little cinnamon with the sugar and dust them with that instead.

1 pound (2 cups or 4 sticks) cold butter
1 pound (about 4 cups) flour
1 cup sweet cream or whipping cream
½ cup sugar
1 tablespoon cinnamon
2 cups finely chopped pecans
Additional sugar

Cream butter in a large mixing bowl. Add flour and sweet cream alternately, mixing well after each addition. Refrigerate dough overnight.

Roll out chilled dough to ¼-inch thickness on a lightly floured surface and cut into 1½ x 2-inch rectangles. Blend the ½ cup sugar and cinnamon together. Sprinkle mixture over dough and press it down very lightly. Sprinkle pecans on top. Roll up each rectangle of dough into a cylinder to resemble a tamale. Place cookies cut side down on a lightly greased cookie sheet. Sprinkle with additional sugar and bake at 275°F for 1 hour, or until cookies are just golden. Remove cookies to paper towels laid over newspaper to cool. *Makes about 6 dozen*

Contributed by Nadine "Dee" Vernell Rosenberg Henneke
Augusta Margeta Kneupper Heitkamp's great-granddaughter
DeWitt County

ee doesn't know the origin of Tamale Cookies, but she thinks the recipe could have come from some of her great-grandmother's neighbors. "At one time, my great-grandparents had a general store, bowling alley, and cotton gin in what was then the small town of Bracken, between San Antonio and New Braunfels," she explains. "They catered to the other Germans in the area and

Augusta Margeta Kneupper Heitkamp (*Gross Oma*)
1860–1945
Comal County

Augusta Margeta Kneupper Heitkamp. Courtesy of Dee Henneke.

also to the Mexican Americans living and working in the area who came in to buy supplies. My grandmother was the postmistress. Both she and my great-grandmother were fluent in English, German, and Spanish.

"These are my favorite cookies because they're not too sweet. My daughter Elizabeth [Boenig] remembers that when she phoned me in 1982 to tell me she was pregnant, I was making these cookies."

Edythe Shafer Jackson (Memommie)

1898–1987

Dimmit, Kleberg, and Guadalupe Counties

Edythe Shafer Jackson. Courtesy of Marianne Hudiburg.

Memommie's Butterscotch Cookies

1 cup (2 sticks) butter
4 firmly packed cups brown sugar
4 eggs
½ teaspoon vanilla
7 cups flour
1 tablespoon baking soda
1 tablespoon cream of tartar
½ teaspoon salt
1 cup chopped pecans

Cream butter and sugar. Add eggs and vanilla and mix well; set aside.

Sift together flour, baking soda, cream of tartar, and salt. Add to egg-butter mixture, ½ cup at a time, mixing well after each addition. Stir in pecans. Shape dough into 2 rolls; wrap in waxed paper and refrigerate overnight.

Cut rolls of dough into thin slices and place on a greased cookie sheet. Bake at 350°F for 10 to 12 minutes. *Makes about 5 dozen*

Contributed by Stacy Shanafelt Johnson and Marianne Shanafelt Hudiburg
Edythe Shafer Jackson's granddaughters
Guadalupe County (both granddaughters)

Edythe was born in Troy, Ohio. In the mid-1920s, she moved from Dayton, Ohio, to Texas, with her husband, Alva Jackson, and her three-year-old daughter, Adele. "My grandfather had earlier gone on an excursion to the Rio Grande Valley, gotten all excited about the area, and bought forty acres of land in Dimmitt County," explains Marianne. "After one year of trying to grow onions, however, he knew the city boy would never make a farmer. He got a job with the State of Texas and moved to town. They eventually settled in Kingsville.

"Memommie was an only child, as was our mother, Adele, so after our grandfather died in 1944, we were her only family — my parents and the five of us kids. She loved having us visit. When we would drive to her house in Kingsville, it was always a big race to see who could get to her candy dish first. It was always filled with green and white Kentucky Mints."

Stacy describes the special way her grandmother served Butterscotch Cookies. "She would mix up the dough for these ahead of time and keep rolls of it wrapped in waxed paper in the fridge. When we got there, she would slice a roll of dough and then bake the cookies. She'd serve them to us — nice and soft and warm, right out of the oven — with ice-cold milk. (We always put ice in our milk.) She would put the leftover cookies — not many, of course — in round tins between layers of waxed paper, along with a few apple slices to keep the cookies moist.

"We always had these cookies at Christmas," continues Stacy, " and we still do. My mother made them after Memommie, and I make them now. It's just a Christmas tradition with our family."

Most cooks know they can rescue brown sugar that has become hard by placing it an airtight container along with an apple slice for a few days. But what if you need it right away? Place the hardened lumps in a microwave-safe bowl, cover them with a damp paper towel, and microwave for about 30 seconds. Repeat as necessary. Make sure the brown sugar completely softens so that you can measure it correctly (by firmly packing it into a measuring cup or spoon).

Honora Sloma Paul

1887–1987

Fayette and Brazoria Counties

Honora Sloma Paul. Courtesy of Jean Paul.

Molasses-Pecan Cookies

1 cup sugar
1 cup shortening
1 cup molasses
1 large egg
1 tablespoon vinegar
4 cups flour
¼ teaspoon pepper
1 teaspoon baking soda
4 teaspoons cinnamon
1 teaspoon salt
2 teaspoons nutmeg
2 teaspoons cloves
1 cup finely chopped pecans

Cream sugar and shortening in a large bowl. Add molasses, egg, and vinegar, mixing well.

Sift flour, pepper, baking soda, cinnamon, salt, nutmeg, and cloves into a separate bowl. Add to molasses-sugar mixture, 1 cup at a time, mixing after each addition. Add pecans and mix well. Divide dough into 6 equal parts. Roll each in floured waxed paper, forming rolls 1½ inches in diameter. Refrigerate for 1 hour.

Unwrap rolls, cut into slices ¼-inch thick, and place on an ungreased cookie sheet. Bake at 375°F for 8 to 10 minutes. Cool slightly on cookie sheet and then place cookies on a wire rack to cool. *Makes 8 to 10 dozen*

Contributed by Jenny Lynn Paul Kier
Honora Sloma Paul's great-granddaughter
Brazoria County

This fourth-generation recipe may well be a fifth-generation recipe. Family members think Grandmother Paul learned the recipe from her mother, Augusta Yeager Sloma, who was born in 1863 in Fayette County. Jenny makes these cookies every Christmas. "They're a favorite of all of Grandmother Paul's

Chapter 2: Recipes

descendants," she says. "In fact, every female in the family has a copy of the recipe. We all make it and look forward to the smell permeating our homes during the holidays. Our younger children say the cookies are 'too hot,' referring to the spices," adds Jenny. "We just smile, knowing they, too, will grow to love this cookie!"

Before measuring molasses or other sticky liquids, coat the inside of measuring cups or spoons with cooking spray. This makes it easier to pour out the molasses.

Syrup Cookies

Margaret Ann Abercrombie Carroll

1850–1930

Cherokee and Sabine Counties

Cane syrup is generally more available in East Texas than in other parts of the state. You can also find it in some specialty stores or on the Internet. If cane syrup isn't available, substitute dark corn syrup. Note that these cookies don't contain eggs.

3 cups flour
1 cup (2 sticks) melted butter, cooled slightly
1 teaspoon baking soda
1 teaspoon salt
1 cup cane syrup (such as Steen's Pure Cane Syrup)
1 teaspoon vanilla
½ teaspoon cloves
½ teaspoon allspice
2 teaspoons ginger
Sugar for sprinkling (about ½ cup)

Margaret Ann Abercrombie Carroll. Courtesy of Peggie Moseley.

Measure flour into a mixing bowl. Make a well in the center of the flour and add melted butter, baking soda, salt, syrup , vanilla, and spices. Using a spoon, whip the mixture, gradually mixing in the flour. When all the flour has been mixed in, turn dough out onto a floured board and knead dough until it can be rolled out.

Roll out dough to ¼-inch thickness. Cut out cookies with a round cookie cutter and place them on a greased cookie sheet. Bake at 350°F for 8 to 10 minutes, or until cookies lose their shine. Sprinkle hot cookies with sugar.

Cool on cookie sheet for 5 minutes; remove to a wire rack to cool completely. *Makes 6 to 8 dozen*

Contributed by Peggie Elizabeth Hogan Moseley
Margaret Ann Abercrombie Carroll's great-granddaughter
Jefferson County

"My grandfather raised sugar cane and made cane syrup every year. There was always a good supply of syrup; therefore, my grandmother and great-grandmother used it a great deal in their baking. During the years of the Great Depression, these cookies were baked for the children of the family to eat. After my great-grandfather died, my great-grandmother lived with my grandparents, and she loved to cook. My mother has many fond memories of her and the delicious foods she cooked. Syrup cookies or tea cakes were always available for big appetites."

Zimtsterne (GERMAN)

Zimtsterne are traditional German Christmas cookies. Also called Cinnamon Stars, the cookies are flavored with cinnamon and traditionally cut into star shapes. The instructions below are for drop cookies ("roundish" in shape), but the dough can also be rolled out and cut into stars before baking.

6 egg whites at room temperature (reserve yolks for another use)
1 pound (about 4½ cups sifted) powdered sugar
½ teaspoon cinnamon
Grated rind of 1 lemon
1 pound shelled pecans, ground (about 3½ cups of ground pecans)

Beat egg whites at high speed with an electric mixer until frothy. With mixer still running, gradually add powdered sugar, cinnamon, and lemon rind. Continue to beat 15 minutes. Remove ⅓ of mixture and reserve for topping.

Fold ground pecans into remaining mixture. Drop by rounded tablespoonfuls onto a lightly greased cookie sheet, flatten cookies slightly, and spread about 1 teaspoon of reserved egg-white topping mixture on the top

Hulda Pfeuffer Weidner
(*Oma*)
1883–1964
Comal County

*Hulda Pfeuffer Weidner.
Courtesy of Dee Henneke.*

Chapter 2: Recipes

of each cookie. Bake at 300°F for about 20 minutes until light beige in color and topping looks glazed and crusty. Do not brown. *Makes about 6 dozen*

Contributed by Nadine "Dee" Vernell Rosenberg Henneke
Hulda Pfeuffer Weidner's granddaughter
DeWitt County

"I've been making Zimtsterne at Christmas for more than fifty years," says Dee. "My husband loved egg-white ('light') cookies. I usually make them as drop cookies, but I've also rolled out the dough and used a cookie cutter to make them in the traditional star shape. I think my grandmother (Oma) got this recipe from her mother [Mina Fuhrmann Pfeuffer] because of the German origin. When Oma made these cookies, she would call in my grandfather to help with the beating, which he gladly did. Today I use a mixer!"

Granny's Master Mix Drop Cookies

Authemia "Tennie" Brown McKey (Granny)

1921–2010

Lavaca, Hardin, and Tyler Counties

2 cups Granny's Master Mix
   (see Granny's Master Mix recipe in Breads section)
¼ cup sugar
1 egg
⅓ cup water
1 teaspoon vanilla
½ cup chopped nuts or chocolate chips

Combine all ingredients and mix well. Drop dough by teaspoonfuls onto a greased baking sheet. Bake at 375°F for 8 to 12 minutes, or until golden. *Makes 3 to 4 dozen*

Contributed by Tasha Harper-Werner
Authemia "Tennie" Brown McKey's granddaughter
Tyler County

To read some of Tasha's memories of her grandmother, see Granny's Master Mix recipe.

Authemia "Tennie" Brown McKey. Courtesy of Tasha Harper-Werner.

A Bounty of Tea Cakes

It turns out I'm not the only Texan who has fond childhood memories of tea cakes. Based on the number of offerings I received for "my grandmother's tea cakes recipe" while working on this project, I would say that it's by far the most common third-generation (and older) Texas recipe. The five recipes I included were passed down from grandmothers or great-grandmothers who lived in areas ranging from the Panhandle to Central Texas to far East Texas. One contributor says that according to family legend, her tea cake recipe came over on the boat with her English ancestors when they immigrated to America in 1840.

Family legend could be correct. Mark H. Zanger writes in *The American Ethnic Cookbook for Students* (Oryx Press, 2001), "Tea cakes came over from England with founding-stock English settlers. After the Civil War, southerners began to think of tea cakes as a symbol of Anglo-American gentility and northeners lost interest in them. But from the 1900s to the 1960s, African-Americans migrating from the South to northern cities began to cherish tea cakes as symbols of how far they had come, from being the cooks of those tea cakes in the Old South, to where they could serve them to their own guests."

Elbert Mackey, an African American businessman with a passion for cooking, has done his part to keep the tea cake tradition alive. In 2006, a desire to re-create his aunt Maggie's tea cakes led the Cedar Park resident to launch a website called the Tea Cake Project (www.teacakeproject.com) in which he solicited tea cake recipes, poems, and remembrances. He writes in his subsequent book, *The Tea Cake Roundup: Preserving a Baking Legacy for Future Generations* (Infinity Publishing, 2009), "After [a *USA Today* article about the website] appeared in 2006, I received an overwhelming outpouring of feedback." The cookbook includes more than 130 recipes from cooks across the country, with Texans well-represented. "Over 60 recipes and anecdotal stories came from Texas—more than from any other state," says Elbert. And yes, "Aunt Maggie's Resurrected Tea Cake Recipe" made it into the book, too. (For updates on the Tea Cake Project, see www.theteacakeroundup.com.)

Recipe contributor Harold Odom had a similar obsession with replicating his grandmother's tea cakes, and he, too, was successful (see Big Mama Addie Odom's Tea Cakes), which is lucky for readers of this cookbook. Lucky for me, too, because Harold sent me a package of these special cookies. They just might be better than Grandma's.

Addie Jane Lewis Odom (Big Mama)

1893–1987

Newton County

Addie Jane Lewis Odom.
Courtesy of Harold Odom Jr.

Big Mama Addie Odom's Tea Cakes

You'll need an extra-large bowl or clean dishpan, as well as a large work surface and plenty of extra flour, to mix this batch of cookies.

2 cups buttermilk
2 teaspoons baking soda
2 eggs, beaten
2 teaspoons vanilla extract
1 teaspoon pineapple extract
1 teaspoon lemon extract
2 cups sugar
1 (2-pound) bag of flour plus extra flour for rolling out dough
2 teaspoons baking powder
1 stick (½ cup) butter, softened
1 stick (½ cup) shortening

Pour buttermilk in a bowl and stir in baking soda. Add beaten eggs and flavorings; mix well. Add sugar and mix well. Set aside.

Combine the 2-pound bag of flour and baking powder in an extra-large bowl; mix well. Add softened butter and shortening to flour mixture and cut in with a pastry cutter until no lumps of butter or shortening remain and mixture has a fine texture. Add buttermilk mixture and mix well, until dough has a fairly smooth texture.

Turn out dough onto a floured board and knead the dough, adding more flour to the board and sprinkling it around the dough until it no longer sticks to your hand or the board (a maximum of 5 minutes).

Pinch off dough in amounts that will fit on the board and roll out to a little less than ¼-inch thickness. Lightly dusting the board with flour will make the dough easier to roll. Cut with a pizza wheel or knife into 3-inch squares or use cookie cutters in the shape you prefer. Place cookies on a cookie sheet that has been lightly greased (use the butter left on the butter wrapper) and dusted with flour. Bake at 325°F about 15 minutes, or until

Chapter 2: Recipes

bottom of tea cake is medium brown. (Longer baking times make the tea cakes crispy, but do not allow them to burn.) *Makes about 3 dozen*

Contributed by Harold Odom Jr.
Addie Jane Lewis Odom's grandson
Fort Bend County

*H*arold's grandmother, Big Mama Addie Odom, was well known for her tea cakes. "As a result, she earned the name 'Tea Cake Lady' in her Shankleville community and throughout Newton County," says Harold. "On one visit with Big Mama, the two of us sat and calculated the number of tea cakes that she'd made over her lifetime, and we came up with more than 250,000. She made them every day for her kids to take to school in a syrup bucket with a piece of sausage for lunch. When her grandchildren came along, she'd make them for us, but she'd never give us more than one tea cake at a time. We would crawl on our bellies to get to the ceramic cookie jar where she kept them, and every time we touched the lid, she would hear and get on us, then give us another.

"Several of her granddaughters tried to learn the recipe and the process she used, but when Big Mama would taste the cookies they made, she'd say, 'You ain't got it.' She had the habit of baking a batch of tea cakes whenever she'd visit her children and/ or grandchildren, and during a 1984 visit she made to Houston for treatments at MD Anderson Cancer Center, I videotaped her making a batch at my house. I studied the tape and, through trial and error, finally 'got it.' I then reduced the process to a recipe, and today at the biennial A. T. and Addie Odom Family Reunion, I teach a tea cake–making class for family members.

"I don't know where Big Mama obtained the tea cakes recipe, but I know it did not come from her mother [Jessie Gatlin Lewis] because she told me that Grandma made molasses tea cakes, not the ones in this recipe. I've been asked to add things like nuts and other flavors, but my creed is that 'you don't adulterate Big Mama Addie Odom's Tea Cakes.'"

Harold makes the tea cakes at least once a month. "I send batches to all of the uncles and aunts in the family and some cousins," he says. "My Sunday School class demands them at least once a quarter. My grandkids and all of the Odom family love them. My golfing buddies look in my lunch bag to see if I brought any to share."

Thanks to Harold, Big Mama Addie Odom's Tea Cakes will continue to delight Odom descendants for generations to come. When he teaches the class at family reunions, Harold insists that the cookies be referred to as "Big Mama Addie Odom's Tea Cakes." He has two recipes — one version calls for two pounds of flour and makes about three dozen tea cakes. The other version calls for five pounds of flour and makes about ten dozen. "We do the two-pound version in the class," says Harold. "I usually have five or six participants each time. Some of them are 'remedial students' from previous classes."

The biennial family reunions are held in Shankleville on the grounds of the Addie L. and A. T. Odom Homestead, which was listed in the National Register of Historic Places in 2012. For details about the site, see the Shankleville Historical Society's website, www.shankleville.org. (For another grandchild's memories of Addie Jane Lewis Odom, see the Purple Hull Peas recipe in the Vegetables and Sides section.)

Addie Jane Lewis Odom.
Courtesy of Harold Odom Jr.

Shankleville: A Love Story

While Harold Odom Jr. celebrates his grandmother's legendary tea cakes, he also takes pride in another remarkable family legacy. His great-great-great grandparents Jim and Winnie Shankle were the founders of Shankleville, a freedmen's community in Newton County with a poignant, romantic origin.

Jim and Winnie were both born into slavery in the early 1800s. They fell in love while together on a Mississippi plantation. According to the Shankleville Historical Society website, "After Winnie and her three children were sold to a Texan, Jim ran away from his Mississippi owner. He traveled by night, foraged for food, swam streams (including the Mississippi River), walking out of sight [under cover of darkness] the 400 miles to East Texas. At dusk one day, he found Winnie beside her master's spring. After slipping out food to Jim for several days, Winnie told her master, who arranged to buy Jim."

The article goes on to say that the couple raised Winnie's three children (by her slave masters) and had six of their own. After Emancipation, they began buying land, and with their son-in-law Steve McBride, eventually owned more than four thousand acres. They became local leaders in the freedmen's community that sprang up and was named for them. An annual Shankleville Homecoming has been held since 1941. For more information about the Shankleville community's heritage, see the Shankleville Historical Society website (www.shankleville.org).

Grandmother's Tea Cookies (ENGLISH)

1 cup shortening, melted
1 cup sugar
3 eggs
3 cups flour
¼ teaspoon salt
2 teaspoons baking powder
1 teaspoon vanilla

Combine melted shortening and sugar and mix until blended. Add eggs and beat well. Add remainder of ingredients and mix until smooth. Roll out dough to about ⅜-inch thickness on a floured surface and cut out cookies. Place on a lightly greased cookie sheet and bake at 450°F for about 8 minutes. Remove to a sheet of waxed paper to cool. *Makes 3 to 4 dozen*

Contributed by Mary Alice Graves Liles
Carolyn Tate Drum's granddaughter
Bailey County

*A*lice has been told all her life that this recipe came over on the boat with her English ancestors, the Cornforths, when they immigrated to America in 1840. "The Cornforths were from the London area, and they were my grandmother Drum's great-grandparents," she says. "After arriving in the United States, they settled in St. Louis, Missouri, and bought a textile factory in Mexico, Missouri, about 120 miles away." Alice knows little about the family's life in the United States except that the factory was later burned by the Union army after the discovery that it was manufacturing material for Confederate uniforms. The first American-born Cornforth, Maria Louise Cornforth (1844–1931), was Alice's great-great-grandmother.*

Whether the recipe originated in England or not, Grandmother's Tea Cookies have a long history in Alice's family. "My mother [Jack Louise Drum Graves] made these cookies, but I remember eating them more often at my grandmother's house in Olney," says Alice. "I've been making them as long as I have been married and doing my own cooking — more than fifty years.

Chapter 2: Recipes

"Grandmother's original recipe didn't call for a specific amount of flour. It just said 'add enough flour to make rolling consistency,' which to me is typical of a past generation of cooks who never seemed to need a recipe and just 'cooked by heart.' I've found that three cups of flour is just about right. Sometimes I add food coloring, swirling two or three colors in the dough without completely blending the colors, which gives the cookies a marbleized look. I also have fun making these cookies for various holidays and using cookie cutters appropriate to the season. But I usually just make round ones using Grandmother's original biscuit cutter.

"When I asked Grandmother for this recipe back in the late 1960s, she typed it for me on an index card using the old family manual typewriter, whose keys were a bit worn out from years of use and didn't always put the letters right on the line. And she did it in her hunt-and-peck style, which didn't always produce a perfect copy. Over the years, the original index card has had quite a lot of use and has yellowed with age and become spotted with a few food stains, so I finally retired it, making another copy in my handwriting and laminating the original so it could be preserved. The copy will be handed down to my kids and perhaps used for another lifetime."

Carolyn Tate Drum with
her husband, Richard Drum.
Courtesy of Alice Liles.

Grandma's Old-Fashioned Tea Cakes

½ cup (1 stick) butter
1 cup sugar
2 eggs
1 teaspoon vanilla
2 teaspoons lemon zest or 1 teaspoon lemon extract (optional)
2 cups sifted flour
2 teaspoons baking powder
½ teaspoon salt

Cream butter and sugar in a large bowl. Add eggs and beat well. Stir in vanilla and lemon zest, if using. (Grandma's recipe called for lemon zest, but she sometimes omitted it.)

Blend flour and remaining ingredients together and add to butter mixture; mix well. Place dough on a floured board and roll out to ¼-inch thickness; cut into 2-inch rounds. Place cookies on a lightly greased baking sheet and bake at 375°F for 10 to 12 minutes, or until edges are golden brown. Remove to wire racks to cool. *Makes about 3 dozen*

Ailcy Elizabeth "Bessie" Hall McKey with her husband, Claud McKey.
Courtesy of Helen McKey

164

Chapter 2: Recipes

Contributed by Nola McKey (author)
Ailcy Elizabeth "Bessie" Hall McKey's granddaughter
Travis County

I described how I rediscovered Grandma McKey's tea cakes recipe and my subsequent epiphany in chapter 1, but I didn't mention that my "heirloom recipe" consisted of only a list of ingredients. No mixing or rolling-out instructions, no baking time or temperature. Cooks in Grandma's day didn't need this information — everyone "knew" how to make tea cakes. And because she always baked them before we arrived, I never saw her make them.

Because of this omission, I've tried making the recipe several different ways. The method given here results in pretty cookies, and they have the same flavor that Grandma's did. However, Grandma's tea cakes weren't always pretty. In fact, they were a little haphazard. (Remember, she made them all the time for years!) They were rectangular, not round, and sometimes the rectangles looked more like parallelograms or trapezoids, and they had a dusty, floury texture. So when I really want to "visit Grandma," I make them the way I think she did: I roll out the dough on a floured board and cut it into rectangles with a sharp knife. Then I use a spatula to transfer them to the baking sheet. When the cookies come out of the oven, voilà: perfect imperfection. I'm back at Grandma's oilcloth-covered table, and all is right with the world.

These rather plain cookies offer a canvas for any number of alterations. Try rolling the dough into 1-inch balls and then rolling those in sugar, a mixture of sugar and cinnamon, or chopped pecans; place the balls on a baking sheet and press each one with the bottom of a glass before baking. If you want a more pronounced lemon flavor, double or triple the amount of lemon zest, or use the amount called for in the recipe but press additional lemon zest into the top of each cookie before baking. You can also make the cookies according to the recipe and decorate the tops with colored icing after baking.

*Jerusha "Jo" Love Clark
Schnitz. Courtesy of Jean
Schnitz.*

Nanny's Tea Cakes

2 "large eggs" of Crisco (½ cup Crisco)
2 cups sugar
2 extra-large eggs
2 teaspoons vanilla or lemon extract
1 cup milk
5 cups flour
¼ teaspoon salt
4 teaspoons baking powder

Cream Crisco and sugar in a large bowl. Add eggs and beat well.

Stir vanilla or lemon extract into milk and set aside.

Sift together flour, salt, and baking powder in another bowl. Add to Crisco mixture alternately with vanilla-milk mixture, mixing well after each addition. Drop by spoonfuls onto a lightly greased cookie sheet and bake at 350°F for about 10 minutes. *Makes about 6 dozen*

Contributed by Nancy Walters Powell
Jerusha "Jo" Love Clark Schnitz's granddaughter by marriage
Bexar County

"*My husband, Therrell [Powell], has loved these cookies since he was a little boy," says Nancy. "Nanny always enjoyed telling me about Therrell lying on the floor underneath the table that she was using for her ironing surface and kicking it while yelling, 'I want tea cakes! I want tea cakes!' She said it sure made for bumpy ironing.*

"When Nanny gave me the recipe in the late fifties or early sixties and I came to the instructions to roll out the dough and cut out cookies, I said I couldn't do that — chasing my one-year-old, three-year-old, and four-year-old took most of my time. So she revised the recipe so that I could make drop tea cakes. Today Therrell still loves them with vanilla flavoring; I love them with lemon; and my kids, grandkids, and great-grandkids love them with either!

"I always double Nanny's original recipe, which called for '1 large egg of Crisco,'" says Nancy. "That measurement is made by taking a regular tablespoon and scooping it into the Crisco can until it is mounded to the size of a large egg resting in the spoon, about 1½ inches at the highest point. Nanny also said that if I wanted to, I could use a coffee cup for the flour and sugar — approximate measurements worked fine."

The tea cake tradition continues in Nancy's family. Her daughters (Leslie Scirratt and Elaine Bailey) both make the cookies, as well as two of her three granddaughters (Rochelle Bradley and Rhonda Proctor).

Great-Grandmother's Tea Cakes

Stella Baker Dolen Becker

1896–1979

Harris and Travis Counties

½ cup (1 stick) butter or margarine
½ cup Crisco
2 cups sugar
4 eggs
2 teaspoons baking powder
1 to 2 teaspoons vanilla
4 cups flour plus additional for rolling out dough

Combine all ingredients except flour in a large bowl and mix well. Add flour gradually. Roll out dough on a lightly floured surface to about ¼-inch thickness and cut out cookies. Place on a lightly greased baking sheet and bake at 400°F for 12 to 15 minutes. Remove to a wire rack to cool. *Makes about 6 dozen*

Contributed by Tracy Becker Thronburg
Stella Baker Dolen Becker's great-granddaughter
Travis County

"This is my father's favorite cookie," says Tracy. "You can also make it with all butter or margarine or all Crisco. Sometimes I add a little black pepper to the recipe for a savory variation. Other than that, I make it just the way my great-grandmother wrote it out for my mother more than forty years ago."

Pies and Cobblers

Bessie Kolonko McClosky (Bomo)

1895–1975

Bexar County

Bomo's Cheese Pie (POLISH)

Using small-curd cottage cheese results in a smoother pie; however, some people prefer to use the large-curd variety for the different character and texture it produces.

1 (16-ounce) carton large-curd or small-curd cottage cheese
½ cup sugar
2 eggs
1 unbaked (9-inch) pastry shell
Freshly grated nutmeg or ground nutmeg
Fresh fruit or berries (optional)

Mix cheese and sugar together by hand with a large spoon. Add eggs and mix again. Pour mixture into pastry shell and sprinkle with nutmeg. Bake at 400°F for 5 minutes. Reduce temperature to 350°F and bake 45 minutes to 1 hour, or until a knife inserted in center of the pie comes out clean. Let cool on a wire rack 1 to 1½ hours. Serve with fresh fruit or berries, if desired. Makes one 9-inch pie

Contributed by Toni McCloskey Gustafson
Bessie Kolonko McClosky's granddaughter
Bexar County

"*This was one of my favorite desserts when I was a child," says Toni. "And it was among the first recipes I received from Mama [Judy Giannini McCloskey] as a young bride. She herself had received it from her mother-in-law, Bomo. It reminds me of old-time Texas cooking and echoes similar recipes from Silesia, Poland, whence Bomo's grandparents emigrated in the 1850s.*

Chapter 2: Recipes

"My Silesian-Polish-American grandmother – who went by Bessie – was born Bronislava Kolonko in the Polish community of St. Hedwig, east of San Antonio," says Toni. "Her Silesian family arrived in Texas in the mid-1850s. My grandfather Frank McClosky, along with his family, emigrated from Poland to the United States in 1890. Before they came to the United States, the family name was Mikołłajczyk. How the children of a Polish immigrant family ended up with an Irish name is another story!" (Like many immigrants' names, the original was "Americanized" during the immigration process; Toni says it was incorrect even on the ship's manifest.) Toni goes on to explain that "McClosky" further evolved into "McCloskey" when her father (Gene McCloskey) served in the US Navy during World War II. "Daddy's family line – his children and grandchildren, et cetera – uses the McCloskey spelling," she says. "The rest of the family still uses 'McClosky.'

"In Bomo's youth, the St. Hedwig community was quite cohesive, and the Polish language survived well into the twentieth century," says Toni. "I remember Bomo speaking Polish with her sisters on the phone when I was a little girl. I do not know when she obtained this recipe. To me, it 'always existed.' Bomo was a wonderful, plain, and simple cook and baker. I loved her dearly. As an adult, I had to learn how to make this pie. When I lived in New York, my friends enjoyed it so much that I passed the recipe along to several of them.

"My schedule does not allow a lot of time for cooking these days, but Bomo's Cheese Pie remains my favorite dessert. In her later years, my mom made it for my birthday instead of a cake. To see it and taste it after experiencing its aroma brings Bomo back, as well as my mom. When I compiled our intrafamily cookbook [a collection of recipes from the Frank McClosky and Bessie Kolonko McClosky family] two decades ago, it was the first recipe I typed up. We have a large, close-knit, long-lived family, and now the recipe has been passed on to younger generations."

Bessie Kolonko McClosky holding her granddaughter Frances McCloskey. Courtesy of Toni Gustafson.

Thelma McKey Williams
1916–2000
Brown, Lavaca, Victoria, and Gonzales Counties

Thelma McKey Williams.
Courtesy of Helen McKey.

Aunt Thelma's Chess Pie

This simple dessert has deep Southern roots and features ingredients that rural cooks would likely have had on hand in the nineteenth and twentieth centuries.

4 eggs, well beaten
½ cup (1 stick) butter, melted and cooled
1 cup milk
1 teaspoon vanilla
1 tablespoon flour
1½ cups sugar
Aunt Thelma's Favorite Pie Crust (recipe follows) or ½ (15-ounce)
    package refrigerated pie crusts

Combine eggs, butter, milk, and vanilla and blend well. Add flour and sugar and mix until smooth. Set aside.

Fit pie crust into a 9-inch pie plate. Fold edges under and crimp as desired. Pour mixture into crust, leaving ¼-inch room below rim. Bake at 325°F for 10 minutes. Place pie crust shield on top of pie and continue baking for about 40 minutes, or until a knife inserted in the center comes out clean. *Makes one 9-inch pie*

Aunt Thelma's Favorite Pie Crust
1 cup flour
⅜ teaspoon salt
⅓ cup shortening
About 2½ tablespoons ice water

Sift together flour and salt. Cut in shortening with a pastry blender. Slowly sprinkle enough ice water over mixture to hold ingredients together. Mix with a fork to form a ball. Turn pastry out onto a floured board and roll to ⅛-inch thickness. *Makes enough crust for one 9-inch pie*

Contributed by Kaitlyn "Kaitie" Marie Braddock
Thelma McKey Williams's great-niece
Brazoria County

Author's Note: Chess pie has a round-robin history in my family. It probably originated with my grandma (Bessie McKey), but we know that several other family members also made it, including my mother (Helen McKey). She baked many of these simple, delicious pies in the late 1960s, when my family moved to the El Toro area (near Edna) and raised cows and chickens. Even though she worked full-time as a public health nurse, she would bake chess pie and pack slices of it in Daddy's lunch box. The beauty of chess pie is that it uses a lot of eggs and milk, which they had in abundance.

After I began working on this cookbook, my sister Becky Braddock found a handwritten recipe for chess pie among my late aunt Thelma's keepsakes. My niece Kaitie, a college student who likes to bake, made the pie for Thanksgiving one year and then did what college students do—she took a picture and promptly texted it to four friends. Thanks to her iPhone, this old-fashioned Southern dessert has new standing in the digital world.

Kaitie's great-aunt Thelma would be pleased. She loved to cook, almost as much as she loved her numerous nieces and nephews (great and otherwise). She and my uncle Pete had no children of their own, but she often babysat the youngest family members and spent much time with the older children, sometimes involving them in her numerous hobbies, such as crocheting, basket making, woodworking, painting, and jewelry making. Like many women of her generation, she raised a garden and canned her own fruits and vegetables. At one time, she and her husband had a peach orchard near Harwood, which probably accounts for her descendants' wistful memories of the jars of sweet, delicious peaches always on her table. Sometimes she would make peach pies, no doubt using the other handwritten recipe my sister found among her papers, My Favorite Pie Crust. It's given as an option with the chess pie recipe.

Aunt Thelma's Chess Pie was delicious, but my aunt Tennie (Authemia McKey) made one that was truly remarkable. Her granddaughter Tasha Harper-Werner wrote about it in "McKey Stories," a booklet my sister Laura McKey compiled for the 1997 McKey reunion (adapted here by permission).

"Brother Weigel [the pastor at Sublime Baptist Church, near Hallettsville] used to stay at church members' homes on weekends so that he didn't have so far to drive on Sundays. One such weekend, he was going to stay with Dewey and Authemia [my grandparents] and Pam [my mother, who was eight or nine at the time]. While preparing Saturday's supper, Authemia realized that she didn't have any sugar for her chess pies. She sent Pam over to Granny McKey's kitchen [next door] to get some. Pam knew right where to get it, so she didn't bother to ask for help.

"That evening after supper, Granny brought out that troublesome pie. She served up a nice piece for Brother Weigel, who ate it all up with many compliments. When Dewey took his first bite, he realized what had happened. Pam had gotten salt instead of sugar. [Granny McKey kept flour, sugar, salt, and other staples in big tins in her cupboard.] Shocked, Authemia went to apologizing, but was cut short by Brother Weigel, who declared, 'No, no. It was simply scrumptious!'"

So far, no one in the family has made a chess pie that tops that one.

if you do not have a pie crust shield, fold strips of aluminum foil in half, open folds slightly, bend strips to fit around the pie, and place them over the edge of the pie crust.

Edith "Egy" Nolting
Karoline Glaeser Goodrich

1900–1984

Uvalde and Bexar Counties

Aunt Egy's Mock Apple Pie

1 cup sugar
½ cup firmly packed brown sugar
3 tablespoons cream of tartar
½ teaspoon salt
Juice of 1 lemon
1¾ cups water
18 saltine crackers
1 unbaked (8-inch) pastry shell
Cinnamon
Topping (recipe follows)
Vanilla ice cream or sweetened whipped cream (optional)
Dash of nutmeg (optional)

Combine sugars, cream of tartar, salt, lemon juice, and 1¾ cups water in a small saucepan. Boil 3 minutes, stirring occasionally. Set aside.

Break crackers by hand into fairly large pieces into pastry shell. Sprinkle generously with cinnamon. Pour cooked mixture evenly over cinnamon

Chapter 2: Recipes

and crackers. Sprinkle Topping on pie. Bake at 400°F about 30 minutes, or until browned. Cool slightly before slicing; serve warm. Top with a scoop of vanilla ice cream or sweetened whipped cream and sprinkle with nutmeg, if desired. *Makes one 8-inch pie*

Topping
½ cup firmly packed brown sugar

3 tablespoons flour

1 tablespoon butter or margarine

Combine sugar, flour, and butter in a small bowl and mix until crumbly. *Makes enough topping for one 8-inch pie*

Contributed by Nancy Helen O'Bryant Puentes
Edith "Egy" Nolting Karoline Glaeser Goodrich's great-niece
Travis County

Edith "Egy" Nolting Karoline Glaeser Goodrich (left) and her niece Helen Lydia Pearce O'Bryant. Courtesy of Nancy O'Bryant Puentes.

"*J* don't make this pie too often, but it's quite good," says Nancy. "I've been known to play a joke on people by telling them I'll make a special apple pie and they have to guess the secret ingredient. No one has ever guessed that it uses saltine crackers instead of apples! I don't know why this recipe works, but it does.

"Aunt Egy was always my favorite great-aunt. She had red hair, blue eyes, and a feisty personality. Her name came from her initials – E.G. – and that's how we pronounced it. She was the second-youngest daughter in my maternal grandmother's family of twelve children. When she was born, my great-grandmother, no doubt swamped with the tasks of raising her already large brood, as well as running a Sabinal farm household requiring three large and nourishing meals daily for the men who farmed the fields, 'gave' her to my grandmother with the charge that she was responsible for raising her.

"Aunt Egy was the first person anyone in our family knew who was divorced. As a divorcée, she took a job at Joske's [department store] in San Antonio, where she worked for many years. Everyone there knew her as E. G. also, but when she gave a gift to a young co-worker departing to get married and included a card signed 'Egy,' the young woman was totally puzzled. 'Eggy?' she queried. 'But I don't know anyone named Eggy!'"

Ethel Juanita Hunter Weiss (Gran)

1917–1995

Coryell, McLennan, Travis, Bexar, Comal, and Smith Counties

Gran's Peach Pie

6 to 8 peach halves (fresh peaches taste best)
1 unbaked 9-inch pastry shell
½ cup sugar
⅛ teaspoon salt
2 tablespoons cornstarch or flour
¼ teaspoon nutmeg
½ teaspoon vanilla
½ cup heavy cream
3 tablespoons sliced almonds
Freshly grated nutmeg

Place peach halves in pastry shell. Set aside.

Combine sugar, salt, cornstarch or flour, nutmeg, vanilla, and cream and stir well. Pour over peaches. Sprinkle peaches with almonds and nutmeg. Bake at 400°F for 45 to 55 minutes, or until browned. Check midway; if edges of crust are browning too quickly, place pie crust shield over pie. *Makes one 9-inch pie*

Contributed by Tracy Becker Thronburg
Ethel Juanita Hunter Weiss's granddaughter
Travis County

Tracy has been baking this pie since she was a little girl. "Gran taught me how to make it," she says. "She was not known as a good cook, but this pie was always good. She probably got the recipe from someone in her bridge club in New Braunfels. The peaches probably came from Stonewall or Johnson City."

Chapter 2: Recipes

Peach Custard Pie

Note that this recipe makes two pies. If you want to make only one, use two small or medium eggs and divide the other measurements in half. If you have excess water after cooking the peaches, you can use it to replace part of the milk in the recipe.

2 unbaked 10-inch pastry shells
1 pound dried peaches
3 eggs
1½ cups sugar
2 scant tablespoons cornstarch
2 tablespoons butter, softened
1 teaspoon vanilla
1 cup milk
Freshly ground nutmeg

Line 2 10-inch pie plates with pastry and partially prebake crusts at 425°F for 10 minutes. Set aside.

Combine peaches and enough water to completely cover the peaches (about 4 cups) in a large saucepan. Bring mixture to a boil, reduce heat, and simmer over low heat, covered, about 20 minutes, or until peaches are very tender. Drain any excess water. Mash peaches to a fine pulp (use a food processor if available) and set aside.

Beat eggs in a large bowl until mixed but not foamy. Combine sugar and cornstarch and stir into eggs. Add butter, vanilla, and milk, and mix well. Set aside.

Place half of the mashed peaches in each pastry shell (layer should be about ¾-inch thick). Smooth top but *do not pack*. Pour egg mixture over peaches, dividing evenly between pastry shells. Sprinkle with nutmeg. Bake at 325°F for about 30 minutes, or until a knife inserted in the center comes out clean. If edges of crusts brown too quickly, cover them with pie crust shields. *Makes two 10-inch pies*

Melissa Alice Autrey West (Momie)

1876–1927

Tarrant County

Melissa Alice Autrey West and her daughter Thelma Ulala West Shannon. Courtesy of Anne Isham.

Contributed by Anne Shannon Lewis Isham
Melissa Alice Autrey West's great-granddaughter
Travis County

*S*ometimes a family recipe gets lost for a while and then reappears, as
was the case with Peach Custard Pie. "This recipe came from my great-
grandmother," says Anne, "but we didn't discover it until after Munnie (my
grandmother) died and we were going through her recipes."

Both Anne and her late sister, Joanie, began making the pie, and each added a
few changes over the years. For example, the original recipe called for additional
sugar to sweeten the peaches, but Anne finds that the pie is sweet enough
without it. She also makes her own pie crust and substitutes one tablespoon of
whole-wheat flour for one tablespoon of white flour. The resurrected recipe now
includes notes from four family cooks, which makes it even more of a culinary
heirloom. It's also something of an inspiration. "Just reading the recipe gives me
a serious craving for Peach Custard Pie," says Anne.

**Recipes for custard pies often call for prebaking (also called blind baking) the
crust to prevent it from becoming soggy from the filling that will be added later.
Line the crust with a sheet of aluminum foil or parchment paper, fill with dry
beans, and bake at 425°F for 15 minutes. Remove and discard aluminum foil or
parchment paper and beans, prick the crust all over, and allow to cool.**

Lillie Loucindy Lee McKey

1887–1973

**Bastrop, Lavaca, and
Wharton Counties**

Grandma's Coconut Pie

*Whipped cream or whipped topping can be substituted for the meringue; just let
the filling cool first and skip the final baking.*

2½ cups milk
2 eggs
1½ cups sugar
3 tablespoons flour
1 cup sweetened flaked coconut
2 tablespoons butter

1½ teaspoons vanilla
1 baked 9-inch pastry shell
3 egg whites (reserve yolks for another use)
Additional ½ teaspoon vanilla
¼ teaspoon cream of tartar
Additional 6 tablespoons sugar

Place milk in a medium saucepan and slowly bring to the boiling point.

In the meantime, beat eggs in a medium bowl. Add the 1½ cups sugar and flour and mix well. Stir egg mixture into milk gradually and cook over low heat a few minutes, or until mixture thickens. Stir in coconut, butter, and the 1½ teaspoons vanilla. Pour into pastry shell.

Beat egg whites, the additional ½ teaspoon vanilla, and cream of tartar at high speed with an electric mixer until soft peaks form. Gradually add the additional 6 tablespoons sugar, beating until sugar is dissolved, mixture is glossy, and stiff peaks form. Spread meringue over filling, sealing to the edge. Bake at 350°F for 12 to 15 minutes, or until lightly browned. *Makes one 9-inch pie*

Contributed by Vada Marie Morton Wolter
Lillie Loucindy Lee McKey's granddaughter
Wharton County

"Grandma's original recipe made enough for two pies," says Vada. "With eight children in my family, making two pies was necessary. When I lived in El Campo during the 1970s, I baked this pie a lot for birthdays and special occasions."

*Lillie Loucindy Lee McKey.
Courtesy of Vada Wolter.*

Lillie Loucindy Lee McKey

1887–1973

Bastrop, Lavaca, and Wharton Counties

*Lillie Loucindy Lee McKey.
Courtesy of Vada Wolter.*

Grandma's Raisin Pie

This old-fashioned pie features plumped raisins and a meringue topping.

2 cups raisins
2 cups milk
3 eggs, beaten
1 cup sugar
3 tablespoons flour
1½ teaspoons vanilla
1 baked (9-inch) pastry shell
3 egg whites (reserve yolks for another use)
Additional ½ teaspoon vanilla
¼ teaspoon cream of tartar
Additional 6 tablespoons sugar

Place raisins in a medium bowl, pour boiling water over them, and let them sit about 10 minutes. Drain and set aside.

Pour milk into a medium saucepan and slowly bring to the boiling point.

In the meantime, beat eggs in a medium bowl. Add the 1 cup sugar and flour and mix well. Stir mixture into milk gradually and cook over low heat, stirring constantly. When mixture begins to thicken, stir in drained raisins and vanilla. Continue cooking about 5 minutes longer, or until mixture has the consistency of a cream filling. Pour mixture into baked pastry shell.

Beat egg whites, the additional ½ teaspoon vanilla, and cream of tartar at high speed with an electric mixer until soft peaks form. Gradually add the additional 6 tablespoons sugar, beating until sugar is dissolved, mixture is glossy, and stiff peaks form. Spread meringue over filling, sealing to the edge. Bake at 350°F for 12 to 15 minutes, or until lightly browned. *Makes one 9-inch pie*

Contributed by Vada Marie Morton Wolter
Lillie Loucindy Lee McKey's granddaughter
Wharton County

Chapter 2: Recipes

"$\mathcal{I}$, remember as a very young girl going to Grandma McKey's home and eating this pie," says Vada. "She would always have a bouquet of flowers in the center of the table . . . usually from her garden or from along the roadside."

Sweet Potato (or Pumpkin) Pie

Canned sweet potatoes work fine in this pie, but using the fresh-baked version results in better flavor. (For ½ cup mashed sweet potatoes, pierce 1 large or 2 small sweet potatoes with a fork and bake at 350°F for about 45 minutes, or until tender.) To make pumpkin pie, substitute mashed pumpkin for mashed sweet potatoes.

1 cup sugar
½ teaspoon pumpkin pie spice
½ teaspoon cinnamon
½ cup mashed sweet potatoes
2 eggs
1 (12-ounce) can evaporated milk
½ teaspoon vanilla
1 unbaked 10-inch pastry shell
Whipped cream (optional)

Mix first 7 ingredients together in a large bowl and pour into pastry shells. Bake at 425°F for 15 minutes. Lower heat to 350°F and bake for an additional 35 minutes, or until center is firm. Let pies cool. Garnish with whipped cream. *Makes one 10-inch pie*

Contributed by Cheryl Jean "CJ" Stephenson
Onie Lee Johnson Cooper's granddaughter
Lubbock County

Onie Lee Johnson Cooper
1903–1969
Lubbock and Lynn Counties

Onie Lee Johnson Cooper with her husband, Duffie Cooper. Courtesy of Cheryl Stephenson.

"My great-grandmother died when my grandmother was just a toddler," says Cheryl, "so she was raised by her aunt and uncle and grew up with several cousins on a farm in Georgia. She did a lot of cooking at a young age. My grandfather worked for her uncle. Part of his attraction to my grandmother had to be that she was such a wonderful cook. After they married, they moved to Texas. Their first child — my mother — was born in New Home, a small community near Lubbock.

"My grandmother passed down this recipe to her middle child, my aunt Faye, who made it with fresh sweet potatoes. Aunt Faye then passed it along to me. I usually use canned sweet potatoes or pumpkin." Cheryl has made this pie for both Thanksgiving and Christmas. "One year I was hosting our extended family for a holiday meal and had put two pies on the lower level of a serving cart," she says. "Our schnauzer, Barkley, got into the house and had eaten half of one of the pies before my brother-in-law alerted me. Needless to say, Barkley was banished to the backyard."

Estelle Morton's Pumpkin Pie

Check edges of crust while pie is baking. If browning too fast, place pie crust shield on top of pie. Remove shield during last 15 to 20 minutes of baking.

1 cup sugar
1 tablespoon flour
½ teaspoon cinnamon
Dash of salt
1 cup canned pumpkin
2 eggs
2 cups evaporated milk
1 teaspoon vanilla
1 unbaked (9-inch) pastry shell
Whipped cream or Cool Whip
Pecans or walnuts (halves or chopped)

Combine sugar, flour, cinnamon, and salt in a large bowl. Stir in pumpkin. Set aside.

Beat eggs in a medium bowl. Stir in milk and vanilla. Add to pumpkin mixture and mix well. Pour into pastry shell. Bake at 450°F for 10 minutes. Lower heat to at 400°F and cook an additional 10 minutes. Lower heat to 350°F and cook 20 to 25 minutes longer, or until knife inserted in center of pie comes out clean. Cool pie completely. Top with whipped cream and nuts as desired. *Makes one 9-inch pie*

Contributed by Vada Marie Morton Wolter
Estelle Reese Morton's granddaughter
Wharton County

ada has been making this pie for Thanksgiving for more than fifty years. "Grandma Morton made her own pie crusts; I use Marie Callender's pie shells," she says. "She used whipping cream; I use Cool Whip. It doesn't seem to matter. At my house, there's never enough of this pie for everyone."

Estelle Reese Morton
1898–1974
Wharton County

Estelle Reese Morton. Courtesy of Vada Wolter.

Rita Cook McClain
1882–1961
Williamson County

Rita Cook McClain.
Courtesy of Meredith McClain.

Angel Lemon Pie

This "pie" features four layers — crisp meringue squares topped with sweetened whipped cream, a lemon filling, and more sweetened whipped cream.

4 egg whites at room temperature (reserve yolks for Lemon Filling)
¼ teaspoon salt
1¼ cups sugar
1 tablespoon white vinegar or lemon juice
Lemon Filling (recipe follows)
1 cup heavy cream
2 tablespoons additional sugar
Toasted pecans (optional)

Line an 8 x 8 x 2-inch baking pan with brown paper (or parchment paper) so that bottom and sides of pan are covered and paper extends 1 inch above the rim.

Whip egg whites with salt until soft peaks form. Add the 1¼ cups sugar slowly, alternating with a few drops of vinegar or lemon juice at a time. Beat continuously about 1 minute, or until very stiff. Spread meringue evenly in the paper-lined pan and bake at 275°F for 1 hour, or until meringue is crisp but not browned. While meringue is baking, prepare Lemon Filling (recipe follows).

Remove pan from oven and lift out meringue carefully (it will be very brittle and light), using the paper extensions as handles, and place on a cutting board. Gently push meringue off the paper onto the board. When it is completely cool, use a serrated bread knife (with a gentle sawing motion and very little pressure) to cut meringue into 9 equal squares. Then reassemble these into a large square on a serving dish. (If exposed to moist air for several hours, the squares may become sticky, so proceed promptly with the rest of the recipe.)

Whip cream until soft peaks form. Add the 2 tablespoons additional sugar gradually and continue whipping until soft peaks form again. Spread half of this mixture onto the cooled and reassembled meringue squares. Then spread all of the Lemon Filling on top. (Don't worry if it mixes a bit with the cream layer below.) Then spread remainder of sweetened whipped cream on top of filling. Chill for 4 to 6 hours, but no longer. Serve with a spatula and pass a bowl of toasted pecans as an accompaniment. *Makes 9 servings*

Lemon Filling
4 reserved egg yolks
⅓ cup sugar
1 tablespoon grated lemon rind
3 tablespoons lemon juice
Pinch of salt

Beat egg yolks and add sugar; beat thoroughly. Stir in lemon rind, lemon juice, and salt. Cook mixture in the top of a double boiler until thick; let cool. If mixture is too thick, add a little extra lemon juice. *Makes enough filling for Angel Lemon Pie*

Contributed by Meredith McClain
Rita Cook McClain's granddaughter
Lubbock County

*A*ngel Lemon Pie is a lost-and-found recipe. *"My brother Martin and I loved our grandmother's Angel Lemon Pie during our childhood,"* says Meredith. *"Somehow, after her death in 1962, we lost track of the recipe. Then in 1973, the Georgetown Garden Club published its first* San Gabriel Garden Cook Book. *Louise Wilcox, one of the editors, honored Grandmother by submitting from her own private recipe file 'Rita McClain's Angel Lemon Pie.' Our mother, Rosamond Martin McClain, who was active in the Garden Club, sent copies of the cookbook to both Martin and me."*

Adapted from the Angel Lemon Pie recipe, that appears in the *San Gabriel Garden Cook Book*, compiled by the Georgetown Garden Club. First edition 1973 and reprinted in 1983.

If a recipe calls for both lemon zest and lemon juice, zest the lemon first, avoiding the white part just beneath the peel. Then roll the lemon on a hard surface, applying a little pressure, before slicing it and extracting the juice.

Bertha Lee Hester Bustin (NanNan)

1899–1974

Williamson and Travis Counties

NanNan's Lemon Pie

1 large lemon
3 tablespoons flour
1 cup sugar
1 cup boiling water
3 whole eggs
1 tablespoon butter
1 baked 9-inch pastry shell
3 egg whites (reserve yolks for another use)
½ teaspoon cream of tartar
Additional 6 tablespoons sugar

Zest lemon and extract juice; set aside (separately) lemon zest and juice.

Combine flour and the 1 cup sugar in a medium saucepan and mix well. Stir 1 cup boiling water into mixture and cook over medium heat, stirring constantly until thickened. Stir in lemon juice and remove from heat.

Beat the 3 whole eggs together in a small bowl. Stir about one-fourth of the hot mixture into eggs and then add that to the remaining hot mixture, stirring well. Return saucepan to stovetop and cook over medium heat until mixture thickens again. Remove from heat and stir in butter and reserved lemon zest. Cool slightly and pour into baked pastry shell.

Beat 3 egg whites and cream of tartar at high speed with an electric mixer until foamy. Gradually add the additional 6 tablespoons sugar, beating until stiff peaks form.

Spread meringue over filling, sealing to the edge. Bake at 350°F for 10 to 15 minutes, or until golden brown. *Makes one 9-inch pie*

Contributed by Tracy Becker Thronburg
Bertha Lee Hester Bustin's great-granddaughter
Travis County

Chapter 2: Recipes

"*This is my grandfather's favorite pie,*" *says Tracy. "I've been baking it for more than fifteen years, and I've never made any changes in the recipe. Don't mess with a good thing!"*

Tracy's mother, Marti Becker, made NanNan's Lemon Pie for a dinner party soon after she married in 1965. "This was her first dinner party," says Tracy. "She baked the pie as per the recipe, but the custard would never set. She called NanNan, who told her to keep baking it. Well, the pie never set, and they wound up eating the pie out of bowls. A funny ending for her first dinner party."

Grandma Lucy's Lemon Meringue Pie

Note that the filling recipe is for one pie and the pie crust recipe makes enough pastry for two. If not making a second pie, freeze the extra dough in a zip-top plastic freezer bag for future use.

Grandma Lucy's Pie Crust (recipe follows)
1½ cups sugar
5 tablespoons cornstarch
½ teaspoon salt
1½ cups boiling water
4 eggs
2 teaspoons butter
Zest of 1 lemon
½ cup lemon juice
¼ teaspoon cream of tartar
Additional ¼ cup plus 2 tablespoons sugar

Prepare Grandma Lucy's Pie Crust. Fit pie crust into a 10-inch pie plate, fold edges under, and crimp as desired. Prick bottom and sides of crust with tines of a fork and bake at 450°F until golden. Set aside.

Mix the 1½ cups sugar, cornstarch, and salt together in a saucepan. Stir in boiling water. Cook over low heat, stirring constantly, until mixture boils. Remove from heat.

Lucille "Lucy" Aletha Crider Harrison (Grandma Lucy)

1916–2005

Falls, Jones, Llano, and Victoria Counties

Lucille "Lucy" Aletha Crider Harrison. Courtesy of Candy Spaulding.

Separate eggs, reserving egg whites for meringue. Beat egg yolks in a medium bowl. Temper egg yolks by whisking in a small amount of the hot mixture into the eggs and then whisking a small amount of the egg mixture into the hot mixture. Repeat several times, working quickly. When original egg mixture has warmed, add it to the original hot mixture, whisking constantly. Stir in butter. Cook over low heat for 2 minutes, stir in lemon zest (reserve a small amount for garnish, if desired) and lemon juice, and continue to cook until thick. Pour filling into pie crust and set aside.

Beat reserved 4 egg whites and cream of tartar at high speed with an electric mixer until foamy. Gradually add the additional ¼ cup plus 2 tablespoons sugar, beating at high speed until sugar is dissolved and stiff peaks form. Spread meringue over pie filling, sealing to the edge. Bake at 350°F for 12 to 15 minutes, or until lightly browned. Garnish with reserved lemon zest, if desired. *Makes one 10-inch pie*

Grandma Lucy's Pie Crust
3 cups flour
½ teaspoon salt
1 cup plus 3 tablespoons shortening
1 egg, beaten
1 teaspoon vinegar
3 tablespoons ice-cold water

Combine flour and salt in a large bowl. Cut in shortening with a pastry blender until mixture resembles coarse crumbs. Add beaten egg, vinegar, and ice-cold water and mix until dough forms a ball. Divide dough in half. Place 1 portion of dough on a floured board and roll out into a round ⅛-inch thick. If making only one pie, freeze remaining dough in a zip-top plastic freezer bag. *Makes enough pastry for two 10-inch pies*

Contributed by Candy Spaulding
Lucille "Lucy" Aletha Crider Harrison's granddaughter
Victoria County

"*I think this picture of my grandma was taken in the summer or fall of 1942, shortly after my mom's older sister was born,*" says Candy. "*Fourteen months later, she had my momma. My grandparents lived at this house in Stamford during World War II. My grandpa had been in the Army Air Corps at Randolph Field in San Antonio, but his service was 'bought out' so that he could train army aviation cadets through a civilian flight school at Arledge Field in Stamford. (In those days, the military had to get creative in order to mobilize so many young men for service, and it depended on the private sector to provide primary flight training.) My grandma had to deal with ration books while obtaining milk for babies.*

"*Mom says that she can't remember a time when my grandma didn't make this pie, but I would think that the ingredients would have been a luxury during wartime. I once heard my grandma talking to an elderly friend about living on cornmeal mush during the Great Depression. Her favorite meal during that time was pinto beans with chocolate cake — eaten together, no frosting on the cake. Evidently, both women had enjoyed this combination during the Depression years.*

"*While Grandma had a real talent for cooking, I think living through the Depression and World War II served to make her more resourceful in life, and this was evidenced in what she would dare to tackle in the kitchen. I think this was true of many cooks in her generation. They had this gift of adaptability and — in some cases — the ability to make something great out of next to nothing. I hope we as a society don't lose this gift.*"

Candy says that although her grandma was a Texan, "*she spent some time during the 1950s in Cimarron, New Mexico, where she was very resourceful in earning money to support the family after my grandpa injured his back.*" She adds, "*Grandma took in washing, cut and sold firewood, baked bread, and did anything else she could to make ends meet. For two summers, she rented a building in nearby Ute Park and operated a restaurant that catered to tourists. She served this pie [and her Chocolate Meringue Pie] for dessert. She made ten-inch pies so that customers would get good-sized portions.*"

The pies came into play later, too. "*There was a time when I was a young girl that Grandma Lucy lived more than one thousand miles away,*" says Candy. "*My mom really missed her, so she would bake these pies and we would all feel closer to her. In her late eighties, Grandma gave up cooking and moved from Llano to Victoria to be closer to my family. She enjoyed letting me cook for her.*

Lucille "Lucy" Aletha Crider Harrison. Courtesy of Candy Spaulding.

[Candy has been cooking since she was seventeen.] When I baked these pies, she always got a particular twinkle in her eye and had to have a small piece of each! I always felt we had a strong connection when it came to cooking. For Grandma, cooking was sometimes a real necessity but always a joy. Now she's in heaven, but her joy is deeply rooted in me, and I can still feel close to her by making these pies and sharing them with those I love." (See Grandma Lucy's Chocolate Meringue Pie.)

Adding eggs or egg yolks to a hot mixture calls for a technique called tempering. This involves stirring a small amount of the hot mixture into the eggs so that the temperature of the eggs rises gradually. Then the egg mixture can be added slowly to the remaining hot mixture without worrying that the eggs will curdle.

Lucille "Lucy" Aletha Crider Harrison (Grandma Lucy)

1916–2005

Falls, Jones, Llano, and Victoria Counties

Lucille "Lucy" Aletha Crider Harrison. Courtesy of Candy Spaulding.

Grandma Lucy's Chocolate Meringue Pie

The original recipe gave the choice of replacing the 2 cups of milk with 1 cup powdered milk mixed with 2 cups water, probably a reflection of shortages during wartime years or the Great Depression. Peanut butter–and–powdered sugar crumbles were added in the 1960s; this option makes the chocolate flavor more intense.

Grandma Lucy's Pie Crust (recipe follows)
⅓ cup peanut butter (optional)
¾ cup powdered sugar (optional)
½ cup cocoa
1 cup sugar
2 tablespoons flour
½ cup Crisco or softened butter or margarine
4 eggs
2 cups milk
Pinch of salt
1 teaspoon vanilla
¼ teaspoon cream of tartar
Additional 6 tablespoons sugar

Chapter 2: Recipes

Prepare Grandma Lucy's Pie Crust. Fit pie crust into a 10-inch pie plate, fold edges under, and crimp as desired. Prick bottom and sides of crust with tines of a fork and bake at 450°F until golden.

If adding peanut butter–and–powdered sugar crumbles, combine peanut butter and powdered sugar in a small bowl and mix with a fork until crumbly. Sprinkle most of the crumbles over bottom of baked pie crust, reserving a few for garnish, if desired. Set aside.

Mix cocoa, the 1 cup sugar, and flour together in a saucepan. Add Crisco or softened butter or margarine and mix thoroughly.

Separate eggs, reserving egg whites for meringue. Beat egg yolks and add to cocoa mixture, mixing well. Stir in milk, salt, and vanilla. Cook over low heat, stirring constantly, until mixture thickens.

Spoon filling into pastry shell (over crumbles, if using) and set aside.

Beat reserved 4 egg whites and cream of tartar at high speed with an electric mixer until foamy. Gradually add the ¼ cup plus 2 tablespoons sugar, beating at high speed until sugar is dissolved and stiff peaks form. Spread meringue over pie filling, sealing to the edge. Bake at 350°F for 12 to 15 minutes, or until lightly browned. When pie cools, garnish with reserved peanut butter–and–powdered sugar crumbles, if desired.
Makes one 10-inch pie

Grandma Lucy's Pie Crust
3 cups flour
½ teaspoon salt
1 cup plus 3 tablespoons shortening
1 egg, beaten
1 teaspoon vinegar
3 tablespoons ice-cold water

Combine flour and salt in a large bowl. Cut in shortening with a pastry blender until mixture resembles coarse crumbs. Add beaten egg, vinegar, and ice-cold water and mix until dough forms a ball. Divide dough in half. Place 1 portion of dough on floured board and roll to ⅛-inch thickness. Freeze remaining dough in a zip-top plastic freezer bag if not making two pies. *Makes enough pastry for two 10-inch pies*

Contributed by Candy Spaulding
Lucille "Lucy" Aletha Crider Harrison's granddaughter
Victoria County

"Grandma made several kinds of pies, but her Chocolate Meringue Pie is one of my favorites," says Candy. "I usually make it and her Lemon Meringue Pie at the same time and use her pie crust recipe, which makes enough for two pies. I like to bake them as a surprise for special friends.

"While my grandma passed down the basic recipe for this pie, it was my mother [Maurine Spaulding] who came up with the idea of sprinkling the peanut butter–and–powdered sugar crumbles over the bottom of the crust. It has been a yummy addition to the recipe ever since." (For more about the pie-baking tradition in Candy's family, see Grandma Lucy's Lemon Meringue Pie recipe.)

NanNan's Chocolate Icebox Pie

Bertha Lee Hester Bustin (NanNan)

1899–1974

Williamson and Travis Counties

1 cup sugar
3 tablespoons flour
2 cups milk
1 to 1½ squares (1 ounce each) unsweetened chocolate
3 egg yolks (reserve egg whites for another purpose)
1 tablespoon butter
1 teaspoon vanilla
1 baked (9-inch) pastry shell
1 cup whipping cream
½ teaspoon almond extract
½ cup sifted powdered sugar
Additional 1-ounce square unsweetened chocolate, grated (optional)

Mix sugar and flour together in a medium saucepan. Gradually stir in milk. Bring mixture to boil over medium heat, stirring constantly, for 2 minutes. Remove from heat. Whisk in 1 to 1½ squares unsweetened chocolate until melted.

Beat egg yolks in a small bowl. Whisk about one-fourth of the hot mixture into egg yolks and then add that to the remaining hot mixture, stirring well. Return mixture to a boil, stirring constantly, and cook for an additional minute, or until mixture is very thick. Remove from heat and stir in butter and vanilla. Cover with waxed paper and let cool in refrigerator. When completely cooled, spoon into baked pie shell.

Combine whipping cream, almond extract, and powdered sugar and whip until light and fluffy. Spread over pie filling. Grate chocolate over pie if desired. *Makes one 9-inch pie*

Contributed by Tracy Becker Thronburg
Bertha Lee Hester Bustin's great-granddaughter
Travis County

"My great-grandmother [NanNan] was the second-oldest of thirteen or fourteen children," says Tracy. "She and her sister Annie were born in Tennessee; the other children were born in Texas. Her father (my great-great-grandfather), Paul Hester, was one of the early settlers of Round Rock. All of the Hester women, including my great-grandmother, were outstanding cooks and seamstresses. NanNan's chocolate pie is one of my family's favorite desserts. We always have it at Thanksgiving and Christmas."

Frankie Jones Gerhard (Aunt Frankie)

Born in 1930

Wharton, Matagorda, Jackson, Harris, and Lavaca Counties

Aunt Frankie's Pecan Pie

This pie works best baked in a glass pie plate using either a homemade crust or one of the rounds in a package of refrigerated pie crusts. A frozen pastry shell is usually not large enough to hold all the filling.

Crisco
½ (15-ounce) package refrigerated pie crusts
   (reserve remaining crust for later use)
1 cup pecan halves
3 tablespoons butter, cut into pieces
3 eggs
½ cup sugar
1 cup white corn syrup
Dash of salt
1 teaspoon vanilla

Grease bottom and sides of a 9-inch glass pie plate with Crisco. Unroll pie crust and fit into pie plate. Fold edges under and crimp as desired. Set aside.

Place pecans in a microwave-safe dish and dot with butter. Cook on High for 25 to 30 seconds, or until butter begins to melt. Stir well and spoon melted butter over pecans. Set aside.

Beat eggs in a mixing bowl. Add sugar and mix well. Add corn syrup, salt, and vanilla and mix well. Add melted butter and pecans and pour into pie crust. Bake at 350°F for 35 to 40 minutes, or until set.
Makes one 9-inch pie

Contributed by Anna Volkmer Zahn
Frankie Jones Gerhard's great-niece
Wharton County

"*My mom has been making this pie as long as I can remember,*" *says Anna. "I've been making it since I got married a few years ago, and my husband loves it. I make it once or twice a month — everyone in my family loves Aunt Frankie's Pecan Pie. We live in the country and have pecan trees growing around our house, so I use pecans from our trees to make the pecan pies. We like to spread a blanket out in front of the TV, shell the pecans, and spend time together. When finished, we just shake out the blanket outside. This makes for great family time.*"

Author's Note: Frankie says she obtained this recipe from her late sister-in-law Martha Kubecka about twenty years ago. She has since adapted the recipe — adding more butter and heating the pecans with the butter in the microwave before she puts them in the filling.

I once made this pie to take to a lunch function at work. I rushed the baking time that morning and it didn't set. I left the pie at the appointed place anyway and went on to my office, where I worked until noon. When I joined my co-workers for lunch, some of them had already begun eating dessert, including my pecan pie. I began apologizing for my failed attempt, but several of them cut me off immediately. They had had to resort to eating the pie with spoons, but they loved it and told me I could bring that "horrible" pie back anytime. I took an empty pie plate home; not a bite was left.

Frankie Jones Gerhard.
Courtesy of Frankie Gerhard.

Big Mama's Syrup Pie

There's usually a little more filling than the pastry shell will hold. The recipe contributor has a solution for that — it's a family tradition.

6 eggs
2 cups sugar
½ cup butter, melted and cooled
1½ cups light corn syrup (Karo red label)
1 teaspoon nutmeg
1½ cups pecan halves (optional)
1 unbaked 9-inch pastry shell

Beat eggs well in a medium bowl. Add sugar, butter, corn syrup, and nutmeg and mix well.

If using pecans, place them in bottom of pastry shell. Pour egg mixture into pastry shell. Bake at 375°F for 30 to 40 minutes, or until set.
(If crust begins to brown too quickly, place pie crust shield over pie.)
Cool completely before serving. *Makes one 9-inch pie*

Contributed by Cynthia "Cindy" Robinson English
Ima McKey Fenner's granddaughter
Nueces County

"*I almost always add pecans when I make this pie,*" *says Cindy,* "*although when my daughters were younger, they requested the plain syrup pie.* "*I usually make it several times a year — definitely at Thanksgiving and Christmas. I don't remember my grandmother ever saying much about it, but she baked it fairly often, usually with pecans, when my family was visiting her at her home in Speaks. One of Big Mama's neighbors once served me this pie as well; perhaps it was a regional favorite in Lavaca County.*
 "*When I was younger, I was teased because I loved eating Syrup Pie for breakfast. Well, I still do. Another tradition in our family is to bake a mini syrup pie with the leftover filling — there's always a small amount that doesn't fit in the*

Chapter 2: Recipes

pie crust. I just put it in a Pyrex custard dish and bake it along with the pie. My mother did the same thing. I don't recall Big Mama doing this, but I'll bet her pie dish was deeper than ours."

Ribbon Cane Syrup Pie

Claudia Stripling Strickland (Mama)

1905–1997

Nacogdoches County

A type of syrup that was once common throughout the South, ribbon cane syrup is difficult to find in stores today. Ribbon cane once made up the majority of sugar cane grown in the United States, but it fell out of favor and is now grown only by small, local farmers. In East Texas, you sometimes see the syrup sold at roadside stands, farmers' markets, and festivals. Ribbon cane syrup is also available through Fain's Honey Company in Llano (www.fainshoney.com) and Anthony Syrup Company in Philadelphia, Mississippi (800–844–7052), as well as through other Internet sites. You can also substitute a pure cane syrup such as Steen's; however, the pie may need to bake longer and the flavor will not be the same.

Claudia Stripling Strickland. Courtesy of Wilma Halbert.

3 eggs
½ cup sugar
1 tablespoon flour
½ teaspoon salt
1 cup ribbon cane syrup (such as Fain's, Uncle John's, or Ryan's Favorite)
¼ cup butter, melted
1 unbaked 9-inch pastry shell

Whisk eggs in a medium bowl and set aside.

Combine sugar, flour, and salt; add to eggs and whisk together. Stir in syrup and beat until smooth. Stir in melted butter. Pour mixture into an unbaked pastry shell and bake at 350°F for 40 to 50 minutes, or until set. (If using pure cane syrup instead of ribbon cane syrup, pie may take longer to bake.) Let cool before serving. *Makes one 9-inch pie*

Contributed by Suzanne Marie Halbert Wohleb
Claudia Stripling Strickland's granddaughter
Jefferson County

"*My grandmother (I called her 'Mama') made this pie for many years,*" says Suzanne. "*I understand that many East Texas women made some form of this recipe during the late 1800s and early 1900s. The syrup they used was produced from the type of sugar cane that grew in this area. Mama stopped making the pie when I was young. She always said that there were newer and better pies to make. The main problem, though, was that she no longer had easy access to the good, thick ribbon cane syrup that East Texas farmers had produced at home for so many years. You can still find it at roadside stands and farmers' markets in East Texas, but it's not widely available. My mom [Wilma Halbert] likes this pie a lot — she says it brings back childhood memories.*"

One of the best sources for ribbon cane syrup is the Heritage Syrup Festival, which takes place annually the second Saturday of November in Henderson. You will have a front-row seat for watching ribbon cane syrup being made in the old-fashioned way, complete with antique equipment and mule power. Other activities include demonstrations of traditional crafts such as basket making, lace making, broom making, spinning, blacksmithing, and wood carving. Folksingers, cloggers, square dancers, and other performers provide musical entertainment. Hayride shuttles, arts and crafts booths, children's activities, an antique and classic car show, and an antique tractor show round out the offerings. And be sure to buy some syrup from local vendors. Call 866-650-5529 or see www.visithendersontx.us.

Dewberry Cobbler Pie

2 unbaked 9-inch deep-dish pastry shells
4 to 5 cups dewberries
1½ cups sugar
½ cup flour
½ teaspoon salt
2 eggs, beaten
½ cup evaporated milk
Streusel Topping (recipe follows)

Fill each pastry shell to the rim with 2 to 2½ cups
dewberries. Combine sugar, flour, salt, eggs, and milk
and mix well. Pour half of mixture over dewberries
in each pastry shell. Sprinkle half of Streusel Topping
over each pie. Bake at 350°F for 1 hour. Check edges
of pie crust about midway; if browning too quickly,
protect them with aluminum foil or a pie crust shield.
Makes two 9-inch pies

Streusel Topping
½ cup sugar
½ cup flour
¼ cup butter

Mix ingredients with a fork or pastry blender until crumbly.
Makes enough topping for two 9-inch pies

Contributed by Amy Grones Snelgrove
Anastasia Caroline Svetlik Sevcik's granddaughter
Brazos County

*A*my says she has fond childhood memories of visiting her grandparents
on their Vsetin farm, near Hallettsville, during dewberry season in early
spring. "Stasie would send all the grandkids to collect the berries," she explains.
"We'd return with buckets of dewberries and wait for the pies to be ready. They

**Anastasia Caroline Svetlik
Sevcik (Stasie)**
1919–2009
Lavaca County

*Anastasia Caroline Svetlik
Sevcik with her husband,
Adolph "A. C." Sevcik.
Courtesy of Patsy Weiser.*

made all the scratches we got from picking the berries worth it. I believe Stasie made up this recipe — she was full-blooded Czech and never used recipes. The only reason we have it is because we made her write it down for us." Amy has been making the pie herself for more than twenty years. *"Each spring during dewberry season, we go as a family to the old farm place and pick berries, and then we come home and make Dewberry Cobbler Pie,"* she says. *"My children love the tradition as much as I do."*

Mary Francis Parker Graves (Mama)

1891–1972

Garza, Scurry, and Young Counties

Mama's Green Grape Cobbler

This cobbler originally featured wild mustang grapes, which still grow in many parts of Texas. If you opt to gather mustang grapes, wear a long-sleeved shirt and gloves and be sure to pick them early in the season, when they are small and green and the seeds haven't yet developed. Seedless varieties of other types of grapes can also be used.

Pie Crust, rolled and cut into 2-inch strips (recipe follows)
5 cups stemmed and washed wild mustang grapes (*picked green*)
½ cup butter
1 to 1½ cups sugar (depending on the tartness of the grapes)

Place pie crust strips lengthwise in the bottom of a 13 x 9-inch pan, leaving a little space between strips and reserving enough to put on top. Spread grapes over crust. Dot with pats of butter. Distribute sugar over grapes. Place remaining pie crust strips crosswise on top of grapes, leaving a little space between strips. Bake at 400°F for about an hour, or until crust is golden brown. *Makes one 13 x 9-inch cobbler*

Chapter 2: Recipes

Pie Crust

1½ cups flour
½ teaspoon salt
¾ cup Crisco
½ cup cold tap water

Mix flour and salt together. Cut in shortening with a fork or pastry blender. Slowly sprinkle water over mixture and mix with a fork to form a ball. Turn pastry out onto a floured board and roll to ⅛-inch thickness. *Makes enough crust for 1 cobbler, 1 double-crust pie, or 2 single-crust pies*

Note: Although this pie crust recipe doesn't call for ice water, the contributor stores her flour in the freezer between uses, which has the same desired effect of chilling the dough.

Contributed by Mary Alice Graves Liles
Mary Francis Parker Graves's granddaughter
Bailey County

*M*uleshoe photographer, freelance writer, and blogger Alice Liles has never picked wild mustang grapes, having adapted her grandmother's recipe for Green Grape Cobbler to use the seedless grapes produced by the domestic vines in her backyard. However, she has fond childhood memories of her mother making the original version to please Alice's father, who loved the pie as a boy and as an adult was still willing to pick the wild grapes it required. Over the fifty-plus years Alice has been making the recipe herself, Green Grape Cobbler has engendered a few more family memories, many of them associated with the seemingly simple pie crust that goes with it. (To read Alice's blogs on Muleshoe and cactus, see her website, www.aliceliles.com.)

*Mary Francis Parker Graves.
Courtesy of Alice Liles.*

Cobbler, Pies, and Crust Confusion

ALICE LILES

My father, AJ Graves, came from a family of six children, and they often had a hard time making ends meet. The family lived in Garza, Scurry, and Young Counties, eventually settling in Olney. My grandfather held a variety of jobs, and at one point, my daddy quit school to help support the family.

When Daddy was growing up, if he happened upon some wild mustang grapes before they were ripe, he would pick them, and my grandmother (we called her Mama) would make a cobbler with them, adding enough sugar to counteract the tartness of the green grapes. I have no idea where the recipe originated, and I never saw a written recipe. I just learned it from my mother, who used a pie crust recipe that was probably handed down from her mother, Carolyn Tate Drum.

When I was growing up, we lived in Rosenberg, and Daddy would find wild mustang grapevines on the banks of the Brazos River and pick from those vines. Producing the cobbler was a team effort: He would pick and de-stem the grapes, and Mother would make the cobbler. She also made green grape jelly, which Daddy loved, too. I have never tried to make the jelly, though I've eaten a lot of it.

Any kind of seedless grape—green or ripe—can also be used in the cobbler. I use red flame grapes from the vine in my yard that covers an arbor. I use them in varying degrees of ripeness, just adding more sugar to the green batches. I sometimes pick the grapes prematurely to keep the birds from harvesting them ahead of me, or if we will be out of town when they ripen. (If I'm not going to make a cobbler right away, I freeze the grapes with a little Fruit Fresh. The frozen grapes work just fine in this recipe; you don't even have to thaw them.)

My husband likes this pie more than my kids do, but I make it quite often, especially in the summer. Since we have our own grapes, the only expense is the sugar. And it is certainly not hard to make. I have discovered an easy way to dress it up: I use my cookie cutters to cut out pieces of crust, which I arrange on top.

The pie crust I use for the cobbler also has a history in our family. As a newlywed, I wanted to make nice desserts for my husband, Bill. He liked chocolate meringue pie, so I set out to make one for him using my mother's chocolate meringue pie recipe. I had no trouble with the pie filling, but the crust was just awful! I had a terrible time getting the rolled-out dough off the counter and into the pie pan because it was so crumbly and fragile. Then, when I baked it, everything turned out well, except for the crust. Bill would bravely attempt to eat it but usually ate just the filling and meringue, leaving the crust, which was pretty inedible.

Well, time passed and I gamely kept trying to make pies, but with the same results. Finally, I mentioned to Mother how much trouble I was having with the crust and asked her what I was doing wrong. She went through the recipe with me, citing from memory, naturally, and clicked off the ingredients for the crust. When she got to the one-half cup of water, I said, "Water? What water?" To which she answered, "Yes, water. I can't believe you got it to mix at all without the water." So I checked my recipe, and sure enough, I had left off the water. Not surprisingly, the next pie crust worked like magic.

This pie crust seems to delight in causing confusion in our family because we had another incident this past Thanksgiving involving the recipe. I had given it to my son AJ (named for his grandfather AJ Graves), and he, too, had dutifully followed the recipe when he made the chocolate and lemon meringue pies for this dinner. His crusts, however, were thick and tough, prompting my husband to ask me if they were made with my recipe. AJ heard us and chimed in that it was and that he had wondered what had gone wrong. Since we all had done what Bill had done with my first pie crust attempts—eating the filling and meringue and tossing the crust—we were in need of more pies, so the next day we started over, this time with me as the cook so we could figure out what was amiss. I mixed the dough, and as I split it in half and starting rolling out the first crust, AJ motioned to the other half still in the mixing bowl and asked what that was for. "The other pie crust," I told him. He rolled his eyes and confronted me with the fact that I had not bothered to put that little piece of information on the recipe card! (The pie crust strikes again.) After that, almost like magic, two new pies appeared and then rather quickly disappeared, crust and all.

Granny's Miracle Cobbler

You can use stewed fruit such as apples, cherries, or peaches in this dish. Fresh fruit in season also works, of course; just sprinkle it with additional sugar and let it stand 15 to 30 minutes, or until a little juice forms, before pouring it over the batter. If using fresh peaches, stir in a dash or two of cinnamon and nutmeg. For more crunch, sprinkle a little sugar on the top of the cobbler before baking.

½ cup flour
½ cup sugar
1 teaspoon baking powder
½ cup milk
⅛ to ¼ cup butter
1 (16-ounce) can of peaches in light syrup or 2 cups fresh fruit and juice
    (about 3 parts fruit to 1 part juice)
Vanilla ice cream or sweetened whipped cream (optional)

Combine flour, sugar, and baking powder in a small bowl and stir in milk. Dot an 8 x 8-inch baking pan with butter. Spoon batter into pan. Pour fruit and juices over batter. Bake at 400°F for 30 minutes, or until top is nicely browned. (Batter will rise to cover fruit as cobbler bakes.) Best served warm. Top with a scoop of vanilla ice cream or sweetened whipped cream, if desired. *Makes 8 to 9 servings*

Contributed by Nancy Helen O'Bryant Puentes
Ella Wilhelmina Glaeser Pearce's granddaughter
Travis County

*N*ancy says she has been making Granny's Miracle Cobbler *"since forever." Both her grandmother and mother made it often, usually with canned peaches. "I don't have any idea where Granny got the recipe," she adds, "but I'm quite sure it was popular with her and her six German American sisters because you could use canned fruit. This would have made it not only an economical dessert but one that you could make when fresh fruit was out of* season, both practical considerations when cooking for a Sabinal farm family that included twelve children. I don't recall either Granny or Mother ever using fresh peaches. I think we all would have considered that a travesty since fresh peaches are so delicious on their own —— why would you cook them? And since everyone in the family liked the basic dessert so much, they never experimented with any other fruits.

"It's not a 'special occasion' dessert but one to make for everyday, although if you use fresh fruit and top each serving with vanilla ice cream or whipped cream, it can be dressed up. I especially like to make it with fresh dewberries or blackberries. (I use four or five pints, add a generous amount of sugar, and then let them stand for fifteen to thirty minutes so they will form plenty of juice. I also double all the other ingredients and use a thirteen- by nine-inch baking pan.) I serve the cobbler with crème Chantilly (sweetened whipped cream infused with vanilla extract) when I'm ambitious, or just pour heavy cream over it when I'm not."

Although Nancy doesn't remember specifics, she says she's sure that Granny's Miracle Cobbler was served at many family gatherings in previous generations, "including the great-aunts' canasta parties." She adds, "These ran into the wee hours of the morning, and we kids were put to 'bed' in two club chairs pushed together or on a 'Methodist pallet.' No doubt multiple cobblers also served as covered dish contributions for many family funerals in Sabinal. It's a traditional family recipe I sort of always took for granted because it's so good and so easy."

Ella Wilhelmina Glaeser Pearce. Courtesy of Nancy O'Bryant Puentes.

A Quilting Tradition

Ella Glaeser Pearce passed along not only a special cobbler recipe but also her love of quilting to her two daughters and their daughters. Herself a third-generation quilter, Ella taught both Nancy and her cousin Karey Patterson Bresenhan—her other granddaughter—how to quilt at a family quilting bee, where Karey's wedding quilt was quilted. (It had been pieced for Karey earlier by Ella's mother, who pieced quilt tops for all her grandchildren and great-grandchildren.) Although the cousins had grown up with quilts on every bed, that was the first time they themselves had quilted.

The cousins' love of quilting was also influenced by Karey's other grandmother, Myrtle Loomis Patterson, who was like a "third grandmother" to Nancy. Myrtle was also a prolific quilter. Both grandmothers had high standards for quilting. For instance, Myrtle would "inspect" the quilting after a quilting bee at her house and rip out any stitches she felt were not up to par. (See Gran's Childress Cookies recipe for more about Myrtle.) This is indeed a family of quilters—both Nancy's and Karey's mothers were also fine quilters, as were their great-aunts.

As adults, the cousins turned their love of quilting into a patchwork of successful quilting-related enterprises. Their flagship company, Quilts, Inc., produces several quilt shows annually, including the International Quilt Festival in Houston. Founded by Karey in 1974, the festival is the largest quilt show, sale, and quiltmaking academy in the world and attracts more than sixty thousand people annually. In November 2011, the cousins marked two major accomplishments, timed to coincide with the state's 175th anniversary: They published *Lone Stars III: A Legacy of Texas Quilts 1986–2011* (the last in their trilogy of volumes that chronicles 175 years of quilting in Texas), and they opened the Texas Quilt Museum in La Grange.

Housed in two historic downtown buildings that were painstakingly renovated, the ten thousand–square-foot museum offers a stunning showcase for works that range from traditional pieced and appliqué quilts to contemporary "art quilts." The offerings include four changing exhibits each year, a library, museum store, and period Texas garden, as well as space for lectures and presentations. For more about Quilts, Inc. and the Texas Quilt Museum, respectively, see www.quilts.com and www. texasquiltmuseum.org.

Mamaw's Fruit Cobbler

If you want to skip making pie crust, use two 15-ounce packages of refrigerated pie crust. (Each package contains two rounds, which is enough for one rectangular crust.) See note below for variation featuring green mustang grapes.

Mary Elois Kelly Bresenhan (Mamaw)

1912–1991

Falls, Harris, Hidalgo, and Denton Counties

Mary Elois Kelly Bresenhan. Courtesy of Karey Bresenhan.

Pie Crust (recipe follows)
18 small peaches, peeled, pitted, and sliced or 3 pints dewberries or
    blackberries, washed and drained
2 cups sugar
Pinch of salt
½ cup butter, cut into small pieces
¾ cup water
Juice of ½ lemon
2 teaspoons additional sugar (for sprinkling on top crust)
2 tablespoons additional butter, cut into pieces
Whipping cream (optional)

Roll out half of dough into a large rectangle and fit it into a 13 x 9-inch pan. Be sure dough extends over the sides of the pan. Set aside.

Spread sliced peaches over bottom of crust. Combine the 2 cups sugar, salt, the ½ cup butter (cut into pieces), water, and lemon juice; pour mixture over sliced peaches.

Roll out other half of dough into a second rectangle and place it over the fruit; pinch edges of crusts together or seal by pressing a fork around the edges of the cobbler. Perforate top crust several times. Sprinkle with the 2 teaspoons sugar and dot with the 2 tablespoons of butter (cut into pieces). Bake at 375°F for 35 to 45 minutes, or until top crust is browned. Pour a bit of whipping cream (unwhipped) over the top of each serving, if desired. *Makes 12 to 15 servings*

Pie Crust
3 cups flour
1 teaspoon salt
1¼ cups shortening

1 egg, beaten
6 tablespoons water
1 teaspoon vinegar

Sift flour and salt together. Add shortening and mix with a fork until crumbly. Combine egg, water, and vinegar and add to mixture. Form dough into 4 balls and chill in refrigerator about 30 minutes. Each ball makes one crust. Two balls are needed for each top and bottom crust of a 13 x 9-inch cobbler. *Makes enough crust for one 13 x 9-inch cobbler, two double-crust 9-inch pies, or four single-crust 9-inch pies*

Note: To make a green mustang grape version, you will first have to find mustang grapes growing wild; guard them jealously. Wear a long-sleeved shirt and gloves and pick grapes when they are small and green, before seeds have formed. Follow previous recipe except for preparation of filling: Combine 3 cups washed and stemmed grapes with 1 cup sugar and 1 cup water and simmer until grapes soften. Add a pinch of salt, ½ cup butter, and 1 tablespoon flour and mix until butter melts.

Contributed by Brandy Bresenhan Craig
Mary Elois Kelly Bresenhan's granddaughter
Harris County

Brandy says she makes the peach version of this cobbler every summer, when the fruit is in season. "I don't make homemade pie crust," she adds. "I just use the refrigerated pie crust from the grocery store. I have a tip for serving the cobbler, too: Let it set for a while after you take it out of the oven so that some of the juices are drawn into the crust. There's too much liquid if you serve it right away."

While Brandy has never made the green grape version herself, she says she remembers her Mamaw's green grape cobbler from when she was a little girl. She says, "My aunt Karey told me that each spring before Mamaw retired from teaching, she would watch the mustang grapes that grew wild on a fence behind Hamilton Junior High School, where she taught in Houston. She waited to snitch them at just the right time — when they were still small and green — so she could make her green grape cobbler. Aunt Karey said she'd known my grandmother to make a one hundred–mile drive to buy a bushel of good tomatoes. This was a woman who took her food seriously!"

Puddings

French Plum Pudding

The first thing you need to know about this plum pudding is that it contains nary a plum. The name originated in centuries past, when "plums" referred to raisins and other fruits. To make this rich dessert, you will need either a 3-quart pudding basin or two 1½-quart pudding molds. You will also need a good measure of fortitude. Read Anne Isham's account of the first time she made her great-great-grandmother's pudding before you start. She includes some shortcuts that make the process easier.

Butter
1 cup flour
1 teaspoon salt
1½ teaspoons cinnamon
1 teaspoon allspice
½ teaspoon cloves
1 teaspoon freshly grated nutmeg
Grated zest of 1 orange
Grated zest of 1 lemon
1½ cups raisins (sultanas are best)
1½ cups dried currants
2 ounces candied ginger, finely chopped
1 pound blanched almonds, chopped
8 ounces dates, sprinkled with flour and chopped
8 ounces fresh beef suet (ask your butcher for this)
2 cups fresh fine bread crumbs
4 eggs, separated
1 cup sugar
1 cup cognac
Additional ⅓ cup cognac for flaming pudding
Hard Sauce (recipe follows)

Marie Sophie Victoire Lebel Commins Stewart

1842–1915

Galveston, Tarrant, and Palo Pinto Counties

Marie Sophie Victoire Lebel Commins Stewart. Courtesy of Anne Isham.

Generously grease pudding mold with butter. Cut a piece of aluminum foil a couple of inches wider than the diameter of the mold and butter one side of it. (This, along with a plate, will serve as a lid while the pudding steams.) Set aside.

Mix together flour and next 7 ingredients in a large bowl. Stir raisins and next 4 ingredients into flour mixture.

Finely chop beef suet, removing any red or pink parts as well as any papery membranes. Place suet in a medium bowl and mix with bread crumbs. Stir suet mixture into flour-fruit mixture.

Combine egg yolks and sugar and beat until light in color. Stir in the 1 cup cognac. Pour egg mixture over flour-fruit-suet mixture and stir only until mixed.

In another bowl, beat egg whites until stiff but not dry. Fold egg whites into batter. Pour batter into prepared mold, leaving about 1 inch at the top for the pudding to expand. Place aluminum foil buttered-side down over top of mold, crimp foil down around the edges, and place a plate on top of the foil. Place mold inside a large pot on a wire rack or a folded kitchen towel. Carefully pour boiling water into the pan about ⅔ of the way up the side of the mold. Put the lid on the pot and simmer for about 3½ hours (or 2 hours, if you're making two smaller puddings). Pudding should be firm on top.

Remove pot from heat but leave the pudding inside to keep warm for 2 to 4 hours. Using oven mitts, remove the mold from the pot. Let the pudding cool at room temperature for about 20 minutes. Invert the pudding onto a heatproof plate.

Prepare the Hard Sauce while the pudding cools completely.

To flame the pudding, warm the ⅓ cup cognac. Pour the warm liquor over the pudding, stand at arm's length, and carefully light liquor with a long match. Serve with Hard Sauce (recipe follows). *Makes 10 to 16 servings*

Hard Sauce

2 cups (4 sticks) butter
3 cups powdered sugar
¼ cup cognac

Cream butter in a medium bowl. Gradually add powdered sugar and beat until mixture is fluffy but still thick enough to hold its shape. Continue beating, gradually adding cognac. "Sauce" will be the consistency of buttercream frosting. *Makes enough sauce for French Plum Pudding*

This pudding can be made up to a month in advance; it gets better with age. To store, let it cool completely in its mold. (Do not make sauce in advance.) Remove the pudding from the mold and wrap tightly in plastic wrap; then wrap it again in aluminum foil. Store in refrigerator. To reheat the pudding, return it to its original well-buttered mold, seal it, and steam it (1½ hours for a large pudding, or 1 hour for smaller puddings).

Contributed by Anne Shannon Lewis Isham
Marie Sophie Victoire Lebel Commins Stewart's great-great-granddaughter
Travis County

Although plum pudding originated in England, Marie Sophie's version has a decided French twist. "I like to think she made this dish to please her English husband but modified it to suit her French soul," says Anne who has made this elaborate pudding for more than twenty-five years. "Usually at Christmas, maybe once every five years," she says. "Friends and family like the drama and display. And those who like fruitcake really love the pudding."

As someone who appreciates family history, Anne first tried to make the pudding by following the recipe exactly as she received it from her great-aunt Nene, Marie Sophie's granddaughter. "I think her memory of ingredients was on the mark, but the method was a little off," says Anne. (See Anne's account below.) After trying different methods over the years, she has found that if she uses two smaller molds rather than one big one, two large Crock-Pots are ideal for steaming the puddings. She notes that you can also steam the pudding in a large roasting pan at 325°F (2 hours for a large pudding; 1½ hours for two smaller puddings).

In addition, she has started using a food processor to chop the candied ginger and almonds (she first tosses them with the flour and spices and then pulses the mixture a few times). "The dates are too sticky to chop properly in a food processor," she notes, "so you have to chop those by hand."

She also replaces the suet with the same amount of cocoa butter, which she orders online. "Butter and shortening don't work well in steamed puddings because they melt at a lower temperature than suet does," explains Anne. "Cocoa butter remains solid longer than butter or shortening. The pudding needs time for the flour to bind with liquids and set before the fat begins to melt. The fat melting later leaves lots of tiny cavities, which results in a lighter pudding. Besides, cocoa butter is so much better for you." The author of Eat (More) Chocolate, Lose Weight (Anyway): The Chocoholic's Survival Guide and Practical Handbook *(Pandora McShannon Press, 2007), Anne is a staunch proponent of cocoa butter. Her book includes a wealth of information about the health benefits of chocolate.*

Marie Sophie Victoire Lebel Commins Stewart.
Courtesy of Anne Isham.

Chapter 2: Recipes

Making French Plum Pudding
with My Favorite Ancestor

ANNE SHANNON LEWIS ISHAM

My great-great-grandmother, Marie Sophie Victoire Lebel Commins Stewart was very tall, even by today's standards—ultimately six feet, two inches. Born March 23, 1842, in the village of Villeneuve-l'Archevêque in Bourgogne, southwest of Paris, she was the daughter of the town miller. In France, as in most of Europe at that time, it was the custom for large families to send one child to the church to be a priest or a nun. This was done partly for financial reasons, and it was especially common if the family had an unmarriageable daughter. That girl was certain to draw the black bean and be assigned to a life of hard work and isolation in a convent.

By the time Marie Sophie was in her late teens, it was evident that she would be much taller than the average girl. When she reached more than six feet tall, her parents, thinking that poor Marie Sophie would never be able to snare a husband, sent her to a convent of Belgian nuns who were famous for their culinary skills and fine, skilled needlework.

As a novice in the convent, Marie Sophie learned to cook and sew; to make beautiful, delicate lace; and to crochet intricate patterns. It must have been a very repressive existence for a high-spirited, resourceful young woman. After a few years, the prospect of spending her entire life confined within the walls of the convent became unbearable. So Marie Sophie and an English friend, a much smaller girl equally determined to have a life outside the convent, scaled the walls and escaped to Texas by way of a sailing vessel headed from Le Havre, France, to Galveston. Her friend's brother joined them on the ship at Portsmouth, England.

Ultimately, Marie Sophie married her English friend's brother, then divorced him and married again, but not before she learned to make plum pudding and added her own touches. She used fresh lemon and orange zest rather than candied fruit, and she insisted on bracing it with cognac rather than the sherry or brandy used in traditional plum pudding recipes. Marie Sophie eventually had two daughters and a son. She owned and operated the Fairfield Inn, an inn and spa in Mineral Wells, and spent the rest of her life in Texas.

My great-aunt Nene, who as a child lived near my great-great-grandmother, told me about one of the inn's Thanksgiving-dinner customs. In addition to being a great cook, Marie Sophie had a flair for drama. In her later life, she made herself a white dress of handkerchief linen and handmade lace. It was covered in cutwork and, of course, all done by hand. Marie Sophie had snow-white hair and must have cut quite a figure in her voluminous white dress. She wore it only for special occasions and hired two very tall, very dark-skinned black men to help her serve. She had the men wear black evening clothes (tuxedos). All this was designed for effect.

At the end of Thanksgiving dinner, the three of them would walk in—Marie Sophie in the middle in her white dress, her white hair piled high on her head, and the two dark men in their elegant formal wear, each carrying a tray of flaming plum puddings into the darkened dining room.

Aunt Nene helped her grandmother make the plum puddings and remembered everything in vivid detail. She was very clear on the ingredients and the method of steaming the puddings, even though she was probably only about ten at the time. Aunt Nene remembered that the puddings were made in individual sizes for these special dinners. Marie Sophie's method, as told to me seventy-five years later, was to tie up about a cup of the pudding batter in a square of cheesecloth and suspend each pudding from a wire rack in a pot of boiling water. I learned the hard way how they must have been suspended above the boiling water.

The first time I tried making Marie Sophie's plum pudding, I did exactly as I was told and went to great lengths to find and buy fresh spices and suet. (The butcher at Whole Foods did not want to sell me the suet, as it is beef fat and an arterial disaster. I assured him that I needed it for historical accuracy in the recipe. Reluctantly, he gave me the half pound of suet.) I brought everything home, ground all the spices, grated the nutmeg, chopped the suet, raisins, dates, and nuts, poured the cup of cognac into the batter, and then proceeded to boil the individual puddings for a couple of hours. When they were done, I unwrapped one and tasted it. It tasted like cardboard. The water the puddings were boiled in, however, was sweet and flavorful, redolent as it was of fine cognac and fresh spices. In retrospect, I figured out that Aunt Nene couldn't have been tall enough to see into that pan. The puddings were surely steamed *above*, not in, the boiling water.

It took me a year to steel myself to make another run at plum pudding. This time I did some research and made it as one large pudding. That was in the early 1980s. Since then, I've made it occasionally for Christmas. The method has evolved for convenience. I now cheerfully use a food processor and a couple of Crock-Pots, but I haven't tinkered with Marie Sophie's recipe, except for replacing the suet with cocoa butter. It feels good to stir up the same batter as my favorite ancestor.

Elsie Mae Brice Hill
1885–1960
Victoria County

Elsie Mae Brice Hill. Courtesy of Linda Mozisek.

Rice Pudding (SCOTTISH)

This pudding bakes in a hot-water bath, or bain-marie. You don't need a special piece of kitchen equipment, but you will need two ovenproof casserole dishes, one smaller than the other. The smaller one holds the pudding and the larger one holds the water, as well as the smaller dish, during baking. Be careful when adding the water so that it doesn't slosh over the side of the smaller dish.

2 loosely packed cups cooked rice (either instant or regular)
½ cup sugar
½ cup raisins (optional)
½ teaspoon vanilla
1 egg, beaten
1½ cups milk

Choose a casserole dish that will easily fit inside a 13 x 9-inch glass casserole dish (be sure there's ample room around the smaller dish), and spray the inside of the smaller dish with Pam. Combine rice, sugar, raisins (if using), and vanilla in the smaller dish. Beat egg and milk together. Add to rice mixture and mix well.

Line the bottom of the larger dish with a towel. Place the smaller dish in the larger dish and carefully add enough water to the larger dish so that water level is one-third of the way up the side of the smaller one. Bake at 350°F for about 1½ hours. *As the pudding bakes, stir it occasionally to prevent the raisins from sinking to the bottom.* The pudding is done when it has a custardlike thickness. Serve warm. *Makes 6 to 8 servings*

Note: Sometimes, despite doing all the above steps carefully, the pudding will separate slightly from the rice and become too liquid. Just stir and enjoy anyway.

Contributed by Linda Frances Hill Mozisek
Elsie Mae Brice Hill's granddaughter
Victoria County

*L*inda's Scottish grandmother came from Oklahoma to Texas in 1919, traveling with her husband (Albert Hill), and three little boys in a Model T Ford. "They came here to start a fruit orchard, and they bought land at Telferner, near Victoria," says Linda. "My grandfather had read that Texas was the right climate for this. They found fairly quickly, though, that they had not gone far enough south for a successful orchard, so they started a nursery instead. The nursery business was hard but rewarding work; it provided for three families for many years and remains in the family today.

"I've been eating this pudding all my life," she continues. "I used to watch my grandmother and mother make it when I was a little girl. I remember that Grandma had a special pan called a bain-marie that held the water bath and small bowls (ramekins) in which she put the pudding. I just use two glass casserole dishes, one larger than the other, and cook the pudding in the smaller one. The pudding still cooks in a water bath. Although I've been making it for almost fifty years, I only recently measured the ingredients. It's a pretty forgiving recipe."

A traditional bain-marie is a large pan that holds small containers (such as custard cups) in place with ample room for water to be poured around the containers. It is used for cooking delicate foods such as custards and puddings. When the bain-marie is placed in the oven, the water creates steam that helps the food cook evenly and prevents it from cracking or curdling. However, you can assemble a bain-marie that achieves the same effect by using two similar ovenproof containers of different sizes. Just make sure the outer container is large enough to allow the water level to reach at least one-third of the way up the side of the smaller container, which holds the food.

Lena Belle Hill Shelton
1889–1970

Smith, Anderson, and Kleberg Counties

Grandma's Banana Pudding

4 cups milk, divided
3 heaping tablespoons cornstarch
6 eggs, separated
1¾ cups sugar, divided
2 tablespoons butter
2 teaspoons vanilla
1 (11- to 12-ounce) box vanilla wafers
7 to 8 bananas

Mix ½ cup of the milk and cornstarch with a fork until blended. Set aside.

Combine egg yolks, remaining 3½ cups milk, 1 cup of the sugar, and cornstarch mixture in a saucepan and mix well. Cook over medium-low heat, stirring constantly, until very thick. Remove from heat. Stir in butter and vanilla; set aside.

Beat egg whites until soft peaks form; add remaining ¾ cup sugar 1 tablespoon at a time and continue beating until very stiff peaks form. Set aside.

Line a 13 x 9-inch glass dish with wafers. Slice bananas over the top. Pour pudding over cookies and bananas. Top with meringue, sealing to edges. Bake at 400°F for 10 to 15 minutes, or until meringue is browned on top. Serve warm. *Makes about 12 servings*

Contributed by Nancy Walters Powell
Lena Belle Hill Shelton's granddaughter
Bexar County

Chapter 2: Recipes

"*This has been the traditional dessert for all special occasions in my family for more than seventy years,*" *says Nancy. "My mother [Gertrude Shelton Walters] loved to tell about the afternoon when I was about eighteen months old, and instead of napping as I was supposed to, I crawled out of bed and into the kitchen. Mother found me in the middle of the floor surrounded by the peels of a dozen bananas. She had bought them for a banana pudding that she planned to make for a family visit the next day."*

For years both Nancy's mother and grandmother made this pudding by just dumping ingredients into a bowl; there was no written recipe. "Finally, one afternoon when Mother was about to make the pudding, my daughter Elaine took matters into her own hands," says Nancy. "She hounded her with measuring cups and stopped her periodically so that she could measure each ingredient. So then we had a recipe that everyone could use, myself and my sisters included."

Elaine put the recipe to good use. A few years ago, she took the pudding to a dessert auction held by her bowling league, and it sold for forty dollars, the highest amount paid for any dessert. Nancy notes that when Elaine (and her sister Leslie) began making the dish, Grandma's Banana Pudding became a fourth-generation recipe. However, the tradition doesn't stop there. One of Nancy's granddaughters, as well as two great-grandsons, prepare it, making Grandma's Banana Pudding a sixth-generation recipe.

Lena Belle Hill Shelton (right) and her daughter Gertrude Walters. Courtesy of Nancy Powell.

Other Desserts

**Karrina "Carrie"
Swenson Knudson**

1865–1952

Bosque County

Grandma Knudson's Rosettes (NORWEGIAN)

The original recipe called for deep-frying the rosettes in lard, which is not widely available today. Whatever type of fat you choose, it is essential to use a heavy pot when making these crispy treats. You will also need a rosette iron. Expect to do some experimenting before turning out well-formed rosettes.

2 eggs
1 teaspoon sugar
1 cup flour
1 cup milk
¼ teaspoon vanilla
Crisco (or a combination of ½ Crisco and ½ canola oil)
Powdered sugar

Line a shallow pan with paper towels and set aside.

Beat eggs lightly in a small mixing bowl. Add sugar, flour, milk, and vanilla and stir until blended. Set aside.

Place enough Crisco in a heavy pot to deep-fry rosettes (about 2 or 3 inches of melted fat); heat until the oil is very hot (about 375°F). Heat rosette iron in the hot oil until it is very hot (*if the iron isn't hot enough, the batter will stick to it*); drain excess oil and dip the hot iron halfway into the batter. Then return the iron to the hot oil. Rosette should slip off the iron as it starts to fry. (If necessary, use a fork to gently loosen it.) Cook rosette about 30 seconds, or until golden brown. Remove rosette with a slotted spoon and drain well on paper towels. Dust rosette with powdered sugar, using a sifter.

Karrina "Carrie" Swenson Knudson and her granddaughter Geneva Allen. Courtesy of Geneva Allen Finstad.

Reheat iron and repeat procedure with remaining batter. As you become more experienced, you can fry several rosettes at a time, but don't crowd them. *Makes about 30 rosettes*

Contributed by Geneva Allen Finstad
Karrina "Carrie" Swenson Knudson's granddaughter
Bosque County

"I've been making rosettes from the time I was big enough to help my mother and grandmother," says Geneva. "I make them several times a year, often for fund-raisers such as the Bosque County Norwegian Society of Texas booth at the annual Texas Folklife Festival in San Antonio. I also make them for my family at Christmastime.

"My great-grandmother [Marit Moen Swenson] brought the recipe from Norway when she came to America in 1851, as well as many other Norwegian recipes not written down, just memorized. My mother gave me the heavy pan she used to make the rosettes and the irons to dip in the batter. She said, 'They will not turn out good if you use any other pan.' So I use the same pan she did. But any heavy pan will work. Making pretty rosettes takes a lot of practice. I avoid making them when the weather is rainy.

"Mother made many dozens of these cookies to fill a gallon container for each of her grandchildren for Christmas. They loved them so much as they grew up and had their own families; they would hide Grandma's cookies to save them and make them last longer."

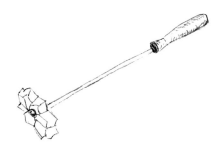

Apple Strudel (CZECH)

This recipe makes two strudels, with half the filling going into each one. Note that it is important not to mix the filling ingredients together but to layer them onto the dough in the order listed. Although "melted butter" isn't listed in the ingredients for either the dough or the filling, you'll need about a cup (2 sticks) of it for use in various steps. Don't skimp on this crucial component—it has a lot to do with the deliciousness of this Old World dish.

STEP 1: MAKE THE DOUGH.

Dough
1½ cups flour, plus more if needed
⅛ teaspoon salt
3 tablespoons butter, softened but not melted
1 egg yolk
½ cup milk

Measure flour and salt into a large bowl. Work in softened butter, using your hands or a pastry blender, until crumbly.

Beat egg yolk with milk and add to flour mixture; mix well. Knead dough, using a *small amount* of flour, for at least 5 minutes, or until smooth and not sticky. If necessary, add a *little* more flour and continue kneading until smooth. (Too much flour will make the dough tough.) Divide dough into 2 parts and form into balls; wrap each ball in plastic wrap or aluminum foil. Let stand at room temperature (*do not refrigerate*) in a covered dish overnight or for at least 4 hours.

STEP 2: ROLL OUT THE DOUGH.

After the dough has rested as described earlier, roll out *one-half* of the dough on a clean, lightly floured cloth into an 18-inch circle. Brush surface with melted butter. *Repeat with remaining half of dough.* Set aside.

STEP 3: GATHER INGREDIENTS FOR FILLING
(*DO NOT MIX TOGETHER*).

Filling

8 large apples (Red Delicious or another sweet variety), peeled, cored,
and sliced, divided

2 cups vanilla-wafer crumbs (or graham-cracker crumbs), divided

1½ cups sugar and 2 level tablespoons cinnamon, blended well
and divided

1 cup shredded coconut, divided

1 cup raisins, divided

1 cup chopped pecans, divided

STEP 4: MAKE THE TOPPING.

Topping

5 tablespoons sugar

1 teaspoon cinnamon

Blend ingredients together and set aside.

STEP 5: ASSEMBLE STRUDELS.

Sprinkle filling ingredients (*use one-half of each ingredient*) in the
order listed over the surface of 1 circle of dough. Using a pastry
brush, drizzle filling generously with melted butter 6 times.
Roll up dough like a jellyroll, holding corners of one end of the
cloth underneath it to flip dough over several times in the same
direction. Seal ends of dough. Brush strudel with melted butter
and place on a greased cookie sheet. *Repeat, using other circle of
dough and remainder of filling ingredients.*

*Emily Novosad Patek with her
husband, Joseph Patek. Courtesy
of Barbara Lloyd.*

STEP 6: BAKE STRUDELS.

Bake strudels at 350°F about 45 to 50 minutes, or until browned.

Remove strudels from oven and brush tops with melted butter. Sprinkle
one-half of Topping mixture over top of each strudel. Cut into 1-inch
slices and serve warm. *Makes 2 strudels (about 12 to 14 servings each)*

Note: *To freeze one strudel and bake later,* place prepared strudel on a greased sheet of heavy-duty aluminum foil (instead of on a greased cookie sheet), brush strudel with melted butter, wrap well, and freeze. *To bake frozen strudel,* do not thaw before baking. Unwrap aluminum foil and turn down at sides immediately after removing strudel from freezer. Place strudel (and aluminum foil) on a cookie sheet and bake at 275°F for 30 minutes. Increase oven temperature to 350°F and continue baking an additional 45 to 50 minutes, or until browned. Remove strudel, brush top with melted butter, and sprinkle with remaining half of the sugar-cinnamon mixture.

Contributed by Janice Lloyd Schacherl and Josie Lloyd Davis
Emily Novosad Patek's granddaughters
Lavaca County (both)

The list of people in Emily Patek's family who still use her Apple Strudel recipe today includes not only her granddaughters but also two daughters, three daughters-in-law, and three great-granddaughters, making it a fourth-generation recipe. Emily's daughter Barbara Patek Lloyd says Emily always credited her good friend Annie Dusek Bolech with giving her the recipe. Annie was a little older than Emily, but like Emily, she was of Czech descent and lived most of her life in Lavaca County. In addition to being a good friend, Annie worked in the café that Emily and her husband, Joseph, owned and operated in Shiner (now Patek's Grocery and Market).

Barbara started making strudel with her mother and her sister, Rosalie Vrana, for Thanksgiving and Christmas beginning sometime after she married in the early 1960s. "I didn't help make it when I was growing up because I worked in my family's grocery, market, and café business from an early age," she explains.

Considering how many strudels Barbara has made since the 1960s, you might think she's been making up for lost time. Not only has she passed along the recipe to her descendants; she has adapted it for quantity cooking and passed it along to the congregation of her church, Sts. Cyril and Methodius Catholic Church in Shiner. For more than two decades, the parish has held a Strudel Bake each November, a fund-raiser for the church that involves making some twenty-four hundred strudels using Emily's basic recipe. Preparations ——slicing the apples, mixing the dough, combining the sugar and cinnamon that top the apples ——last several days, with men, women, and children all working together to put on the event. Barbara and about a dozen other family members are always among the volunteers. It's a safe bet that Emily would be proud of her legacy and amazed if she knew how many people have enjoyed her Apple Strudel over the years.

Want to buy a strudel in Shiner instead of making one? While the Strudel Bake is always held on the second Saturday of November, strudel orders have to be placed by the previous Thursday. See www.sscmshiner.org for details.

The most difficult part of making strudel is rolling it up. With the (unrolled) strudel before you on a counter or table, hold a corner of the cloth underneath the strudel in each hand, step back a little so that the cloth is slightly taut, and flick the cloth several times in the same direction so that the dough wraps around the filling. The goal is to form something that resembles a slightly flattened jellyroll. At first, it feels a bit like trying to perform a magic trick, but with practice, you'll produce a strudel ready for the oven.

L ike the church in Dubina with the same name, Shiner's Sts. Cyril and Methodius Catholic Church is a "painted church," one of more than twenty such churches in Texas painstakingly decorated by early Czech and German settlers. In addition to its annual Strudel Bake, the Sts. Cyril and Methodius Catholic Church parish holds a Spring Picnic (on the Sunday before Memorial Day) and a Fall Picnic (on the Sunday before Labor Day). Activities include dancing, a country auction, country store, cake walk, bingo, and children's games, as well as Czech Picnic Stew and other foods. To arrange a tour of the church and obtain details about the picnics, call 361–594–3836 or see www.sscmshiner.org.

Dora Ann Love Stripling

1869–1961

Sabine and Nacogdoches Counties

Dora Ann Love Stripling. Courtesy of Wilma Halbert.

Fried Apple Pies

Dried peaches and other dried fruit may also be used in this recipe. You may also substitute your favorite pastry recipe (make enough for 3 crusts) or use refrigerated pie crusts.

1 (10-ounce) package dried apples
About 1 cup sugar
¼ cup butter
Pastry (recipe follows)
Crisco for frying

Line a shallow pan with paper towels and set aside.

Cut away any hard places from dried apple slices. Rinse apples and place in a saucepan. Add just enough water to cover and cook over medium heat, stirring occasionally, about 20 minutes, or until apples are tender. Watch carefully and add a *little* additional water, if necessary, so that apples don't scorch.

When apples are tender, drain any excess liquid from the saucepan. Add sugar and butter and partially mash apples with a fork. Set mixture aside to cool.

Roll out pastry to ¼-inch thickness on a heavily floured surface and cut into rounds about 4 inches in diameter (an empty 1-pound coffee can works well for this). (For smaller pies, use a biscuit cutter or glass and cut into approximately 2-inch rounds.) Place 1 tablespoon apples (about half that if making smaller pies) to one side of each pastry round. Moisten edges of pastry with water, using fingertips; fold one side of pastry over to cover filling; and crimp edges with a fork. Repeat until all rounds are formed into half-moon-shaped pies.

Place enough Crisco for deep-frying in a heavy pot and fry a few pies at a time until golden. Remove pies with a slotted spoon and drain well on paper towels. Best served warm, but good cold, too. *Makes 12 to 16 (4-inch) pies or 16 to 20 (2-inch) pies*

Chapter 2: Recipes

Pastry

3 cups flour
½ teaspoon salt
1 cup shortening
About 10 tablespoons ice-cold water
Additional flour for rolling

Combine flour and salt in a large bowl. Cut in shortening with a pastry blender. Add water gradually, stirring with a fork. Gather dough into a ball. *Makes enough pastry for 12 to 20 fried pies, depending on size*

Contributed by Wilma Dell Strickland Halbert
Dora Ann Love Stripling's granddaughter
Jefferson County

ilma's grandmother was born into a large family in Sabine County in far East Texas. After she married Zachariah Stripling, the couple lived on a farm about ten miles from Etoile in southern Nacogdoches County. Zachariah and his father had earlier preempted (homesteaded) a large tract of land through laws in effect designed to attract settlers. They lived in an unpainted dogtrot house and raised three children; another died in infancy.

"I watched my grandmother and my mother [Claudia Stripling Strickland] make these pies together as a child," says Wilma. "They were using what they had on hand, and that usually included dried fruit, either apples or peaches. Grandma usually made the pies with biscuit dough. My mother later used pie crust. Mom's fried pies were thicker and heartier than the version I make today, though; I use a thinner and flakier crust.

"I think fried fruit pies were common in the South, including East Texas, when I was growing up. Each cook had her own variations in the fruit and dough, but hog lard was always used both in the pastry and for frying the pies. That's what Grandma used, as did my mother until her later years, when she switched to shortening.

"This recipe is a favorite in my family," says Wilma, "especially since my husband and children have memories of my mother making the fried pies often. I make them infrequently. Mom would cook the apples or peaches and keep them in the fridge so she could make a batch quickly. My daddy carried fried pies in

his lunch pail every day when he worked for lumber companies in the East Texas pine forests. I remember that he would often ask Mom to include extras for his friends. She used to joke that she got tired of frying pies for so many people. They were very popular."

Dora Belle Lee Scudder (Grandmama)

1874–1970

Comanche, Palo Pinto, Baylor, Hale, Lubbock, Harris, Taylor, Victoria, Jim Wells, Willacy, Cameron, and Bee Counties

Dora Belle Lee Scudder. Courtesy of Jean Schnitz.

Taffy (For Pulling Teeth Out)

The title gives fair warning: This is a very sticky candy, best enjoyed without chewing. That said, it has a delicious flavor and is fun to make as a group. To "pull" taffy, one person begins stretching the slightly cooled mixture until it is several inches long. Then two people—one holding each end—continue to stretch the candy while it's still warm. (If you have enough pullers, you can divide the work.) Once the taffy is cold, it's time to cut it into pieces because it can no longer be stretched.

½ cup sugar
1 cup molasses
1 tablespoon vinegar
⅛ teaspoon baking soda, plus enough water to make a smooth paste
1 tablespoon butter

Combine sugar, molasses, and vinegar in a heavy saucepan. Bring to a boil and cook over medium heat, stirring almost constantly, until mixture reaches hard-ball stage (when a few drops of mixture forms a hard ball when dropped into cold water), or until a candy thermometer registers 255°F to 260°F. Remove from heat, add baking soda–water paste and mix well. Stir in butter. Pour mixture into a well-greased shallow pan and allow to cool slightly.

As soon as taffy is cool enough to handle, butter (clean) hands and pull taffy until light in color. Form into ropes ½ inch to 1 inch in diameter. Cut with scissors into 1- to 2-inch pieces. Wrap in squares of waxed paper.
Makes 2 to 3 dozen pieces

Chapter 2: Recipes

Contributed by Jean Granberry Schnitz
Dora Belle Lee Scudder's granddaughter
Bexar County

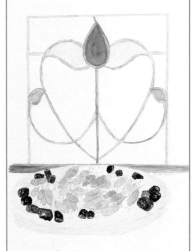

"*Grandmama and my mother [Lena Belle Scudder Granberry] would make taffy usually in the wintertime – unless it was needed in the summer," says Jean. "I always thought this was more fun to make than it was to eat. We gathered in the kitchen, which was the warmest room in the house and pulled the taffy with clean, well-buttered hands. (We made our own butter in those days.) I can remember Daddy and Grandpapa both helped pull the taffy because an entire batch needed to be pulled pretty quickly when the temperature was right. If it got too cold, it didn't pull!*

"I specifically remember that this was actually used on several occasions when my brother Billy or I had loose teeth that were ready to come out. It was a sneaky – and practically painless – way to get loose teeth to go ahead and come out! The problem was that we didn't always realize the tooth had come out before it had been swallowed along with the candy. The tooth fairy always came anyway.

"After my uncle Hollis died in 1938 and my grandparents' house burned the same year, Grandmama and Grandpapa lived the rest of their lives with either my family or my aunt Flora Mae. We made this taffy most often when they lived with us in Victoria (1936–1944). I think we also made it – for the specified purpose – when we lived in Alice from 1944 to 1946."

Jean's relatives weren't the only ones who used taffy for extraction purposes "back in the day." Jean says, "My husband, Lew [Schnitz], once had a dentist give him a piece of taffy to pull off a crown on a tooth that needed more work. I also remember that someone in my family once lost a filling to a nice sticky piece of taffy. It's best not to chew it if you want your fillings and crowns to stay intact. Besides, it lasts longer if you pretend it's a lemon drop!"

Lorene Scott Hulse. Courtesy of Courtney Braddock.

Chocolate Delight

½ cup (1 stick) butter, melted
1 cup flour
1½ cups chopped pecans
8 ounces cream cheese (low-fat or regular)
1 cup powdered sugar
12 ounces Cool Whip, divided
1 (6-ounce) package instant chocolate pudding
1 (6-ounce) package instant vanilla pudding
3 cups cold milk
Grated chocolate (optional)
Additional chopped pecans (optional)

Mix butter, flour, and pecans together and spread evenly in a 13 x 9-inch pan. Bake at 350°F for 20 minutes. Remove from oven and chill until firm.

Beat cream cheese and powdered sugar together with an electric mixer until smooth. Add half of the Cool Whip and fold into mixture. Spread mixture on chilled crust.

Combine pudding mixes and milk and beat well with an electric mixer until thick. Spread mixture over cream cheese mixture.

Spread remaining Cool Whip over top of pudding mixture. Sprinkle grated chocolate and additional chopped nuts over top of dish, if desired. Chill thoroughly before serving. *Makes about 20 servings*

Contributed by Courtney Crawford Braddock
Lorene Scott Hulse's great-granddaughter
Tarrant County

*C*ourtney has been making this recipe eight to ten years for occasions ranging from potlucks to company meals. "My husband loves it," she says, "but my kids love it more! We don't use the nuts anymore due to a child with nut allergies, and I usually adapt the recipe to make it gluten-free for me. Just use a *gluten-free blend in place of the regular flour. The crust will be crumbly and will mix with the first layer a little bit, but that's okay. You can't tell the difference once it's all put together. Most of the time we sprinkle mini chocolate chips over the top. My great-grandmother (we called her Mama) got this recipe from a friend and passed it down to me. My three daughters make it with me, so I guess it's on its way to becoming a fifth-generation recipe."*

Granny's Master Mix Gingerbread

Authemia "Tennie" Brown McKey (Granny)

1921–2010

Lavaca, Hardin, and Tyler Counties

2 cups Granny's Master Mix (see Granny's Master Mix recipe)
¼ cup sugar
½ teaspoon cinnamon
½ teaspoon ginger
½ teaspoon cloves
1 egg, beaten
½ cup water
½ cup molasses

Combine 2 cups Master Mix, sugar, cinnamon, ginger, and cloves and blend well; set aside.

Mix egg, water, and molasses together. Stir into first mixture and mix well. Pour batter into a well-greased and floured 8 x 8-inch pan. Bake at 350°F for about 40 minutes. *Makes 9 to 12 servings*

Contributed by Tasha Harper-Werner
Authemia "Tennie" Brown McKey's granddaughter
Tyler County

To read some of Tasha's memories of her grandmother, see Granny's Master Mix recipe.

Authemia "Tennie" Brown McKey. Courtesy of Tasha Harper-Werner.

Extras

Watermelon Rind Pickles

It's always a good idea to wash the outside of a watermelon before you cut it, especially when you're planning to use the leftover rind to make pickles. (The rind is easier to wash when the watermelon is whole.) This recipe is for refrigerator pickles, so it doesn't require a boiling-water canner, but you will need three (1-pint) canning jars, lids, and rings, as well as some pickling lime, a small piece of cheesecloth, and a short string. Making the pickles is a two-day process.

About 2 pounds watermelon rind (½ of a round watermelon
    generally yields about 2 pounds of rind)
1 tablespoon pickling lime
1 gallon water
4 cups sugar
2 cups vinegar
2 cups additional water
1 lemon, thinly sliced
1 tablespoon whole cloves
3 sticks cinnamon bark
1 tablespoon whole allspice

Using a cheese slicer or vegetable peeler, trim off the dark green parts of the rind. Use a knife to trim off the pink parts, leaving only the white parts. Cut rind into 1-inch cubes.

Add pickling lime to the 1 gallon water and mix until dissolved. Add the cubed rind and soak it overnight.

The next day, drain rind and rinse several times. Place rind in a saucepan and cover with cold water. Cook until just tender; drain rind and set it aside.

Bertha Heitkamp Rosenberg

1887–1961

Bexar and Comal Counties

Bertha Heitkamp Rosenberg with her husband, Wesley Rosenberg. Courtesy of Dee Henneke.

Combine sugar, vinegar, the additional 2 cups water, and lemon slices in the saucepan. Place cloves, cinnamon bark, and allspice in a small piece of cheesecloth, fold it into a bag, and tie it with string; add spice bag to the saucepan. Simmer the mixture for 10 minutes. Remove and discard the spice bag; add reserved watermelon rind. Bring the mixture to a boil, then simmer about 10 minutes, or until mixture is clear. Ladle mixture into hot, sterilized jars, leaving ½ inch of headroom. Place sterilized lids on top of jars, and screw on sterilized metal rings tightly. Store in refrigerator and use within two weeks. *Makes 3 pints*

Contributed by Elizabeth "Liz" Henneke Boenig
Bertha Heitkamp Rosenberg's great-granddaughter
Brazos County

"*All of my German grandmothers and great-grandmothers made Watermelon Rind Pickles*," *says Liz. "My great-grandma Bertha evidently was particularly fond of watermelon. She would float a watermelon in the lake to cool while she fished." Liz's mother (Dee Rosenberg Henneke) explains: "My grandmother Bertha Rosenberg loved to go fishing at Lake Dunlap on the Guadalupe River between New Braunfels and Seguin. She and my grandpa Wesley had a cabin there. Grandpa Wesley didn't particularly like to fish, but he would go with her if a lady friend who lived near the lake couldn't go. I went fishing with her as a young girl.*

"*She always wore a big sunbonnet when she fished. She used a cane pole and baited the hooks with Castile soap. (She used the same thing to bait the hooks when she set out a trotline.) She liked to fish in the lily pads, and my line would always get tangled. Hers never seemed to tangle.*

"*She often put a watermelon in the lake to cool while we were fishing. We'd usually start eating it while we were still on the lake. It was fun to spit the seeds out into the water. We'd eat the remainder of the watermelon when we got back to the cabin, either outside or on the screened-in porch. I would really love it when we'd get in their boat and Grandpa Wesley would motor upstream a way, and then he'd cut the motor and we'd eat our supper while drifting down the lake on the gentle current of the river.*"

Chapter 2: Recipes

Liz has been making Watermelon Rind Pickles for more than twenty-five years. "I make them in the summer, of course, when watermelons are in season," she says. "They're a favorite of everyone, especially the men in the family."

Some recipes for watermelon-rind pickles call for leaving a thin ring of pink watermelon meat attached to the white part of the rind. It's a matter of personal preference.

Blue-Ribbon Wild Mustang Grape Jam

To make this jam, you'll need a potato ricer or a large strainer, as well as the equivalent of four (1-pint) jelly jars (with lids and rings). Jar sizes can be mixed, but do not use any jars larger than a pint. (Smaller sizes allow for more sharing.) Do not double the recipe. Unless the jam is expected to be used within two months, you'll also need a boiling-water canner. If you've never picked wild mustang grapes before, the recipe contributor offers a few tips: It's a good idea to wear boots, gloves, and long sleeves when picking grapes since snakes and wasps frequently seek shelter among the grapevines. Another hazard to watch for is poison ivy.

1 (3-gallon) bucket of ripe wild mustang grapes (this is more than
   enough to yield the required 1 quart of prepared juice)
7 cups sugar
1 (3-ounce) packet Certo (or other commercial fruit pectin)

Wash grapes in several changes of water. Wear latex or nitrile gloves to keep hands from becoming itchy and irritated from handling the grapes and leaves. Pull the leaves and branches from the grapes and remove any dried-up or rotten fruit. *There is no need to remove the grapes from the stems.* When the grapes are removed from the last rinse water, shake them slightly and place them in a large, deep pot.

Using a wooden spoon or potato masher, mash the grapes slightly. Add about ¼ cup water to moisten the bottom of the pot so that the grapes will not scorch before the juice is rendered from the grapes. Bring the grapes and water to a boil and then simmer for 20 minutes, occasionally mashing the grapes against the bottom and sides of the pot.

Savannah Barnes Clark
1862–1943
Gonzales County

Savannah Barnes Clark.
Courtesy of Jean Schnitz.

Place a thick layer of newspaper on the floor and on the cabinet. Put a layer of waxed paper or plastic on top of the newspaper on the cabinet. Wear old clothes or an old apron — *grape juice stains*!

Pour or ladle grapes carefully into a ricer or strainer that is sitting over a large bowl. (If using a strainer, it should be large enough to allow juice to drain into the bowl as grapes are mashed with a wooden spoon to extract the maximum amount of juice.) Press grapes through the ricer until most of the pulp is pushed into the bowl, but *before the seeds begin to get through*. Carefully discard the seeds, stems, and peels. Continue until all grapes have been used.

Measure 4 cups of juice and pulp into a clean, stainless-steel pot that will be large enough to allow the jam to come to a full, rolling boil without boiling over. (Store any remaining juice and pulp in the refrigerator for 2 to 3 weeks if jam isn't going to be made immediately.)

Prepare enough jars and lids to hold 4 pints of jelly. Use pint or half-pint jars. Place jars and lids in the dishwasher and wash with the hottest cycle available, timing them to be still hot when the jelly is ready. (You may also sterilize the jars and lids in a boiling-water canner, following the manufacturer's instructions. For more details, see instructions at nchfp. uga.edu/publications/uga/using_bw_canners.html.) *It is important that the jars be very hot when the hot jam is poured into them.*

Add the sugar to the 4 cups of grape juice. Cook over medium heat and bring the mixture to a full rolling boil, stirring frequently. (You'll notice that the bubbles on the surface of the jam are large at first.) Continue boiling jam for at least 5 minutes, watching for bubbles to become somewhat smaller. (Before Certo existed, it was very important to cook the jam until the bubbles grew quite small; this ensured that the jam was sufficiently cooked to gel properly.) While the jam is still at a full, rolling boil, stir in Certo and continue boiling another 3 to 5 minutes.

Remove the jam from heat and skim the bubbles from the top. Put the skimmed jam in a saucer to save the good part that comes off with the bubbles. Taking care not to get burned, immediately ladle jam into the hot jars, leaving ¼-inch of headroom. Place the sterilized lids on the jars and screw the outer lids on tightly. Invert jars for 5 minutes, then allow to cool several hours. Tighten the lids again before storing. Use within 2 months. *Makes about 4 pints or 8 half-pints*

Note: If making jam that won't be used within two months, process jars of jam in a boiling-water canner according to the manufacturer's directions, or see instructions at nchfp.uga.edu/publications/uga/using_bw_canners.html.

Contributed by Jean Granberry Schnitz
Savannah Barnes Clark's granddaughter by marriage
Bexar County

"My mother-in-law, Jo Clark Schnitz (I called her Nanny), taught me to make wild mustang grape jam in 1954. She, in turn, learned to make it from her mother, Savannah Barnes Clark. When Savannah taught her daughters to make this jam, there was no such thing as Certo or commercial fruit pectin, so she taught them to make it without it. They always picked two or three small bunches of pink, slightly ripened grapes to be sure the jam would have enough natural pectin to gel properly. She also taught her daughters how to judge whether or not the jam had cooked long enough by watching the size of the bubbles on the surface while it was boiling. Nanny used Certo after it was on the market, but she also taught me how to make grape jelly without it.

"Savannah and Seaborn Lewis Clark were close neighbors near what is now County Road 114 West between Nixon and Seguin. They married in 1882. Neighbors married neighbors in those days. My father-in-law grew up about a quarter-mile away, at the juncture of Gonzales, Guadalupe, and Wilson Counties. There's a big, red rock marking that spot. If you stand on that rock, you're standing in three counties! I still pick grapes on the same land where my mother-in-law and her mother also picked them."

Jean has won many blue ribbons with her mother-in-law's (and Savannah's) recipe at the Kendall County Fair in Boerne. She says, "When I win a blue ribbon, I laminate it, put it with a bouquet of flowers, and place it on Nanny's grave in the Dewville Cemetery in Gonzales County with a note: 'This one is yours, Nanny.'" Savannah and Seaborn Clark are buried about ten feet away, so perhaps Savannah shares in the glory, too.

Thalia Pauline Pearson Chasteen Windham

1917–2005

Taylor, Tarrant, Dallas, Dallam, Lubbock, and Upton Counties

Thalia Pauline Pearson Chasteen Windham. Courtesy of Anne Duke.

Wild Pear Preserves

If you're lucky enough to have access to a Kieffer pear tree, watch for the fruit to ripen (turn yellow) sometime in mid-September to mid-October, depending on rainfall and other factors, and gather the pears then. (They're sometimes available at farmers' markets, too.) You'll need five (1-pint) canning jars and lids, as well as a stovetop boiling-water canner to process the preserves. Tongs, a jar funnel, and a jar lifter also come in handy. Home-canning kits (e.g., Ball Fresh Preserving Kit) are a handy all-in-one alternative. For detailed information about boiling-water canning, see nchfp.uga.edu/publications/uga/using_bw_canners. html.

12 to 14 fresh, ripe Kieffer pears (or enough to yield 12 cups peeled, cored, and sliced pears)
6 cups sugar
Fruit Fresh (optional)

Wash, peel, and core pears. Cut into approximately ½-inch slices and measure out 12 cups (1 whole pear generally yields 1 cup sliced pears). Place pears in a large container and cover with 6 cups sugar. (If necessary, divide pears into small batches; just keep the ratio of pears to sugar at 2:1 and be sure sugar coats pears.) Sprinkle with Fruit Fresh, if desired. Place plastic wrap directly over pears to help preserve color and let rest outside the refrigerator overnight.

The next day, place pear mixture in a heavy-bottomed saucepan and heat slowly to boiling. Cook mixture until sugar has completely dissolved and pears are slightly transparent at the edges. (The mixture should have turned a peach color.) Ladle pears into sterilized jars, leaving ¼ inch of headroom. Use tongs to place sterilized lids on top of jars, then screw on sterilized metal rings tightly. Process jars in a water-bath canner according to the manufacturer's directions. *Makes 5 pints*

Contributed by Jill Mickelson Henderson
Thalia Pauline Pearson Chasteen Windham's granddaughter
Tarrant County

Chapter 2: Recipes

"One of my family's traditions is making pear preserves together," says Jill. "We make them with what we call wild pears, since the pear trees we like apparently germinate from the pear cores spread by animals, birds, or the wind. The actual name for this type of pear is Kieffer, and it never really gets soft. A ripe Kieffer turns yellow and has quite a bit of juice." Jill's mother, Anne Chasteen Keller Duke, notes that Wild Pear Preserves is actually a fourth-generation recipe. She explains, "The tradition began in the 1920s with my grandmother Fannie Burleson Pearson, when she and my grandfather lived in Rotan."

Anne goes on to say, "From about 1970 until the early 1990s, my mother [Pauline Windham] and step-dad would travel each fall — usually in mid-September — from our home in McCamey (and later in Abilene) to my aunt Dorothy and uncle Bill Ellis's house in Shamrock. They had the Kieffer pear trees. The two families would spend an entire week together visiting, playing cards, and making pear preserves, using approximately one hundred pounds of sugar.

"The recipe for preserves is simple: pears and sugar. The 'making,' however, is very labor-intensive. This was always a labor of love, and the many pints and quarts we canned were shared with both family and friends. We carry on the tradition today at my home in Arlington, except that today we get our Kieffer pears from a friend's ranch in Oklahoma.

"We always make the preserves using the boiling-water canning method. In good years when the pears are juicy, we have extra pear-sugar syrup, and we can this, too, to use on pancakes and waffles. Of course, the preserves are also good on pancakes, as well as on biscuits and rolls."

For anyone planning to harvest wild pears, Anne offers this advice: "Ripe Kieffer pears are a favorite of many species of wildlife, including deer. However, there's no way you can pick the pears early — you'd never be able to peel them. You just take your chances and hope you have a large enough crop to share with the animals."

Wild Mustang Grape Wine

There are other, more complicated methods of making mustang grape wine; however, this recipe is delightful in its simplicity and makes a good, sweet wine that you can store in the refrigerator for a year or more. The only piece of equipment you need is a 1-gallon glass jar (a wide-mouth jar works best) and a lid.

4 cups wild mustang grapes
4 cups sugar
Nonchlorinated water

Remove stems from grapes, rinse lightly, and put them in a 1-gallon glass jar. Add sugar; then add water almost to the top. Stir well and seal jar loosely.

Place jar in a dark, un-air-conditioned place. Let sit for 6 weeks.

Strain wine off the grapes and discard them. Rinse the jar and put wine back into the same jar. Strain through a clean cloth daily for about 5 days, or until the wine is clear. Place wine in refrigerator during straining process. (There may still be a little sediment on the bottom, but the wine on top should be clear.) Wine can be stored in refrigerator about a year. *Makes 1 gallon*

Contributed by Denver Lee Weiser
Adolph Charles "A. C." Sevcik's grandson
Fayette County

*Adolph Charles "A. C." Sevcik.
Courtesy of Patsy Weiser.*

Chapter 2: Recipes

A.C.'s daughter Patsy Weiser doesn't know where her father learned how to make Wild Mustang Grape Wine, but she says he always picked the grapes in the woods on his farm near Vsetin in northeastern Lavaca County. "He was born on that farm and lived there all of his life, except for the last year and a half," says Patsy. "He died at age ninety-five. He stored his wine on a shelf in the smokehouse and shared it with family and friends."

Patsy's son Denver makes the wine today, averaging about twenty gallons a year. "I make it because I enjoy doing it," he says. "It's fun." While the wine is fermenting, Denver leaves it in a shed in the backyard. "You want it to be in a place that's not air-conditioned," he says. "It doesn't matter how hot it gets."

Sometimes Denver multiplies the recipe and makes the wine in a big, five-gallon water jug. Once the wine is made, he stores the jars in a refrigerator in the garage. On occasion, people have bought the supplies and picked the grapes and had him make the wine for them. Like his grandfather, he enjoys giving away the fruits of his labor.

Author's Note: Not long ago, I stopped at an old-fashioned hardware store somewhere between Cuero and Austin and asked the clerk if he had any one-gallon glass jars, explaining that I needed one to make this recipe. He didn't have any, but an older gentleman followed me out to my car and said that he knew a likely spot to find such a jar. He mentioned a certain barbecue restaurant in a nearby town and said the owners usually had leftover one-gallon pickle jars that were perfect for making mustang grape wine. The reason he knew? He said that he makes gallons of wine himself every year. This chance encounter convinced me that aficionados of mustang grape wine aren't as rare in Texas as you might think.

3

Preserving Heirloom Recipes

*Those handwritten recipe cards [from my grandmother] —
along with more I inherited from my mother — are some of
my most treasured possessions.*

— Bob Ruggiero Jr.
(contributed recipes for Ham Pie, Spinach-Sausage Pie, and Hot Antipasto)

I begin this chapter with a cautionary tale. When I was gathering recipes for this project, I heard a common refrain: "Third-generation recipes? Oh, I wish I had asked my grandmother for some of hers before she passed away. She made the best [fill in the blank—stuffed peppers, cinnamon rolls, chocolate pie]! But unfortunately, she never wrote anything down—the recipes were all in her head, so now they're lost forever." Sound familiar? I hope not. But if you want to be sure the special dishes in your family live on after your loved ones are gone, you have to make preserving these culinary treasures a priority. No one lives forever, memories fade, and even written recipes get lost. In other words, procrastination is the enemy.

Getting Started

So maybe you've decided to take on the task (since no one else is going to do it!) of organizing and preserving the recipes for your family's favorite dishes. There is no magic formula, but there is also no *right* way to do it, either. I picked up a number of tips from the cooks who shared their heirloom recipes with me, as well as some from other sources. They may help you get started.

Back to that magic formula for a moment. A number of publishing companies (Morris Press and Wimmer Cookbooks, for example) specialize in family and community cookbooks. For a fee, they'll take you by the hand and make the process relatively pain-free. You can also find cookbook templates on the Internet that will streamline the publishing process.

But preserving heirloom recipes involves more than just creating a cookbook. You first have to find, uncover, or discover the recipes. Sometimes an elderly relative's signature dish has never been written down. It then becomes your job to do some detective work and get the details on paper (or in a secure computer file). Sometimes this is as simple as sitting down and recording the recipe as your relative rattles off the ingredients and instructions. However, some cooks can't actually tell you how much of an ingredient they use or how they put a dish together—they just "do" it.

In this case you follow the cook around the kitchen with a pen and paper (and measuring cups and measuring spoons, if necessary) as Nancy Powell's daughter Elaine did when she wanted to learn how to make a favorite dessert (see Grandma's Banana Pudding recipe). Note that some cooks are more open to this intrusion than others. Harold Odom Jr. resorted to videotaping his grandmother as she made her legendary tea cakes. After studying the video, he was finally able to replicate the elusive cookie through trial and error (see Big Mama Addie Odom's Tea Cakes recipe).

When recording the recipe, include measurements and methods, of course, but also note details like actual can sizes (the number of ounces in a "large" can today will likely differ in future decades), possible substitutions for hard-to-find ingredients, pan sizes, cooking times, baking temperatures, and the number of servings the recipe makes. (Avoid ambiguous phrases like "serves a family of four" since this doesn't necessarily mean that a dish makes four servings. The cook may be allowing extra helpings for some family members.)

The Rest of the Story

After you have a recipe in hand, try to find out a little information about it in relation to the family by talking to the "ancestor cook." Choose a quiet setting without distractions and bring a tape recorder so you can share in the conversation. Bring along a list of questions, but be prepared for the discussion to take off in other directions, too.

You'll want to tailor the questions and temper the pace according to the circumstances (in other words, be sensitive and show respect), but your list might include the following: How did the recipe come to you? Do you know when, where, or how it originated? Do you think it represents any specific ethnic group? Why do you think so? How long have you been making it? How often do you make it? Do you make it for special occasions? Does anyone else in the family make it? Is it a favorite of anyone in the family? Have you made any changes in the recipe since it was handed down to you? Do you have any tips for making it that aren't in the recipe? Are there any interesting family stories that relate to the recipe? Sometimes the answer to this last question proves as rewarding as the recipe itself. (For a handy list of these same questions, see "Collecting Heirloom Recipes: Questions for the Cook" in the resources section.)

Discussions that involve remembering the past invariably take longer than expected, so you may want to spread the questions out over a couple of sessions. It will take patience and persistence on your part, but don't rush the process. Food is a wonderful vehicle for passing along memories, so these conversations may yield valuable slivers of family history. Interviewing family members is also a wonderful way to connect and make new memories. (For a comprehensive guide to collecting oral histories, download a free copy of *Fundamentals of Oral History: Texas Preservation* from the Texas Historical Association's website www.thc.state.tx.us).

Other Sources of Heirloom Recipes

When a relative has passed away and you can no longer ask that person about a dish you remember, don't dismiss the possibility that he or she gave the recipe to another family member or perhaps even wrote it down at some point. Ask around. You might not find the recipe you're looking for but may find another heirloom recipe instead. If there was a recipe file, find out who inherited it and ask to look through it. If your relative had cookbooks, be sure to check those, too. In the early part of the last century, many cooks used the end papers of their favorite cookbooks to record additional recipes. Check the indexes of any community cookbooks you find for recipes your ancestors might have contributed. Don't overlook boxes of letters and mementos. My sister Becky found my late aunt Thelma's Chess Pie recipe, as well as her favorite pie crust recipe, inside such a box.

Don't forget to check with the genealogists in the family; sometimes they have recipes among their collections and don't realize it. These might be a little vague, perhaps nothing more than a description of how a letter writer prepared an abundance of squash from the garden one summer. However, a good cook might be able to translate that description into a viable recipe.

Speaking of vague descriptions, if you do enough recipe sleuthing, you're apt to run across some obscure measurements such as "1 egg of butter" and "1 tea cup of sugar," as well as phrases such as "bake in a slow oven." Home cooks didn't start using standardized measurements until Fannie Farmer popularized them with the publication of *The Boston Cooking-School Cook-Book* in 1896. Standardized baking temperatures came along a few decades later, with the advent of gas and electric ovens. (For a guide to interpreting obscure culinary terms, see "Deciphering Obscure Terms in Older Recipes" in the resources section.)

The Family That Cooks Together . . .

While collecting recipes and talking to contributors, I realized that the more complicated or time-consuming traditional recipes I found—Pork Tamales, Wendish Noodles, Apple Strudel, Cuccidati (Sicilian Fig Cookies), Pizzelle, Taffy (for Pulling Teeth Out), Wild Pear Preserves—are usually made in groups. If one person had to complete all the steps, the recipe might not have survived very long. In the case of Wild Pear Preserves, the recipe contributor's mother, Anne Duke, told me that she couldn't imagine how her grandmother had managed to do everything by herself back in the day. "We do it today as a family," she said, "and it's still a lot of work."

Mexican Americans call their tamale-making gathering a tamalada, and it's a basically a party that takes place in the kitchen (see Pork Tamales recipe). Although the groups who make the other recipes may not have names for their joint culinary efforts, there's an element of camaraderie in their gatherings, too. More hands make the work go faster, and they make it more fun. And when children are involved as well as elders, it's a valuable chance to pass along family traditions and stories. Gwen Carona had that in mind when she started making Cuccidati and Pizzelle with her grandchildren more than a decade ago, and she hopes they'll pass along the traditions in their own families one day.

Maybe there's a dish in your family that would benefit from more hands in the kitchen. You don't have to start with the most complicated recipes to see the rewards. For example, my mother made cornbread dressing for holidays by herself for years. Now all my siblings—and some of the nieces and nephews—pitch in, boiling eggs, chopping vegetables, and crumbling cornbread. We divide up the work and have fun trying to remember exactly "how Grandma did it." Thank goodness we have her recipe. Making it together helps ensure its preservation.

Resurrecting Lost Recipes

Sometimes you don't have that special recipe, or maybe the one you have isn't complete or the instructions aren't clear. If you remember the flavor of a "lost recipe," you can eventually resurrect the dish through systematic experimentation, as Sylvia Cásares tells students in her cooking classes (see Pork Tamales recipe). Take heed, though, from writer Stephen Harrigan's tale. Trying to find a lost recipe can become an all-consuming endeavor.

Several years ago, I heard *New York Times* best-selling author Stephen Harrigan (*The Gates of the Alamo* and *Remember Ben Clayton*, among others) speak on a writers' panel in Austin. When he mentioned in passing an upcoming *Texas Monthly* article about his obsession with kolaches, I listened intently. His story of rediscovering the kolaches of his youth and how the humble pastry led him to new insights about his Czech roots intrigued me. His experience of being transported to his childhood upon eating a kolache for the first time in three decades struck a familiar chord.

Shortly afterward, his article "Where Is My Home?" appeared in the March 2012 issue of *Texas Monthly*. Subtitled "How a Casual Interest in Kolaches Got Totally out of Control," it details his efforts to re-create the kolaches his grandmother (Nana) had made, his transformation into a kolache snob, and his quest to find the kolaches most reminiscent of Nana's. Somewhere along the way, he realized that his quest was more about his long-neglected Czech culture than kolaches per se. His kolache journey eventually took him all the way to the Czech Republic.

The one thing missing in the *Texas Monthly* article was Nana's recipe for kolaches. So naturally, I wrote to the author and asked him if I could include it in my book. He agreed, and we exchanged several e-mails. He also sent me a lovely photo of his grandmother Gladys Lednicky Berney. It was at this point that I discovered that Steve's grandmother had lived in Kansas and Oklahoma, but never in Texas. Nope, she had stopped short of the Red River—Lednicky Kolaches doesn't qualify as a third-generation Texas recipe. However, I offer it here as a bonus, and as an example of the lengths some Texans will go to in order to preserve their heirloom recipes. *Dobrou chut'*!

Kolaches like Nana's

STEPHEN HARRIGAN

As far as I can tell, my grandmother's recipe for kolaches existed only in her head, though sometime in the 1960s, she was persuaded by one family member or another to write it down. The result was a 4 x 6 index card featuring puzzling quantities (a "cube" of butter) and gnomic observations (" + momma died"). Gladys Lednicky Berney was born in Kansas, but her parents had immigrated to America from the Moravian village of Brusperk, just across the Beskydy Mountains from Poland. Her kolaches were dense, dark, gnarly, and round, quite distinct from the pillowy, square-sided variety you find in most Czech bakeries in the United States. They were overpowering to my childhood taste buds, an assault of primal flavors straight out of some haunted Middle European fairy tale.

I was cautioned by one of my uncles never to publish my grandmother's kolache recipe. He didn't say why. He had an imaginative side, and he might have liked the idea of it being forbidden to outsiders. Or he might have just thought that, as a recipe, it was unreliable. In any case I have honored his ban and am not publishing Nana's recipe here—well, not the verbatim recipe anyway. What follows is the distillation of my attempts, Christmas after Christmas for perhaps twenty years, to reproduce the taste, texture, and mystery of my Czech grandmother's prune and poppy seed kolaches.

Lednicky Kolaches

Making kolaches at my house is a time-consuming, four-part process. There's the dough, then two kinds of filling, and then the streusel-like topping known as popsika. I recommend making the dough the day before; otherwise, dealing with all these ingredients at once can be a little overwhelming.

Dough
Dissolve 1½ cubes of compressed yeast into ½ cup warm water. Add 1 teaspoon sugar and let stand 5 minutes. Scald 1 quart whole milk and pour it into another bowl.

Into the bowl with the milk, add 1 cup softened butter or a combination of butter and shortening, 1 cup sugar, 1 teaspoon salt, and 4 to 5 eggs.

Mix in the yeast and 4 to 6 cups flour. (The flour should be added in increments—2 cups at first and then more as it starts to blend in. I often mix it all in by hand with just a spoon, but it's better to use a food processor. When all the flour is blended in, it should make what is called a "shaggy" dough.)

Turn the flour mixture into a well-oiled bowl. Also brush some oil on top. Cover it with a dish towel and place it somewhere warm, like near the oven. Let it rise until it has doubled in size; then punch it down and refrigerate for at least 4 hours.

Prune/Apricot Filling

This part is pretty simple. Dump 3 (9-ounce) packages of seedless prunes and 1 (6-ounce) package of dried apricots (the California variety that come split in half) into a saucepan. This will make probably more filling than you need, but it never hurts to have a surplus.

Add just enough water to cover the prunes and apricots and cook them down over low heat (they're stewed together). Then you can put them through either a grinder or food processor, or—if you're me—just sort of stir them around with a fork until they're blended into one big, purplish mass. You can add sugar if you want, but the fruit should be a little tart, especially since the kolaches are going to have a sweet topping before it's all over.

Allow the mixture to cool.

Poppy Seed Filling

Buy 2 (2.5-ounce) bottles of poppy seeds in the spice section of the grocery store. The poppy seeds are exceedingly small to begin with, but the recipe works better if you grind them in a coffee grinder.

Scald the contents of approximately 1½ bottles of poppy seeds with 2 cups milk. Put the mixture in the refrigerator for at least a couple of hours.

Melt a stick (½ cup) of butter. Into the melted butter stir ½ cup flour, then the poppy seed mixture. Also add ½ cup sugar, ½ cup honey, and a pinch of salt.

Cook all this over low heat, stirring constantly (and I mean constantly) until it's thick. When it cools, it should look like gray cookie dough. Set aside and let cool until you're ready to bake.

Popsika (topping)

For this, you'll need a 10- to 12-ounce box of Vanilla Wafers (real Vanilla Wafers, by the way, not the ersatz kind that say Nilla Wafers). Crush the cookies with a rolling pin until they're sort of powdery, and then turn into a bowl.

Add 1 teaspoon cinnamon, 1 cup sugar, and 1 stick (½ cup) softened butter.

Wash your hands and mush all this together. It should be pasty but still sort of granular.

Baking

Preheat oven to 375°F to 400°F. Turn the dough out onto a lightly floured surface. Punch it down a little bit, but do not knead it. The dough will still be shaggy, so you may need to add a bit of flour so that it's not too sticky to handle.

Lightly grease a couple of large cookie sheets with butter.

For the prune kolaches, squeeze off a golf-ball-sized piece of dough, stretch it out a bit, and put it down on the cookie sheet. Repeat until you've filled the cookie sheet. (Note: I leave space between the pieces of dough so the kolaches don't bunch up as they're rising. I know, I know: for some kolache bakers that's heresy, but as far as I can tell the Lednickys have always belonged to the round-and-brown school).

Make a little pocket in each ball of dough with two fingers, then spoon in some of the prune mixture, and smooth it out with the back of the spoon. Don't worry about them looking neat or uniform. That kind of thing counts in kolache-baking competitions, but I like them a little smeary.

Sprinkle some of the popsika over the top of each kolache. While you're at it, sprinkle a lot. In my opinion the popsika should cover the fruit.

Place in the oven and bake until lightly — or more than lightly — brown.

After you take them from the oven, drizzle melted butter over the tops with a teaspoon.

For the poppy seed kolaches, the basic procedure is a little different. As with the prune kolaches, grab a golf-ball-sized piece of dough, but this time spread it out on the palm of your hand and spoon some of the poppy seed into the center. Then fold and squeeze until the poppy seed is hidden inside the dough.

Set each one onto the cookie sheet, folded side down. Poke them with a fork and sprinkle popsika on top. Bake for 10 minutes or so, and then once again spoon melted butter over them.

That's it. This recipe should make at least 2 dozen kolaches. I'm sure you can find a less daunting recipe in almost any reliable cookbook, and I've had professional Czech bakers look at my kolaches and gasp in horror at how unbeautiful and misshapen they are. But that's not my problem. These are Lednicky Kolaches, and this is the only way to make them.

Family Cookbooks and Beyond

Once you have a few heirloom recipes, it's natural to want to save them in a cookbook. You will probably want to include recipes from younger cooks, too, since they will provide the heirloom recipes of tomorrow. You can create an online cookbook that you can share with the whole family (or at least those who are computer literate). However, most people like the idea of having a "real book" for something that's meant to be handed down through the generations. As mentioned earlier, you can find companies that will publish your cookbook for you. That's a good option, but if you decide to do it yourself, my advice is to keep the process simple. Otherwise, creating the quintessential family cookbook becomes just another item on your to-do (someday) list.

Here's one option for a simple, get-it-done approach. First, send out the word to family members before the next holiday gathering and tell them that you're collecting recipes for a family cookbook. Ask them to bring not only the favorite dishes they usually bring to family events but also the recipes for those dishes. Tell them to write or copy each recipe onto an 8½- x 11-inch sheet of white paper, making sure they include their name, the name of the person who gave them the recipe, and something interesting about the recipe. Ask them to do the same with any favorite recipes they have from older relatives who aren't up to the task or those who have passed away. When the holiday rolls around, you collect the recipes and give any stragglers a tight deadline for getting their recipes to you.

After a short interval, add your own recipes and head to your local copy shop. Make a set of copies for each household. (Parents can make copies for their children later as they think necessary.) Have the clerk punch holes in each set to fit a three-ring notebook. For a little extra expense, you can purchase clear plastic sheet protectors (hole-punched on the side) at an office supply store and insert recipes inside them. Buy the appropriate number of binders and place a set of recipes in each one. It's up to you whether to include a title page, tabs for different types of recipes, a family tree, photographs, stories, or other material.

At the next family event, you deliver the binders (and collect for expenses, if you like). Now each household has its own set of family recipes that can be easily updated as families expand and new dishes also become favorites.

Here's another easy way to collect heirloom or heirloom-to-be recipes: Throw a "long-distance recipe shower" before the next family wedding. Invite family members on both sides and send recipe cards or preprinted recipe forms along with the invitations, requesting that guests mail back one or more of their family favorites. Once the recipes arrive, insert them in the appropriate-size sheet protectors and place them in an attractive binder, perhaps one covered in special paper or fabric. Include a title page with the names of the couple and the date of the wedding, a copy of the shower invitation, and a list of the contributors. However, before you present the gift to the bride and groom (on behalf of the two families), remember to photocopy the recipes from your family so that you'll have the basis of your own family cookbook.

Toni Gustafson, who contributed the recipe for Bomo's Cheese Pie, used the binder method to create an ongoing, intrafamily cookbook some fifteen years ago. Titled *Mazurka* (after the traditional Polish dance and pastry), the large, three-ring binder includes forty-four recipes to date from the Frank and Bomo Kolonko McClosky family. "It's primarily a cookbook," says Toni, "but it also features photo collages, reminiscences, information on specific Polish traditions, and so on. It's a very 'home-made,' eclectic group of family documents."

Toni began the project in 1992, requesting the most "famed" family recipes to add to the ones she already had in her personal collection. "Circumstances demanded that I put the book idea aside for several years," she explains. "Around early 2001, I opened up the box again and restarted the project. I 'released' *Mazurka* at Christmas 2001, giving copies to each of Bomo and Papa McClosky's children." She eventually followed up by giving copies of the cookbook to each of the grandchildren. The great-grandchildren usually receive theirs upon marriage, "or sometimes upon earnest request."

To produce the cookbooks, Toni makes laser color copies of the original photos and photo collages and photocopies the recipes and other text onto good-quality paper. She then inserts the documents into PVC-free sheet protectors and places them in the binders. But the tradition doesn't end there. Toni also distributes insert packets of recipes, photos, and other materials at intervals during large family gatherings at Christmas or Easter. (She has distributed five inserts since the original *Mazurka* was released.) These go to the approximately twenty-five family members on "the list" (those who have received a cookbook). "Once on the list, you're never off the list," says Toni.

Creating the cookbooks and maintaining this tradition obviously require considerable commitment. "This project is important to me," says Toni, "because a family recipe book is a document that captures the cultural history and character of a family. Preserving, sharing, and preparing heirloom dishes associated with specific individuals brings those dear relatives close once more."

Genny Kraus, who contributed the Chicken and Dumplings recipe (see Main Dishes section), didn't compile her Polish family's cookbook, but she cherishes it nonetheless. "My first cousins Rose Mary Kosub McPherson and her brother Jimmy Kosub decided they wanted to put together a book of Kosub family recipes and stories," says Genny. "Rose Mary contacted all the family members—the descendants of Grandpa Leon and Grandma Agnes Kosub—and collected the recipes and stories. Some contributed recipes they had received from relatives who had passed away. Jimmy put all the information Rose Mary collected on the computer, and his wife, Doris, did spell-check. They made copies for everyone and passed them out to the family in 1999." Titled *The Very Best of the Kosub Family Favorite Recipes*, it includes eighty-eight recipes ranging from Grandma Agnes's Kartofle (Polish Potatoes) to Venison Sausage.

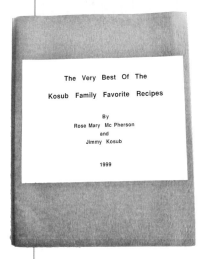

The Very Best of the Kosub Family Favorite Recipes *cookbook. Courtesy of Genny Kraus.*

"The cookbook's not in a hardbound-book form; it's just printed on regular paper and clipped into a paper folder," continues Genny. "Besides recipes, it has copies of a few old pictures, some stories about Grandpa Leon and Grandma Agnes, and the couple's recollections about growing up back then. The cookbook is simple in appearance, but that doesn't matter to us. The fact that we can share family recipes and be able to read the stories and recollections from years ago is the important thing.

"Rose Mary and Jimmy's dad (Tony Kosub) had already passed away before the cookbook was written. Their mom (Mary Kosub) died in September 2006. A couple of months later, my cousins decided to have a special meal with most of their immediate families to pay tribute to Aunt Mary. Each family member was to choose a recipe they liked from the Kosub family cookbook, make it, and bring it to the gathering. When I heard about this, I thought to myself, 'Wow! What a beautiful idea.'

"Others have prepared recipes from the book for their own family celebrations and meals with their friends. Sometimes friends have requested a particular dish from the cookbook because they enjoyed it so much. I am so glad my cousins took the time to get all of us to put our favorite family recipes on paper back in 1999. The Kosub cookbook is even more precious to us now. Our families live so many miles apart that it is a difficult task for all of us to get together. Since the book was put together, our family has lost some of the people—my mom, my two remaining aunts, and several first cousins—who submitted items for it. They are gone and dearly missed, as well as many other family members before them, but they live on because of the stories and recipes they shared with us."

Randy Mallory, another recipe contributor, is the proud owner of a family cookbook that his mother, Betty Smith Mallory (known as Nanee), created in 2007. She surprised each of her children and grandchildren with a copy that Christmas. Titled *From Nanee's Kitchen*, the slim, spiral-bound book contains ninety-eight recipes, including many that Betty

From Nanee's Kitchen cookbook. Photo by Randy Mallory.

recorded in the 1970s as she watched her mother (Mama Smith) cook "by heart." Mama Smith's Cornbread (see Breads section) appears on the cover. The cookbook features other traditional family recipes, as well as an entry on cooking tips designed for the less-experienced grandchildren. Betty's letter to her family at the front includes the following passage: "As you are preparing the [recipes] you wish to use, I hope you will think of family love and traditions."

Another contributor, Tasha Harper-Werner, preserves her grandmother's recipes, too, but not in the traditional way. As a photographer, designer, and owner of a custom-print T-shirt business, she decided to print some of her grandmother's handwritten recipes on dish towels. "My Granny made the best light bread and dinner rolls known to man," she says. "She's in heaven now, and I have a lot of her recipes. (See Granny's Master Mix recipe in the Breads section.) I've decided that these dish towels will be a beautiful way for her to help me in the kitchen, still."

While Tasha's method of preserving heirloom recipes may be the most creative idea I've heard, I like Harold Odom Jr.'s way the best. He not only teaches Big Mama Addie Odom's Tea Cakes baking classes at each family reunion; he makes the tea cakes at least once a month and sends batches to all his aunts and uncles and some of his cousins. Now, that's keeping the tradition alive.

May this collection of third-generation (and older) Texas recipes inspire you to unearth and cherish the heirloom recipes in your family, as well as the traces of history they carry with them.

Tea towel with heirloom recipe. Photo by Tasha Harper-Werner.

Resources

Collecting Heirloom Recipes: Questions for the Cook

In addition to obtaining the recipe for an heirloom dish, you will want to document its provenance, at least since it came into the family. Asking these questions will help you fill in the backstory.

1. How did this recipe come to you?

2. Do you know when, where, or how it originated?

3. Do you think it represents any specific ethnic group? Why do you think so?

4. How long have you been making it? How often do you make it? Does anyone else in the family make it?

5. Do you make it for special occasions? Is it a favorite of anyone in the family?

6. Have you made any changes in the recipe since it was handed down to you or since you began making it?

7. Do you have any tips for making it that are not in the recipe?

8. Are there any interesting family stories that relate to the recipe?

Deciphering Obscure Terms in Older Recipes

Really old heirloom recipes are sometimes riddled with confusing measurements and perplexing phrases that stymie even the most dedicated recipe detective. Here are a few of the most common terms and their equivalents in today's culinary language.

Dry Measurements

Spoonful = 1 tablespoon

Salt spoon = ¼ teaspoon

Pinch = the amount that can be picked up between your thumb and two fingers, about ⅛ teaspoon

Half pinch = the amount that can be picked up between your thumb and one finger, less than ⅛ teaspoon

Butter the size of an egg = ¼ cup

Butter the size of a walnut = 1 tablespoon

Butter the size of a hazelnut = 1 teaspoon

Liquid Measurements

Coffee cup = a little less than 1 cup

Tea cup = ¾ cup

Gill = ½ cup

Wineglass = ¼ cup

Jigger = 3 tablespoons

Pony = 2 tablespoons

Dash = about 6 drops

Oven Temperatures

Slow oven = 250°F to 325°F

Moderate oven = 350°F to 375°F

Moderately hot oven = 375°F to 400°F

Hot oven = 400°F to 450°F

Very hot oven = 450°F to 500°F

From "Heirloom Weights & Measures Conversion Chart," About.com Home Cooking, http://homecooking.about .com/library/weekly/bloldconvert.htm (accessed April 23, 2015); Rick McDaniel, *An Irresistible History of Southern Food: Four Centuries of Black-Eyed Peas, Collard Greens & Whole Hog Barbecue* (Charleston: History Press, 2011), 44–45; and Editors of *American Heritage, The American Heritage Cookbook* (New York: American Heritage Publishing , 1969), inside front and back covers.

Additional Information

If you would like to find out more about your Texas culinary heritage or Texas foodways in general, there are abundant avenues available. These include the usual sources—books, magazines, organizations—as well as sites and events that provide opportunities to learn about cultural traditions in a more direct way.

The sites themselves usually offer displays, ongoing educational programs, and specialized libraries. In addition, they often host events that bring their respective themes to life with music, dancing, games, children's activities, and ethnic foods. Other events (those not associated with a brick-and-mortar site) range from church and community festivals organized by volunteers to city-hosted extravaganzas. Tasting is almost always part of the fun.

The following list of foodways-related sites and events mentioned in the text provides a sampling. It concludes with a few general suggestions for discovering other venues.

Sites and Events

University of Texas at San Antonio Institute of Texan Cultures is the state's largest multicultural museum. It hosts two annual festivals: the Texas Folklife Festival in June and the Asian Festival in January or February. For details about the ITC and the annual Texas Folklife Festival, see Grandma Scudder's Pound Cake recipe. For details about the ITC's annual Asian Festival, see Lucy Wu's Fried Rice recipe.

Texas State Museum of Asian Cultures & Education Center in Corpus Christi recently celebrated its fortieth anniversary. It offers a number of events, including an annual Lunar New Year celebration. For details about the site and its events, see Lucy Wu's Fried Rice recipe.

Texas Czech Heritage and Cultural Center in La Grange. For details about the site and its events, see Grandma Kossa's Homemade Bread recipe.

Czech Center Museum Houston. For details about the site and its events, see Grandma Kossa's Homemade Bread recipe.

Texas Wendish Heritage Museum in Serbin. For details about the site and the annual Wendish Fest in September, see Wendish Noodles recipe.

George Ranch Historical Park near Richmond, a living-history site, offers a Historic Food Program. For details about the site and its events, see Brisket with Chuckwagon Hollandaise recipe.

The Sauer-Beckmann Farmstead is part of the Lyndon B. Johnson State Park & Historic Site near Stonewall. For details about the site, programs, and special events, see Kuni's Homemade Egg Noodles with Chicken recipe.

The Texas Purple Hull Pea Festival takes place each June in the historic freedmen's community of Shankleville. For details, see Purple Hull Peas recipe.

Sts. Cyril and Methodius Catholic Church in Dubina is one of four "painted churches" in Fayette County. Its annual parish picnic takes place in July. For information on touring the church and details about its picnic, see Grandma Kossa's Homemade Bread recipe.

Sts. Cyril and Methodius Catholic Church in Shiner, another "painted church," holds several annual fund-raisers, including its Strudel Bake in November and two church picnics in May and August. For details, see Apple Strudel recipe.

The Heritage Syrup Festival takes place in Henderson each November. For details, see Ribbon Cane Syrup Pie recipe.

For additional museums and other sites related to Texas foodways, search online for cultural centers, living-history museums, and museums with specific ethnic themes. Many of these sites also host one or more annual events. For additional events with food or ethnic themes, see the *Texas Highways Events Calendar* at www.texashighways.com/events.

Books

Barr, Alwyn. *The African Texans*. College Station: Texas A&M University Press, 2004.

Berkley, Ellen Perry, ed. *At Grandmother's Table: Women Write about Food, Life, and the Enduring Bond between Grandmothers and Granddaughters*. Minneapolis, MN: Fairview Press, 2000.

Bernardin, Tom. *The Ellis Island Immigrant Cookbook*: *The Story of Our Common Past Told through the Recipes and Reminiscences of Our Immigrant Ancestors*. New York: Tom Bernardin, 1991.

Brady, Marilyn Dell. *The Asian Texans*. College Station: Texas A&M University Press, 2004.

Brennan, Georgeanne. *The Family Table: A Journal for Recipes and Memories*. San Francisco: Chronicle Books, 2000.

Cooper, Ann, and Lisa Holmes. *In Mother's Kitchen: Celebrated Women Chefs Share Beloved Family Recipes*. New York: Rizzoli International Publishers, 2005.

Daughters of the Republic of Texas, District VIII. *A Pinch of This and a Handful of That: Historic Recipes of Texas 1830–1900*. Austin: Eakin Press, 1988.

Edge, John T. *A Gracious Plenty: Recipes and Recollections from the American South*. New York: G. P. Putnam's Sons, 1999.

Editors of *American Heritage. The American Heritage Cookbook*. New York: American Heritage Publishing, 1969.

Editors of *Cook's Country. America's Best Lost Recipes: 121 Kitchen-Tested Heirloom Recipes Too Good to Forget*. Brookline, MA: America's Test Kitchen, 2007.

Editors of *Cook's Country. From Our Grandmothers' Kitchens: A Treasury of Lost Recipes Too Good to Forget*. Brookline, MA: America's Test Kitchen, 2011.

Elverson, Virginia T., and Mary Ann McLanahan. *A Cooking Legacy: Over 200 Recipes Inspired by Early American Cooks*. New York: Walker, 1975.

Greene, Bob, and D. G. Fulford. *To Our Children's Children: Preserving Family Histories for Generations to Come*. New York: Doubleday, 1993.

Kownslar, Allan O. *The European Texans*. College Station: Texas A&M University Press, 2004.

Kurlansky, Mark, ed. *The Food of a Younger Land*. New York: Riverhead Books, 2009.

Linck, Ernestine Sewell, and Joyce Gibson Roach. *Eats: A Folk History of Texas Foods*. Fort Worth: Texas Christian University Press, 1989.

McConachie, Dorothy. *Our Texas Heritage: Ethnic Traditions and Recipes*. Plano: Republic of Texas Press, 2000.

McDaniel, Rick. *An Irresistible History of Southern Food: Four Centuries of Black-Eyed Peas, Collard Greens & Whole Hog Barbecue*. Charleston, SC: History Press, 2011.

McKenzie, Phyllis. *The Mexican Texans*. College Station: Texas A&M University Press, 2004.

Smallwood, James M. *The Indian Texans*. College Station: Texas A&M University Press, 2004.

Walsh, Robb. *Texas Eats: The New Lone Star Heritage Cookbook*. Berkeley, CA: Ten Speed Press, 2012.

Wilde, Mary Poulos. *The Best of Ethnic Home Cooking*. Los Angeles: J. P. Tarcher, 1981.

Willard, Pat. *America Eats! On the Road with the WPA*. New York: Bloomsbury, 2008.

Wolff, Linda, ed. *"Gone to Texas" Heritage Recipes, Vol. 1 and Vol. 2*. Victoria: Texas Settlement Region, 2002, 2004.

Zanger, Mark H. *The American Ethnic Cookbook for Students*. Phoenix, AZ: Oryx Press, 2001.

Other Media

You'll find regular coverage of Texas foodways in both *Texas Highways* (www.texashighways .com) and *Texas Monthly* (www.texasmonthly .com) magazines.

To download a free copy of the Texas Historical Association's *Fundamentals of Oral History: Texas Preservation Guidelines*, see www .thc.state.tx.us.

"Texas Beyond History: The Virtual Museum of Texas' Cultural History," a project of the Texas Archeological Research Laboratory at the University of Texas at Austin and sixteen partners, interprets and shares the results of archeological and historical research as it relates to the state's cultural heritage. See www.texasbeyondhistory.net and search for "food."

My Grandmother's Ravioli, a program on the Cooking Channel (as of press time), is hosted by Mo Rocca, who regrets that he never learned to make his grandmother's signature Italian dishes. He now visits other people's grandparents in their homes, where they teach him how to make their specialties and give him an earful about ethnic and family traditions. Past episodes have featured dishes from Kimchi to Ham Pie. Although the program has a nationwide focus, many of the ethnic cuisines featured are found in Texas. See www.cookingchanneltv.com/shows/my-grandmothers-ravioli.html.

Organizations

Southern Foodways Alliance. Although based at the University of Mississippi in Oxford, SFA's scope includes Texas. An institution of the Center for the Study of Southern Culture, its mission is "to document, study, and celebrate the diverse food cultures of the changing American South." Call 662-915-3368 or see www.southernfoodways.org.

Foodways Texas is modeled after Southern Foodways Alliance. Its mission is "to preserve, promote, and celebrate the diverse food cultures of Texas." The organization is based in the American Studies Department at the University of Texas at Austin. Call 512-471-3037 or see www.foodwaystexas.com.

Texas Folklife, a nonprofit based in Austin, is "dedicated to the celebration and perpetuation of the folk arts and folklife of the Lone Star State." Call 512-441-9255 or see www. texasfolklife.org.

The Texas Folklore Society, with its office on the Stephen F. Austin State University campus in Nacogdoches, is "dedicated to collecting, preserving, and sharing the folklore of Texas and the Southwest." Call 936-468-4407 or see www.texasfolkloresociety.org.

Index

Recipes are formatted in all capitals.
Ethnic recipes were identified by contributors
  as representative of their ethnic roots.
Other recipes may have lost their original
  cultural identities.

rice
    Dirty Rice (Cajun), 57–58
    Lucy Wu's Fried Rice (Chinese), 83–85
    Mrs. Kelly's Chicken and Rice, 39–40
    Rice Pudding (Scottish), 214–215
Richards, Zelda, 91
Rieken, Kunigunda "Kuni" Schirmer (Kuni), 33–34
Rieken, Reiner, 33
Rieken, Ruth Greenhill, 81
Rieken-Speer, Jeri Lyn, 33–34, 80–81
Roberts, John C., 99
Roberts, Kathryn Nell, 97–99, 129–130
Rocca, Mo, 261
Rodella, Mary, 55
rolls
    Hot Rolls, 21–22
    Jailhouse Rolls, 22–24
Rosenberg, Bertha Heitkamp, 100, 231–233
Rosenberg, Minnie, 143
Rosenberg, Wesley, 231–232
Ruggiero, Bob, Jr., 68–73, 104–105, 241

salami, 68–69
Sargent, Pat, 76
sauces
    Chuckwagon Hollandaise, 61–63
    Hard Sauce, 209
    Microwave White Sauce, 102–103
Sauer-Beckmann Farmstead (Stonewall), 35, 259
sauerkraut
    Czech Sauerkraut, 106
    Dora Scudder's sauerkraut, 128
Scarborough, Peggy Sterling, 3, 57
Schacherl, Janice Lloyd, 221–222
Schautschick, Hattie Mitschke, 90–92
Schnitz, David, 59–60
Schnitz, Herman, 59
Schnitz, Jean Granberry, 59, 125–128, 233–235

Schnitz, Jerusha "Jo" Love Clark (Nanny), 59–60, 166–167, 235
Schnitz, Lew, 227
Schrab, Julie Catherine Puentes, 102–103
Scirratt, Leslie, 167, 217
Scotch-Irish food
    Grandmother's Creamy-Sour Potato Salad (Scotch-Irish), 75–77
    Rice Pudding (Scottish), 214–215
Scudder, Dora Belle Lee (Grandmama), 125–128, 226–227
Scudder, Ira, 126
Sevcik, Adolph Charles "A. C.," 197, 238–239
Sevcik, Anastasia Caroline Svetlik (Stasie), 197–198
Shanafelt, Bessie Hackney (Nana), 111–113
Shang Zhih, 83–85
Shankle, Jim, 161
Shankle, Winnie, 161
Shankleville, Texas, 90, 161, 259
Shankleville Historical Society, 90, 160–161
Shankleville Homecoming, 161
Shannon, Thelma Ulala West (Munnie), 37–38, 175
sheet vs. sheath cake, 113
Shelton, Lena Belle Hill, 216–217
Sicilian food
    Cuccidati (Sicilian Fig Cookies), 134–137
    Sicilian Pizza, 66–67
Silesian immigrants, 169
slaves
    cooks influence on Southern cuisine, 8
    stories of, 161
Sloma, Augusta Yeager, 152
slumgullion, 34
Smallwood, James M., 7
smells, memories from, 2
Smith, Betty White (Mama Smith), 15–16
Snelgrove, Amy Grones, 197–198
Soto, Juanita Cruz, 9, 44–45